This collection brings together the essays of one of the foremost American philosophers of economics. Cumulatively they offer fresh perspectives on foundational questions such as what sort of science is economics? and, how successful can economists be in acquiring knowledge of their subject matter?

In Part I Professor Hausman addresses problems of economic theory and criticizes views, such as those of Karl Popper and Milton Friedman, that see the acceptability of economics as deriving from its predictive success. Instead, the author defends the traditional view that we have reason to believe the conclusions of economic theories because they are deduced from plausible fundamental principles.

The essays in Part II defend the importance of causal notions in theoretical economics, whereas those in Part III concern the structure and development of economic theory. Part IV, together with the general introduction, provides an accessible account of Hausman's general philosophical perspective and of the purposes underlying his reflections on economics.

Essays on philosophy and economic methodology

Essays on philosophy
and economic methodology

DANIEL M. HAUSMAN
University of Wisconsin-Madison

CAMBRIDGE
UNIVERSITY PRESS

CAMBRIDGE UNIVERSITY PRESS
Cambridge, New York, Melbourne, Madrid, Cape Town, Singapore, São Paulo

Cambridge University Press
The Edinburgh Building, Cambridge CB2 8RU, UK

Published in the United States of America by Cambridge University Press, New York

www.cambridge.org
Information on this title: www.cambridge.org/9780521417402

© Cambridge University Press 1992

First published 1992
This digitally printed version 2008

A catalogue record for this publication is available from the British Library

Library of Congress Cataloguing in Publication data
Hausman, Daniel M., 1947–
Essays on philosophy and economic methodology / Daniel M. Hausman.
p.   cm.   ⊦
Includes index and bibliographical references.
ISBN 0–521–41740–6 (hard)
1. Economics.   2. Economics – Philosophy.   3. Economics –
Methodology.   I. Title.
HB34.H28   1992
330′.01–dc20   91–44733
                                                                              CIP

ISBN 978-0-521-41740-2 hardback
ISBN 978-0-521-06014-1 paperback

Contents

Introduction:
What is philosophy of economics?

I wound up doing philosophy of economics almost by chance. As a graduate student in philosophy at Columbia University, I was searching for a dissertation topic when John Eatwell came to town and delivered an exciting series of lectures on the so-called Cambridge Controversy in capital theory. The history he described was so unlike anything suggested by the philosophy of science I had studied that it seemed that there might be something of interest to be said about it. The slogan in philosophy of science at the time was, after all, that one should study what scientists actually do. And applying that slogan to economics seemed particularly interesting, since it was by no means uncontroversial that economics was a science. Furthermore, I had a tremendous resource ready to hand in Sidney Morgenbesser, who knows more about these issues than any other living philosopher. So over the Christmas holidays in 1976 I decided to do a dissertation on philosophy of economics.

It was a lucky choice. I had more than one great teacher in the subject, for Isaac Levi gradually convinced me of the centrality of problems concerning rational choice, and Ronald Findlay generously coached me into a modest competence in capital theory. My timing was perfect, too, for the great wave of contemporary interest in philosophy of economics was just beginning. Hollis and Nell's *Rational Economic Man*, Rosenberg's *Microeconomic Laws: A Philosophical Analysis*, and Latsis's collection *Method and Appraisal in Economics* had just been published, and the authoritative works or collections in the field by Blaug (1980), Boland (1982), Caldwell (1982), Hutchison (1981), Pitt (1981), Samuels (1980), Stegmueller et al. (1982), and Stewart (1979) were shortly to appear. Conferences in 1979 at Virginia Polytechnic Institute and Michigan State University permitted me to meet many of the other philosophers and economists working on issues in economic methodology, and my career was launched.

The essays collected here are a sample of what I have written over the last dozen years, and they reflect the development of my knowledge and perspective. In its most general outline, my view of how economics ought to be practiced has changed relatively little, but I have made and, I hope, corrected many mistakes in the details. Good interdisciplinary work demands an awful lot of knowledge, which I am still acquiring. The few major revisions in my views concern the connections between "positive" economic theory and theories of rationality and welfare. These have come largely from the wide exposure to work on rationality

1

and economic welfare that has resulted from my editing *Economics and Philosophy*.[1] Were I rewriting these essays today, I would not only patch up many details, but I would place greater emphasis on the fact that economics is built around a normative theory of rationality. For, as I argue in *The Inexact and Separate Science of Economics*, that fact is central to an appreciation of the methodological peculiarities of economics.

When a philosopher sets forth upon a career of peering over the shoulders of economists, he or she should expect not only a pinched neck but some loss of identity. For there is no way to immerse oneself in the goings on of one discipline without feeling oneself becoming a part of it. The role of spectator or voyeur can also be frustrating, for after a while one wants to take part. I cannot participate as a full-blown economist, but increasingly I have come to feel that some of the insights and arguments I have developed are of value to economists. Yet with few exceptions the essays included here have appeared in books and journals read mainly by philosophers. One motive in collecting these essays is to make them accessible to economists.

Many of my ideas have been incorporated into my two books – *Capital, Profits and Prices: An Essay in Philosophy of Economics* (1981) and *The Inexact and Separate Science of Economics* (1992) – but some of the discussions, particularly of historical matters and of causality, do not appear in the books and many of the particular arguments may be more accessible and salient when not integrated into a monograph. Since few philosophers or economists are likely to have come across more than a few of the essays collected here, their assembly and republication may be of some value.

ISSUES IN ECONOMIC METHODOLOGY

The essays in this book are concerned with "economic methodology." I use these words to cover everything that bears on how economics ought to be practiced and how the products of economics ought to be appraised. These essays are thus all at least implicitly normative, although the advice and preaching are typically subdued and are grounded in an attempt to appreciate clearly how economists do their various jobs. The first chapter, "Economic methodology in a nutshell," provides a thumbnail sketch of the history and contemporary state of the discipline.

---

1 With Michael McPherson. Another bit of wonderful good luck. Colin Day, then editorial director at Cambridge University Press, was the matchmaker and encouraged us to found the journal. Working with authors, referees, and editorial board, and especially Mike has been a tremendous education.

My writings on economic methodology have been concerned with a wide range of issues, which can be grouped under the following eight headings.[2]

Problems of appraisal, idealization, and inexactness

When most people think of economic methodology, these are the issues that first come to mind. One striking fact about economics is that it is built on generalizations which, if taken literally, are false. People are not able to rank all objects of choice. Their preferences are not always transitive. They do not always want more. Firms do not always attempt to maximize net returns. How can economics contain such claims and still be "good science?" How can economists make these claims and still be "good scientists?" Like everybody else writing on economic methodology, I have a great deal to say about these problems, particularly in Part I, "Theory appraisal." But I would insist that these are neither the only nor necessarily the best questions to focus on.

Up until the 1930s the dominant view of theory appraisal in economics was that economics proceeds by deducing the consequences of well-established generalizations about human behavior and technology when these are conjoined with premises concerning specific circumstances. Since these generalizations concern only the "major causes" of economic phenomena, the deduced consequences will be inexact and sometimes badly mistaken. Such predictive failures are only to be expected, for there are many "disturbing causes" left out of the theory, and the consequences follow only *ceteris paribus*. Since the initial generalizations are well-established by introspection or everyday experience, the failures do not cast doubt on economic theory itself. This is John Stuart Mill's view, which I reformulate and defend in Chapter 3, "John Stuart Mill's philosophy of economics." With various qualifications I still think it is the correct view of theory appraisal in economics.

Over the past fifty years most economists have come to the opposite conclusion. They have repudiated the deductive method, but only in principle, (not) in practice. Some of the reasons for this repudiation have been bad ones. As economic methodologists who have been influenced by the work of Karl Popper have pointed out, *ceteris paribus* claims are not logically falsifiable. They are not logically inconsistent with any possible observation reports. Apparent disconfirmations can always be attributed to some disturbing cause. But as I argue in Chapter

2 One set of important issues that is badly underrepresented both in the methodological literature as a whole and in my writing are those especially concerned with econometrics. Although the status and accomplishments of econometrics are controversial, it is obvious that econometrics links economic theory to statistical data. The practices and problems of econometrics are thus relevant to discussions of the appraisal of economic theories. But writers on economic methodology have typically paid little attention to econometrics, and writers on econometric methodology have often focused on problems of mathematical statistics without explicitly drawing the connections to philosophical problems of theory appraisal.

6, "An appraisal of Popperian methodology," individual theories in science are never logically falsifiable. As I stress both in Chapter 6 and in Chapter 7, "Is falsification unpracticed or unpractisable?" there is no reason to criticize economists for failing to meet a standard that no scientist can meet.

Not all of the reasons for repudiating the deductive method have been bad ones.[3] If observations are capable only of confirming economic theories or of demonstrating the influence of some "disturbing cause," then what can economists learn? And if there is no way to learn from observation, then economics cannot be an empirical science. Any method of theory appraisal that rules out the possibility of learning from experience must be repudiated.

In Chapter 4, "The deductive method," I present and answer this criticism. It is fair to insist that disconfirmation must not be ruled out by methodological fiat, but I argue that the sort of deductive method that economists still cling to does not do so. Anomalous observations count so little in economics, not because of economists' commitment to any unreasonably dogmatic view of theory appraisal, but because these observations constitute poor data with no clear evidential relevance. If the price of wheat goes up and demand for wheat rises, it is more likely that some disturbing cause is at work than that the law of demand is mistaken. When better data are available, as in the case of the preference reversal phenomena discussed in Chapter 15, leading economists are prepared to admit that fundamental postulates of economics are false and should be revised. Some dogmatism remains, not because of any mistaken view of testing or confirmation, but because economists place unjustifiable constraints on which revisions they are willing to consider.

In my view there is nothing particularly remarkable about the views of theory appraisal that most economists accept. As I argue in Chapter 4, "The deductive method," and Chapter 8, "The limits of economic science," the peculiarities of theory appraisal in economics arise from the special circumstances economists must contend with and from the strategies they have adopted. Economists are blessed with good reason to believe their fundamental behavioral postulates, but they are cursed with such problems in experimentation and data gathering that they are largely unable to learn from experience. The strategy they have adopted is to require that the domain of economics be spanned by a single unified theory in which rationality and acquisitiveness have central roles.

Problems of bad philosophy

Writers on economic methodology have, sensibly enough, looked to contemporary philosophy of science for guidance. Unfortunately much of contemporary

3 As Abraham Hirsch and Neil de Marchi helped me to see.

philosophy of science, particularly the grand systems of Popper, Lakatos, and the logical positivists, contains many mistakes and provides poor guidance. Consequently a good deal of methodology has been devoted to undoing the damage done by philosophers and economists under their influence. Chapter 5 is a brief attempt to make vivid exactly what is wrong with the message of Milton Friedman's influential essay, "The methodology of positive economics." Chapters 6 and 7 explore deep difficulties in the Popperian views that have been so prominent among economic methodologists.

Problems of economic modeling

Theoretical economics is devoted to the formulation of economic models and to essentially mathematical inquiry into their implications. Why? What are economic models? What are the differences between models and theories? Is this concern with models a strength or weakness of theoretical economics? These central questions have commanded too little attention in the literature on economic methodology. In Chapter 3, "On the conceptual structure of neoclassical economics," I sketch the view of these matters that I defend (with a few differences concerning details) in both my books. Models are like definitions, and in working on them, economists engage in the sort of conceptual exploration and development which has been essential in the growth of all the sciences. To say that individuals are rational if and only if their preferences are complete and transitive and they choose what they most prefer is to offer a model of rationality. Theories, on the other hand, are sets of lawlike assertions, which employ the concepts developed in the formulation of models. Modeling is ultimately of value in an empirical discipline only insofar as it leads to improvements in theories.

Global theory structure

As philosophers have come to emphasize over the past generation, sciences are not collections of unconnected theories. To the contrary, as philosophers and historians such as Kuhn, Lakatos, Laudan, and Shapere have stressed, one finds enormous continuity in science, and typical day-to-day theoretical work is heavily constrained by a set of shared values, heuristics, models, fundamental laws, and so forth. Since particular theories in orthodox economics – whether concerned with human capital, rational expectations, or economic welfare – show intimate connections, these philosophical insights were eagerly seized upon by economists, who saw a "paradigm" or a "research program" under every economic bush or tree. In my view, which is sketched in Chapter 2 and defended at length in Chapter 6 of *The Inexact and Separate Science of Economics*, the particular characterizations of the global theory structure of scientific disciplines defended by Kuhn and Lakatos do not fit economics very well. And much more importantly, even if they did, they have too little structure to provide one with much help in understanding economics. As I hint in Chapter 3, "On the conceptual structure of neoclassical Economics" and Chapter 12, "What are general equilibrium theories?" it is more useful to see standard economics as developing the implications of a single fundamental theory.

Problems of definition and scope

Classic works on economic methodology such as John Stuart Mill's "On the Definition of Political Economy and the Method of Investigation Proper to It" (1836) and Lionel Robbins's *An Essay on the Nature and Significance of Economic Science* (1932, 1935) devote considerable attention to the definition of economics. To modern readers this emphasis may seem old-fashioned. Surely it is obvious enough what economics is. On the contrary, it seems to me that economists typically accept competing definitions of their subject as concerned with a particular set of causal factors (rational acquisitiveness) and as concerned with a particular realm of social behavior. Central to contemporary economics is the implicit but highly contestable conviction that the two definitions coincide, that (at a suitable level of approximation) the causal factors with which economists are concerned provide a complete theory of their subject matter. The discussion in Chapter 3 of Mill's view of economics as a "separate science" and the inquiry in Chapter 12 into the role of general equilibrium theory broach these issues, but they call for deeper treatment. These same issues are also lurking in Chapter 13, "Arbitrage arguments." I argue in Chapter 6 of *The Inexact and Separate Science* that the core of the methodological distinctiveness of economics lies here.

Problems of social science

Economics is concerned with social phenomena, and the entities with which social theories are concerned are in important ways unlike the entities with which the natural sciences are concerned. In particular, human beings can learn the theories that purportedly describe their behavior and can adjust their behavior in consequence. Second, human beings act for reasons, and their actions can be appraised for their rationality (and morality) as well as causally explained. Irrational action is consequently likely to be unstable. Third, "folk-psychological" accounts of human action (of which standard economic theory is a variant) see action as depending on constraints, beliefs, and preferences, and beliefs and preferences introduce elements of "intentionality." For human action depends not only on the "facts" but on how the facts are viewed by the agents involved. For example, in *Hamlet,* the fact that the wine was poisoned had physiological consequences for

Gertrude regardless of her subjective state. But the fact that the wine was poisoned had consequences for Gertrude's choices only insofar as she was aware of it.

There is a large literature in philosophy of the social sciences concerning whether the distinctive features of social phenomena require that social inquiries differ in crucial ways from inquiries about nature, and this literature finds echoes in writings on economic methodology. I have until recently been inclined to downplay the differences between the natural and social sciences, and in Chapter 14, "Explanatory progress in economics," I offer a partial defense of scientific progress in economics against Alexander Rosenberg's view that the social sciences have not progressed.

Problems of causality

Although many economists, especially those who have been most influenced by logical positivism, are uneasy about the use of causal language, economics is full of causal claims. Over the last two generations only econometricians have been explicitly concerned about causality, and the literature on the topic they have produced is rarely cited by writers on economic methodology. Although the three essays in Part II draw on this econometric literature, they do not attempt to contribute to it. They are instead concerned with theoretical issues in economics to which concepts of causation are crucial. As argued in Chapter 11, "Supply and demand explanations and their *ceteris paribus* clauses," causal concepts are at the bottom of the so-called *Methodenstreit* over demand curves in the 1950s and 1960s. As Chapter 9, "Are there causal relations among dependent variables?" documents, causal questions are particularly pressing and puzzling when addressing macroeconomic problems. Chapter 10, "Classical wage theory and the causal complications of explaining distribution," illustrates how causal problems arise in functional distribution theory and how the classical economists overcame them.

Detailed problems

Finally there are the details, where all the substance and hard work are to be found. Some of these detailed problems, such as, "In what sense does the intersection of an IS and an LM curve determine the rate of interest?" are related to general issues, in this case concerning causation. But there are many puzzles that stand alone, too. For example, abstract general equilibrium theories, which are discussed in Chapter 12, are peculiar. They take the form of mathematical investigations of the existence, uniqueness, stability, and welfare properties of equilibria of nonexistent and indeed typically quite impossible economies, in which, for example, everybody has perfect knowledge of all present and future commodities and prices. What's the point? Chapter 13, "Arbitrage arguments," provides a

7

second example. Economists often are inclined to deny the relevance of findings of irrationality on the grounds that competitive markets will prevent irrationality from having any major consequences. Chapter 13 provides a detailed analysis of the structure of the argument they are relying on.

STRUCTURE AND ACKNOWLEDGMENTS

I have divided the seventeen essays of which this collection consists into four sections: Part I, "Methodology and theory appraisal," is concerned with the issues that many people think of as constituting the whole subject. The section as a whole offers my view of the special problems of theory appraisal in economics and the methods economists do and should employ. Two of the eight essays, "On the conceptual structure of neoclassical economics" and "Why look under the hood?" are published here for the first time. The first is a revised version of a talk delivered to the Allied Social Sciences meetings in 1982. A revised version of the second is incorporated into chapter 9 of *The Inexact and Separate Science of Economics*.

"Economic Methodology in a Nutshell" is reprinted from *Journal of Economic Perspectives* 3 (1989), pp. 115–27.

"John Stuart Mill's Philosophy of Economics" is reprinted from *Philosophy of Science*, 48 (1981), pp. 363–85.

"The Deductive Method" is reprinted from *Midwest Studies in Philosophy*, 15 (1990), pp. 372–88.

"An Appraisal of Popperian Methodology" is reprinted from N. de Marchi, ed., *The Popperian Legacy in Economics*. Cambridge: Cambridge University Press, 1988, pp. 65–86.

"Is Falsificationism Unpracticed or Unpractisable?" is reprinted from *Philosophy of the Social Sciences*, 15 (1985), pp. 313–19.

"The Limits of Economic Science" is reprinted from N. Rescher, ed., *The Limits of Lawfulness*. Pittsburgh: Center for Philosophy of Science, University of Pittsburgh, 1983, pp. 93–100.

Part II, "Causality in economics," documents the importance of causal concepts in theoretical economics. The three essays in this section reveal mistakes economists and sociologists have made as a consequence of supposing that they could avoid making causal claims, and the essays show how causal notions help to resolve disputed issues, such as the nature of the *ceteris paribus* clauses attached to demand and supply functions.

"Are There Causal Relations Among Dependent Variables?" is reprinted from *Philosophy of Science*, 50 (1983), pp. 58–81.

"Classical Wage Theory and the Causal Complications of Explaining Distribution" is reprinted from J. Pitt, ed., *Change and Progress in Modern Science.* Dordrecht: Reidel, 1985, pp. 171–97.

"Supply and Demand Explanations and Their *Ceteris Paribus* Clauses" is reprinted from *Review of Political Economy,* 2 (1990), pp. 168–87.

Part III, "Cases and puzzles," collects four essays which are concerned with detailed questions about particular theories, arguments, episodes, and theoretical developments in economics.

"What Are General Equilibrium Theories?" is reprinted from W. Sieg, ed., *Acting and Reflecting.* Dordrecht: Kluwer, 1990, pp. 107–14.

"Arbitrage Arguments" is reprinted from *Erkenntnis,* 30 (1989), pp. 5–22.

"Explanatory Progress in Economics" is reprinted from *Social Research,* 56 (1989), pp. 361–81.

"On Dogmatism in Economics: The Case of Preference Reversals" is reprinted from *The Journal of Socio-Economics* 20 (1991), pp. 205–25.

Part IV, "Postscripts," is concerned with "meta-methodology." Both essays reflect on the nature and difficulties of the project of doing philosophy of economics.

"How to do Philosophy of Economics" is reprinted from P. Asquith and R. Giere, eds., *PSA 1980.* East Lansing: Philosophy of Science Association, 1980, pp. 352–62.

"Reflections on Philosophy and Economic Methodology" was written especially for this volume, although it draws heavily on "Philosophy and Economic Methodology," published in P. Asquith and P. Kitcher, eds. *PSA 1984,* vol. 2. East Lansing: Philosophy of Science Association, 1986, pp. 231–49.

Although I wrote these essays and am responsible for the errors they contain, I could not have written them without the criticisms and suggestions of virtually everyone who has been working in this area. I have learned from all of my many co-workers in reflecting upon that remarkable human enterprise called "economics."

PART I

Methodology and theory appraisal

The eight essays in this part are concerned with the issues of theory appraisal that dominate writings on the methodology of economics. Chapter 1 offers a general overview of economic methodology and emphasizes that the subject is not exhausted by questions of theory assessment. Chapters 2, 3, 4, and 8 develop my views that the traditional deductive method provides (with some revisions) the best overall basis for assessing economic theories and that the difficulties involving theory assessment in economics result from the complexities of the subject matter economists study and the strategies or heuristics they use to simplify it. Chapters 5, 6, and 7 take issue with the influential views of economic methodology defended by Milton Friedman and Karl Popper.

1

Economic methodology in a nutshell

The literature on economic methodology is concerned mainly with questions of theory confirmation or disconfirmation or empirical theory choice. The central question is usually, "How can one tell whether a particular bit of economics is good science?" Economists would like methodologists to provide the algorithm for doing good economic science – and they want the algorithm to vindicate their own practice and to reveal the foolishness of those who do economics differently. For example, Milton Friedman (1953c) tells economists that good theories are those that provide correct and useful predictions, while Paul Samuelson (1947, 1963) tells economists to formulate theories with "operational" concepts that are, ideally, logically equivalent to their descriptive consequences.

In my view, not only are these (and most other) specific views on theory appraisal mistaken, but the concern with problems of empirical appraisal is exaggerated, for there are also interesting methodological questions to consider – both normative and descriptive – concerning the structure, strategy, goals, and heuristics of various economic theories. For example, few writers on economic methodology recognize that the activities of formulating economic models and investigating their implications are a sort of conceptual exploration. Instead, most mistakenly regard these activities as offering empirical hypotheses and assess them in terms of some philosophical model of confirmation or falsification.

As a tendentious survey of standard methodological literature, this essay will, however, share its preoccupation with the empirical appraisal of theory, microeconomic theory in particular. I shall in particular discuss four approaches to praising or damning microeconomic theory that have dominated methodological discussions. They might be called the deductivist, the positivist or Popperian, the predictionist, and the eclectic. Or to assign representative or striking figures to positions, these are John Stuart Mill's, Mark Blaug's, Milton Friedman's, and Donald McCloskey's views. I shall sketch and assess each position and defend aspects of the deductivist and eclectic views. Along the way I shall have some-

Many of the details in this paper are drawn from earlier works, like Hausman (1984c, 1986b). For a more extensive exposition and references, see Hausman (1987). For more detailed bibliography, see Caldwell (1984) or Hausman (1984d). I would like to thank Bruce Caldwell, Wade Hands, Catherine Kautsky, Michael McPherson, and the editors of the *Journal of Economic Perspectives* for their generous help with this essay.

13

thing to say not only about how to do economics, but also about how to philosophize about economic methodology.

DEDUCTIVISM

John Stuart Mill was both a Ricardian economist and a staunch empiricist, yet his economics seems not to measure up to empiricist standards for knowledge. After all, the implications of Ricardian economics appeared to be disconfirmed (de Marchi, 1970); for example, the share of national income paid as rent did not increase. How could Mill reconcile his confidence in Ricardian economics and his empiricism?

In Mill's view (1836, 1843, bk. 6), a complex subject matter like political economy can only be studied scientifically by means of the deductive method. Since so many causal factors influence economic phenomena, and experimentation is generally not possible, there is no way to employ the methods of induction directly. The only solution is first inductively to establish basic psychological or technical laws – such as "people seek more wealth," or the law of diminishing returns – and then to deduce their economic implications given specifications of relevant circumstances. Empirical confirmation or verification has an important role in determining whether the deductively derived conclusions are applicable, in checking the correctness of the deductions and in determining whether significant causal factors have been left out, but such testing does not bear on one's commitment to the basic "laws." They have already been established by introspection or experimentation. Political economy is in this regard similar to the science of tides, which applies independently established laws.

Mill believed that these established premises state accurately how specific causal factors operate. They are obviously not universal laws; for example, everyone does not always seek more wealth. These basic generalizations are instead statements of tendencies. Since these tendencies are subject to various "disturbances" or "interfering causes," which cannot all be specified in advance, vague *ceteris paribus* (other things being equal) clauses that allow for these disturbances will be unavoidable in formulating them. Economics explores the consequences of these established, but inexact, premises. Since much is left out of the theory, these consequences will not always obtain.

In Mill's view economics is a science, for economists do know the basic causes of economic phenomena. But it is an inexact science, for there are myriad interferences or disturbing causes. Mill's views are almost the opposite of Milton Friedman's, for Mill holds that the confidence of economists in the science of political economy is based on direct and rather casual confirmation of its assumptions, not on serious tests of their implications. Not only were Mill's views adopted by followers such as Cairnes (1875) and early neoclassical methodologists such as

John Neville Keynes (1917), but if one updates the language and the economic theory, one has the view to which, I suggest, most orthodox economists (regardless of what they may say in methodological discussion) still subscribe (see also Stewart 1979).

The transition from classical to neoclassical economics brought not only changes in economic theory, but methodological changes as well, for neoclassical theory focuses much more on individual preferences and decision making than did classical economics. Despite this difference, which was much emphasized by authors such as Frank Knight (1935, 1940), Ludwig von Mises (1981), and Lionel Robbins (1935), early neoclassical economists agreed with Mill that the basic premises of economics are well-justified, and that empirical failures do not cast them into doubt. In defending this view, Lionel Robbins (1935, p. 121) explicitly notes his intellectual debts to Mill, and, by exaggerating the obviousness of the basic assumptions of neoclassical microeconomics, he provides a particularly persuasive formulation of what is essentially Mill's view (pp. 78–79):

The propositions of economic theory, like all scientific theory, are obviously deductions from a series of postulates. . . . The main postulate of the theory of value is the fact that individuals can arrange their preferences in an order, and in fact do so. The main postulate of the theory of production is the fact that there are [sic] more than one factor of production. The main postulate of the theory of dynamics is the fact that we are not certain regarding future scarcities. These are not postulates the existence of whose counterpart in reality admits of extensive dispute once their nature is fully realised. We do not need controlled experiments to establish their validity: they are so much the stuff of our everyday experience that they have only to be stated to be recognized as obvious.

Although Robbins overstates his case, I think that he is basically right.

POSITIVIST OR POPPERIAN VIEWS

To anyone familiar with the methodological literature of the last half-century, such a complacent view of the deductive method must seem perverse. For the theme which has dominated this period is that claims that are hedged with qualifications and *ceteris paribus* clauses are untestable and uninformative. What Mill or Robbins called "tendencies" or "inexact laws" are qualified claims such as, "In the absence of disturbances or interferences, people prefer more wealth," or "*Ceteris paribus*, returns to variable inputs will diminish." Since the content of the *ceteris paribus* clause is not fully specified, it seems that these statements are unfalsifiable and lack definite empirical meaning. Either things are as claimed by the tendency, or there is some disturbance. No outcomes are prohibited, and new evidence never requires economists to alter their beliefs about the basic tendencies.

Fifty years ago, under the influence of logical positivism, Terence Hutchison

15

made essentially just this charge. The statements of "pure theory" in economics are empty definitional or logical truths, he argued, and even applied claims are so hedged that they lack content (1938, esp. ch. 2). Hutchison insisted that economists should start behaving like responsible empirical scientists. Thus, under the guiding star of logical positivism, and later on of Karl Popper (1959), began the first and only major change in economists' official position on the appraisal of microeconomics.

As Hutchison himself partly recognized (1938, ch. 2), this critique can be answered from within the Millian tradition. For one need not regard or employ *ceteris paribus* clauses as blanket excuses (Hausman 1981b, ch. 7). *Ceteris paribus* clauses are part of almost all of science. Rather than condemning them all, one needs to distinguish when one may legitimately employ them and to recognize that rough generalizations can have worth and content despite their vagueness and imprecision. I learned something useful when I was taught that aspirin cures headaches, even though (alas!) this generalization is not a universal law.[1]

Hutchison's attack was still disquieting. Did neoclassical microeconomic theory measure up to the standards for science defended by contemporary (positivist) philosophers of science? Those who first rose to answer Hutchison's challenge, such as Frank Knight (1940), may have aggravated rather than allayed this disquiet, for Knight explicitly repudiated the empiricist or positivist philosophy of science upon which Hutchison's challenge relied. Knight accuses the positivists of overlooking the complexity and uncertainty of testing in all sciences (1940, p. 153) and argues at length that positivist views of science are particularly inappropriate to economics, which, like all sciences of human action, must concern itself with reasons, motives, values and errors, not just causes and regularities. Younger and less philosophically ambitious economists might well have wondered whether there was any way to respond to Hutchison without thus repudiating up-to-date philosophy of science. Indeed, in his review, Knight worries about the pernicious effect Hutchison's book may have on the young (1940, pp. 151, 152). Positivistic recastings of economic theory, such as Samuelson's (1947) "operationalism" and particularly his revealed preference theory, which appeared to provide a behaviorist reduction of talk about preference and utility to observable claims about actions, were beginning to appear. Were they the way of the future? Did logical positivism make traditional neoclassical theory untenable?

Indeed, similar challenges to contemporary economic practice continue in works such as Mark Blaug's *The Methodology of Economics* (1980), which argue that neoclassical economics does not meet Popperian or positivist standards for science.

---

1 I owe this example to Sidney Morgenbesser. Although rough generalizations have statistical implications, they are also not well construed as statistical laws.

Could the profession's high regard for microeconomic theory be squared with the demand that good science be well-confirmed by empirical data?[2]

After World War II, qualms about the empirical standing of microeconomic theory grew, when economists such as Richard Lester attempted to test fundamental propositions of the neoclassical theory of the firm (1946, 1947). Lester's tests, which consisted of surveys sent to various businesses, were not well-designed. But they attracted attention and provoked fierce responses (especially Machlup 1946, 1947; Stigler 1947), partly because everybody knew that Lester was right about one thing: Firms do not behave precisely as marginal productivity theory maintains they do. Indeed one of Lester's sharpest critics, Fritz Machlup, conceded (1956, p. 488), "But we would certainly not find that all of the businessmen do so [maximize profits] all of the time. Hence, the assumption of consistently profit-maximizing conduct is contrary to fact." But does it not follow immediately that neoclassical theory makes false statements and is thus on positivist and Popperian standards inadequate?

Although some, such as Knight and the Austrians, were prepared to deny that the standards of the natural sciences apply to economics, most tried to show that economics satisfies all reasonable demands that one may make of a science. Fritz Machlup's essays (1955, 1960) give some idea of such attempts. Machlup argues that microeconomic theory is compatible with later and more sophisticated logical positivist (or "logical empiricist") accounts of the nature of science, which considerably loosen the connection that is required between theory and observation. Machlup argues that both instrumentalists and defenders of "partial interpretation" views recognize that one need not be concerned about the truth of a theoretical claim such as profit maximization. But the philosophers who defended instrumentalism and "partial interpretation" views were concerned to show how theories that make claims about unobservable entities and properties and thus cannot be directly empirically tested might nevertheless be meaningful and indirectly testable. They never suggested that one should ignore the falsity of a claim — such as "all firms attempt to maximize profits" — on the grounds that such a claim is "theoretical."

2　Given positivist or Popperian standards, the answer is "no." But no science meets these unreasonable standards. In contrast to Samuelson (1963), the early positivists, and (to a lesser extent) Popper, neither the truth nor falsity of theoretical claims can be inferred directly from observation reports. Contrary to Popper's views, intelligent testing requires (inductive) knowledge of how well statements are supported by evidence. Given how poorly supported are the various auxiliary statements needed to derive predictions from economic theories, it is usually not sensible or responsible to follow Blaug's Popperian advice and to regard predictive failures as falsifying economic theories. For a more comprehensive and accurate critique of Popperian economic methodology than is possible here see this volume, Chapter 6.

PREDICTIONISM

The most influential way of reconciling economics and up-to-date philosophy of science was, however, not Machlup's, but Milton Friedman's. In his famous essay, "The Methodology of Positive Economics" (1953c), Friedman offered the apparent way out of the empirical difficulties raised by Lester and others that has proven most popular with economists. It is that apparent way out, not the possible intricacies of Friedman's views, with which I shall be concerned. Although Friedman does not refer to contemporary philosophy of science, he too attempts to show that economics satisfies sophisticated positivist standards.

After distinguishing between positive and normative economics, Friedman begins by asserting that the goals of a positive science are predictive, not at all explanatory (1953c, p. 7). Economists seek significant and usable predictions, not understanding or explanation. The view that science, or at least economic science, aims only at prediction is a contentious one, and one for which Friedman offers no argument. It might reasonably be challenged. But in holding this instrumentalist view of the goals of science, Friedman is in good philosophical company and not obviously mistaken (see Morgenbesser 1969). Since Friedman's methodological views are untenable even if one grants his claim that the goals of economics are exclusively predictive, let us not contest it here.

In Friedman's usage, any implication of a theory whose truth is not yet known counts as a prediction of a theory, even if it is not concerned with the future. Since the goals of science are exclusively predictive, a theory which enables one to make reliable predictions is a good theory. In case of a tie on the criterion of predictive success, simpler theories or theories of wider scope (that apply to a wider range of phenomena) are to be preferred (p. 10).

Friedman stresses that there is no other test of a theory in terms of whether its "assumptions" are "unrealistic" (p. 14). When Friedman speaks of the "assumptions" of a theory, he includes both fundamental assertions (such as the claims that consumers are utility maximizers) and additional premises needed in particular applications (for example, the claim that different brands of cigarettes are perfect substitutes for one another). Although Friedman equivocates with the term "unrealistic," usually he means (as he must if he is to respond to Lester's challenge) that an assumption is unrealistic if it is not true, perhaps not even approximately true, of the phenomena to which the theory is applied.

Friedman can then argue that researchers such as Lester mistakenly attempt to assess the "assumptions" of neoclassical theory instead of its predictions. In dismissing any assessment of assumptions, Friedman is also responding to a critical tradition which extends back to the German Historical School via American Institutionalists, such as Veblen. This critical tradition questions the worth of abstract theorizing and objects to the purportedly unreasonably unrealistic assumptions of neoclassical theory. Friedman apparently enables one to reject all such criticism as fundamentally confused.

But Lester's case cannot be dismissed so easily, for Lester apparently showed that neoclassical theory makes false predictions concerning, for instance, the results of his surveys. The distinction between assumptions and implications is, indeed, a shallow one that rests on nothing but the particular formulation of a theory. Assumptions trivially imply themselves, and theories can be reformulated with different sets of assumptions that have the same implications. Unrealistic assumptions (in the sense of false assumptions) will always result in false predictions, except, perhaps, in the case of assumptions concerning unobservables.

Friedman notices the problem (pp. 26–27) and responds to it by insisting that all that matters is how well a theory predicts the phenomena in which economists are (at least on the particular occasion) interested (pp. 20, 27–28). This odd instrumentalism suggests that falsity of assumptions or of predictions is unimportant unless it detracts from a theory's performance in predicting the phenomena in which one is interested. A theory of the distribution of leaves on trees that states that it is as if leaves had the ability to move instantaneously from branch to branch is thus regarded by Friedman as perfectly "plausible" (p. 20), although of narrower scope than accepted theory. If a theory predicts accurately what one wants to know, it is a good theory, otherwise it is not.

When Friedman says that it is as if leaves move or as if expert billiard players solve complicated equations (p. 21), he means that attributing movement to leaves or calculating power to billiard players leads to correct predictions concerning the phenomena in which one is interested. And a theory which accomplishes this is a good theory, for a "theory is to be judged by its predictive power for the class of phenomena which it is intended to explain" (p. 8). Friedman is not just saying that if a theory "works," then one should use it, but that all one wants of science are theories that work for particular purposes. The realism of the assumptions of microeconomics or the truth of its uninteresting or irrelevant implications is unimportant, except insofar as either restricts the theory's scope. Since economists are not interested in what business people say, but in the consequences of what they do, Lester's surveys are irrelevant.

Yet even if one fully grants Friedman's view of the goals of science, one should still be concerned about the realism of assumptions. For there is no good way to know what to try when a prediction fails or whether to employ a theory in a new application without judging one's assumptions. Without assessments of realism (approximate truth) of assumptions, the process of theory modification would be hopelessly inefficient and the application of theories to new circumstances nothing but arbitrary guesswork. The point is simple: if one wants to use a machine in a new application or to build a new machine out of its components or to diagnose a malfunction, it helps to know something about the reliability of the components of which it is made. Even if all one wants of theories are valid predictions concerning particular phenomena, one needs to judge whether the needed assumptions are reasonable approximations, and one thus needs to be concerned about incorrect predictions, no matter how irrelevant.

I have dwelled on Friedman's views because of their influence and because they illustrate a paradox. Friedman's confidence in "the maximization-of-returns hypothesis" and in neoclassical theory in general purportedly rests entirely on "the repeated failure of its implications to be contradicted" (p. 22; but see pp. 26–30 on indirect testing). On this, Friedman is at one with Popperian methodologists such as Blaug. But the implications of neoclassical theory have certainly been contradicted on many occasions. This would be so even if the theory lived up to its highest praises. All it takes is some disturbance, such as a change in tastes, a new invention or a real or imagined invasion from Mars.[3] Does any economist really accept neoclassical theory on the basis of "the repeated failure of its implications to be contradicted"? Is this not rather a doctrine piously enunciated in the presence of philosophers or of their economist fellow travellers and conveniently forgotten when there is serious work to do?

Those who have noticed that economists do not practice what they preach have most often attacked the practice. Instead of attempting to discover what methodology neoclassical economists actually practice and to think seriously about how that methodology might be justified, these critics (with some notable exceptions, such as Simon 1976) have usually relied on indefensible philosophical theories of science to support broad condemnations (for example, Blaug 1980). There is, of course, nothing mistaken about judging the work of economists – normative concerns are central to economic methodology. But most of these judgments have relied on unreasonable standards that were supposedly vindicated by up-to-date philosophical insight. Philosophers have, however, little to offer by way of informative well-supported systematic theories of the scientific enterprise and that little does not lend itself to mechanical application.

---

3   Objections that readers have voiced to these examples instructively support my point. One objected that neoclassical theory obviously allows for "shocks." But, unless it does so by means of a not-fully-specified *ceteris paribus* clause, there will still be refutations of the kind cited. And if not-fully-specified *ceteris paribus* clauses are permitted, the "repeated failure of its implications to be contradicted" is a cheap triumph. Another reader objected that better examples are those in which the assumptions involved in the particular application of the theory are satisfied. I agree, but this is certainly not a line that Friedman or others who rest everything on the success of predictions can follow. For we are not supposed to pay any attention to whether the assumptions are satisfied – that is, to whether the assumptions are "realistic" for the situation at hand. There are examples in which predictive failures are more puzzling and disturbing than in the cases cited in the text. Consider the fact that even in inflationary circumstances many firms evaluate their inventories on a first in, first out basis or the fact that shares in closed-end mutual funds sometimes sell for less than the value of the assets of the funds (Stiglitz 1982).

ECLECTICISM

Many have by now recognized that there are few good philosophical authorities on matters of theory assessment. Although there is still a great deal to be learned from the judicious study of contemporary philosophy of science, those interested in economic methodology must use their own judgment and their knowledge of the practice of economists to formulate and to defend rational standards for the practice of economics. The situation of a methodologist concerned about understanding and improving economic practice is similar to that of an economist concerned with understanding and improving business practice. Although both may find some of the practices they study mistaken or irrational, both had better show some sense and caution in applying general theories and had better understand thoroughly the actual problems and procedures of the object they study.

Attempts to carry out such a delicate task have varied. Alexander Rosenberg's *Microeconomic Laws: A Philosophical Analysis* (1976) is something of a watershed. Since this book was published Rosenberg's own views have shifted drastically; he denied at one point (1983) that economics is an empirical science at all. But in publishing his first book, and especially in his discussion there of particular aspects of economics, such as the relations between micro- and macroeconomics or the sense in which explanations in economics involve both reasons and causes (ch. 5), Rosenberg is responsible for a growing literature on economic methodology by philosophers of science. This literature is distinctive in its attention to the details of methodological practice and in its cautious use of philosophical models of science.

Among economists the best-known authors in this more eclectic and empirical vein are probably Bruce Caldwell (1982) with his "methodological pluralism" and Donald McCloskey (1985) with his "rhetoric of economics." I do not yet find Caldwell's methodological pluralism to be a clear philosophical position. Sometimes it seems to be intended as the thesis that different economic methodologies must be assessed entirely in their own terms and that no more than internal coherence is to be demanded. But I think that Caldwell should be interpreted more charitably, not as abandoning the normative tasks of economic methodology, but as recognizing that they cannot come first. Since philosophers of science have no gospel for scientific practice, economic methodologists have no prepared sermons. Cast among the heathen, bereft of revealed truth, methodologists must face the bewildering task of attempting to understand and to assess the practices and products of economists. Before judging competing methodological views, one must make a serious attempt to understand and to appreciate them.

Donald McCloskey with his "rhetoric of economics" (1985) also points out that systematic philosophy provides no well-justified code of scientific practice. He proposes that the tools of classical rhetoric and literary criticism are better suited to understanding what economists do. Thus, for example, in discussing a couple of pages from Samuelson's *Foundations of Economic Analysis,* McCloskey (1985, pp. 70–72) finds that Samuelson uses a variety of "rhetorical devices": analogy, appeals to authority, relaxation of assumptions, and hypothetical "toy" economies. Whether any of these may also be construed as good arguments that ought rationally to persuade the reader to accept Samuelson's conclusions is not McCloskey's concern, because he is skeptical about whether there are any detailed standards for what counts as a good argument in economics apart from whatever in fact persuades economists. Like Rosenberg and others, McCloskey encourages careful study of economic argumentation, and in his striking discussions of works by John Muth (ch. 6) and Robert Fogel (ch. 7) he provides memorable models of such study.

But McCloskey offers little solid argument for employing his favored literary tools, and he has a hard time explaining how his proposed successor to economic methodology is supposed to retain any normative role. And the normative role of methodology is unavoidable; whether methodological rules are garnered from imitation, methodological asides, or systematic methodological treatises, there is no doing economics without some standards or norms. Furthermore, if economics is to make any rational claim to guide policy, these standards or norms cannot be arbitrary.

The current literature on theory appraisal in economics and on economic methodology in general is quite eclectic, and I find this development healthy. One finds work as diverse as Abraham Hirsch's and Neil deMarchi's (1986) analysis of how Friedman employs monetary history to argue for his monetary theory, Cristina Bicchieri's (1987) treatment of the epistemological complications of the rational expectations hypothesis, Philip Mirowski's (1990) detailed account of the analogy between classical physics and neoclassical economic theory, or Alan Nelson's (1986) argument that microeconomics is a theory of individual choice. One moral of the past decade of philosophy of science is that the most interesting and substantive methodological work will usually turn on the details of the particular discipline discussed. A dispassionate look at recent methodological studies of economics strongly supports this view.

CONCLUSIONS

Methodological writing is pouring out at an increasing rate. Since the mid-1970s there have been scores of books, hundreds of articles, and even a new journal, *Economics and Philosophy.* This literature is still preoccupied with problems of theory appraisal, although other questions are attracting growing attention. All of the main streams discussed above are represented.

So, first, one still finds positivist or Popperian complaints that neoclassical economists refuse to put microeconomic theory to the test or to heed its disconfirmation. Many of these are from an institutionalist perspective (Eichner 1983; Samuels 1980). Since the models of science upon which these criticisms are based are unacceptable, I am skeptical about the value of these criticisms.

Second, one finds more refutations or rehabilitations of Milton Friedman. It will be a step forward when economists come to regard Friedman's essay only as an historically interesting document.

Third, one finds applications of current trends in philosophy of science – especially work by Thomas Kuhn (1970), Imre Lakatos (1970), and Paul Feyerabend (1975). This literature is almost as disappointing as is positivist or Popperian grumbling or rehashing Friedman. Apart from philosophical difficulties with their views, Kuhn, Lakatos, and Feyerabend have been hard to apply, for they are evasive on questions of theory appraisal, which still interest most of those writing on economic methodology. The most valuable work here (such as E. Roy Weintraub's 1985 Lakatosian account of the structure and history of general equilibrium theorizing) has little to say about issues of appraisal (see also Latsis 1976). There is also a separate technical literature on econometric methods that overlaps too infrequently with the methodological mainstream.[4]

Not surprisingly, I think that the best way forward concerning both theory appraisal and economic methodology more generally is the fourth (eclectic) way, the path I have taken: to focus on the methodology economists practice, making use of whatever tools philosophers of science have had to offer that appear to be well-made and apt for the job (Hausman, 1981a, ch. 12). Although methodologists may find much to criticize, they had better begin by understanding as thoroughly as they can how economists go about their business and why they do what they do. The Popperian/positivist and predictionist interludes in economic methodology have been largely unenlightening. With some restatement and toning down of the overly optimistic conviction that economics starts with the central truths concerning its domain, I think that Mill's views still stand.

The most promising and interesting methodological issues to tackle now are not directly concerned with theory appraisal. The role and significance of general

---

4 Although less familiar, there have also been a number of attempted applications of the views of Joseph Sneed (1971) and Wolfgang Stegmueller (1979). Many of these are to be found in Stegmueller, Balzer, and Spohn (1982). For further references and well-taken criticism, see Hands (1985b). There is also a good deal of methodological discussion written from a specifically "Austrian" perspective. Much of this is concerned with the interpretation of the views of major Austrian figures such as Mises and Hayek and with the defense of views of theory appraisal in economics similar to those of Mill and of Robbins. Caldwell (1982) provides a good discussion of the methodological views of the Austrians. For an interesting collection of essays, see Dolan (1976).

equilibrium theory are still not entirely clear. The implications of rational expectations for the objectivity and logic of economics remain to be explored. The notion of rationality in strategic and uncertain circumstances presents difficult open questions. In tackling problems such as these, I look forward to profitable collaboration between economists and philosophers.

2

On the conceptual structure of neoclassical economics – a philosopher's view

In this chapter I shall discuss two related philosophical issues concerning economics (see Hausman 1981b, chs. 3, 6). First, what is the nature and the significance of *models* in economics? Why does nearly all theoretical work take the form of (unrealistic) model building? How are such models related to things such as laws and theories which are more familiar to philosophers? Second, what is the fundamental theory or model of neoclassical economics? How is that fundamental theory or model related to specific neoclassical theories or models? What is the unit of appraisal of neoclassical economics? I hope to sketch in broad strokes a conceptual map of fundamental neoclassical theory – to provide a consistent and sensible way of seeing the whole enterprise – that is congruent with the actual practices of economics.

1. WHAT ARE MODELS AND WHY ARE THEY SO IMPORTANT IN ECONOMICS?

The models that economists employ should be regarded as complex predicates or concepts or as definitions of such complex predicates or concepts. A model is of the same logical kind as a predicate, such as "is triangular," or as a definition of what it is to be triangular. One thus does not test a model, nor does one say that a model is true (except perhaps in the trivial way in which a definition is true). This is not, of course, to deny that one can use models to make claims about the world which may be tested and which may be true or false. A model of a perfectly competitive economy, for example, itself does nothing more than to define the theoretical term "a perfectly competitive economy." One can then use the term to make claims such as "Japan's economy is not perfectly competitive."

One constructs or presents a model typically by listing a number of "assumptions." These assumptions should be regarded as clauses in a definition. In studying consumer choice, for example, one often begins with the simplified situation in which a consumer spends his or her income on only two commodities, whose prices are given. The various assumptions made in this bit of analysis can be regarded as defining a new concept – call it "a simple consumption system." That is, one can assert that an ordered triple $<A,x,y>$ is a simple consumption system

I would like to thank D. W. Hands and Martin Osborne for helpful comments on an earlier draft.

if and only if (1) A is an agent and x and y are kinds of commodities; (2) A faces a choice between bundles of commodities (q_x, q_y) where q_x and q_y are nonnegative real numbers, quantities of commodities x and y; (3) A's income, I, is fixed; (4) the prices of commodities x and y, p_x and p_y, are fixed and known to A; (5) A's utility function, U, is a strictly semi-concave, increasing and differentiable function of the quantity of x and y A consumes; and (6) A chooses that commodity bundle that maximizes U subject to the constraint that $p_x q_x + p_y q_y \leq I$. One can then prove, for example, that in a simple consumption system with an interior solution that bundle will be chosen for which A's marginal rate of commodity substitution equals the price ratio.

Developing theoretical knowledge is not just a matter of discovering correlations among properties that are already understood. An absolutely crucial part of the scientific enterprise — a part that was underemphasized by the logical positivist philosophers of science who were dominant earlier in this century — is the construction of new concepts, of new ways of classifying and categorizing phenomena. The model of a simple consumption system is such a new concept or way of categorizing phenomena.

Concepts or terms are in themselves of little interest to empirical scientists. They are important only if they enable scientists to say informative things about the phenomena under study. But scientists may nevertheless justifiably wish to *separate* questions concerning the conceptual apparatus with which they study the world from questions concerning the extent to which that apparatus applies to the world. That is, they may sometimes wish to investigate the properties of the models they construct without worrying about whether those models depict or apply to any aspect of reality. One may, for example, wish to study various notions of rationality without worrying about whether people are rational.

In defining a simple consumption system and in proving the theorem mentioned from the six assumptions, one is not necessarily making any claims about the world. Nor need theorists regard themselves as revealing mysterious hypothetical truths concerning hypothetical situations. They are merely constructing concepts and employing mathematical techniques to explore further properties that are implied by the definitions they have offered. Such model-building and theorem-proving does not presuppose that one believes that the particular model is of any use in understanding the world.

Insofar as one is only working with a model, one can reject any questions about the realism of the assumptions one makes. But remember that the reason is that one is saying *nothing* about the world. I am thus not in any way joining in Friedman's (1953c) or Machlup's (1955) blanket defenses of "unrealistic assumptions." Insofar as one is only working with a model, one's efforts and results are purely conceptual or mathematical. One is only exploring and developing a complicated concept or definition.

As soon as one offers some hypothesis about the extent to which some model applies to some bit of reality, one is offering a *theory*. Some contemporary philosophers of science regard scientific theories as just models in the sense defined above (Suppes 1957, ch. 12; Sneed 1971; Stegmueller 1979; Giere 1979, ch. 5, for example), but ordinary usage both within philosophy and within the sciences takes theories as assertions about the world. As soon as one asserts that the triple consisting of George, ice cream, and the composite commodity consisting of everything else George consumes is a simple consumption system, one is asserting that all the assumptions of the model are true of the relevant aspects of reality — that is, one is asserting that ice cream is infinitely divisible, that George possesses a strictly semi-concave, increasing, and differentiable utility function, and so on.

And, of course, this is precisely the point where things become uncomfortable. No assertion about the world of the form "Such and such is a simple consumption system" will be (exactly) true. Commodities are not infinitely divisible. Choices are never between only two commodities. Incomes and prices are not fixed. Probably nobody has a strictly semi-concave and differentiable utility function. But one must be sensible. Even if not strictly true, these assertions may be reasonable approximations (in some sense), and the simple consumption system model may enable one to say true and useful things about the world (Koopmans 1957; Hausman 1981b, ch. 7). But, as I said at the beginning, I am not concerned in this paper with problems of assessment. I mention them here only because they help one to explain the peculiar importance of "unrealistic" models in economics.

In theoretical work, *all* scientists attempt to exclude the various messes and complications that are always present in reality. The only way to theorize is to develop models. But largely because of the possibility of setting up highly simplified experimental circumstances, assumptions in models in the natural sciences may often be regarded as universal laws of nature or as specifications of properties of specific kinds of natural systems. Theorists in the natural sciences may thus not need to divorce their model building sharply from their empirical investigations of nature.

In economics, on the other hand, the problems of application and assessment are much thornier. Even though models in economics need not be as abstract as those which characterize mainstream theorizing, they will never apply to economic reality very simply or cleanly. Insofar as one has any hopes of economic theory, there will always be some need to divorce conceptual development and empirical application. "Unrealistic" model-making is an unavoidable occupation of theoretically inclined economists. But one should remember that models have little value (apart from their mathematical interest) unless they can be applied – unless they enable one to make true or reliable assertions about the world.

2. EQUILIBRIUM THEORY AND THE BASIC EQUILIBRIUM MODEL

I call the fundamental theory of neoclassical economics "equilibrium theory" (which is *not* the same thing as general equilibrium theory). Although economists do not use my terminology, most regard what I call "equilibrium theory" or "the basic equilibrium model" as fundamental to virtually all economic theory. They hope to be able to reduce, or at least relate, macroeconomic theories to equilibrium theory. They hope to be able to augment the basic equilibrium model to deal with questions of economic growth and change. This is the model they rely on in specific empirical research and in many welfare recommendations. When one has succeeded in saying what equilibrium models are, one has largely succeeded in saying what neoclassical economics is.

Among the various assumptions common to different neoclassical models, one can distinguish two different kinds. Some, such as "Agent's preferences are transitive" or "Entrepreneurs attempt to maximize profits," should be regarded as the fundamental "laws" of neoclassical economics – although they are, to be sure, very messy and problematic. Other assumptions such as "Commodities are infinitely divisible" or "Agents have perfect information" have (when taken to be claims about the world) narrower scope and are not regarded as assertions or discoveries of economics.[1] Economists are pleased when these simplifications can be relaxed. Although such simplifications are essential in most economic theorizing and are common constituents of neoclassical models, they are not really assertions of economics, nor are they, I suggest, part of fundamental economic theory or of the fundamental assumptions of equilibrium models. I think one can best understand what neoclassical economics is by focusing on its fundamental laws or behavioral postulates.

"Equilibrium theory" is my name for these fundamental laws or principles. It is helpful to divide them into four groups:

(1) *Utility theory:* Individuals have complete and transitive preferences and choose the option that they most prefer.

(2) *Economic preferences:* Individuals prefer "larger" commodity bundles to smaller. Commodities possess diminishing marginal rates of substitution (or diminishing marginal utility) for all individuals.

---

1 The distinction between "laws" and nonlaws is problematic. It cannot be drawn syntactically, and it is difficult to see how it can be drawn at all in any general and informative way. Yet the distinction is a real one that both laypeople and scientists draw all the time. For a discussion of the philosophical difficulties, see Hempel 1965, pp. 264–70, and 1966, pp. 54–58.

(3) *Production:* Increasing any input (other inputs held constant) increases output at (eventually) a diminishing rate. Increasing all inputs by a certain proportion increases output by more than that proportion. Entrepreneurs or firms attempt to maximize net returns.

(4) *Equilibrium:* An equilibrium exists that reconciles the activities of individuals.

Although utility functions are often immediately defined as ranging over commodity bundles, it is helpful to recognize that utility theory is much more general than economics. It might be regarded as a way of making determinate the idea that people are instrumentally rational. Many economists certainly regard it as, in effect, defining rationality. Utility theory is completely silent on the *content* of preferences and does not imply that individuals are egotistic or that there is any sensation or entity called "utility" that is a goal of individual action. To say that agents are utility maximizers is to say no more than that they do what they most prefer.

"Nonsatiation," the generalization that individuals prefer more commodities to fewer, has the effect of identifying the options that individuals face with commodity bundles. It declares individuals to be self-interested or mutually disinterested. They simply want more. All they care about is the absolute size of the commodity bundle they wind up. "Economic rationality" might be (and often implicitly is) defined as utility theory plus nonsatiation. Diminishing marginal utility is sometimes thought to be part of economic rationality, but I cannot see why. It is simply an empirical generalization about the nature of people's preferences for commodity bundles containing different mixes of commodities.

Diminishing returns to a variable input is, like diminishing marginal utility, a fairly well-founded empirical generalization. Nonincreasing returns to scale, on the other hand, is one of the principles or laws with which economists are least happy. More than any other in the list, it seems to be included largely because it is needed for mathematical proofs of the existence of equilibrium. Profit maximization is a mare's nest of its own. Obviously there is something to it, but there is plenty of evidence of its incorrectness, and it is not obviously compatible with utility-maximizing behavior.

The claim that an equilibrium exists might seem an odd candidate for a fundamental "law" of neoclassical economics, since it is never, or virtually never, stated as an assumption. Instead, the existence of equilibrium is something to be proven. But is not something that incidentally happens to be provable in a great many models. The models are constructed so as to permit one to prove that some sort of equilibrium can or will obtain. Even though the proposition makes its explicit appearance typically as a theorem, it remains a fundamental "law" of neoclassical economics.

The various constituent claims of equilibrium theory might be regarded as the basic principles or laws that neoclassical economists have discovered. Or, if one wants to postpone questions of assessment, one might regard them merely as the fundamental assumptions in neoclassical models and leave aside questions about the applicability of such models. The claims are not all equally central and significant. Various simplifications such as perfect information or infinite commodity divisibility will also be common constituents of neoclassical models, but, as mentioned above, such simplifications are not as essential as are the propositions of equilibrium theory.

Taken as genuine assertions about the world, the four groups of propositions discussed above make up equilibrium theory, the fundamental theory of neoclassical economics. They are an articulation of a basic vision of economic life that was around long before neoclassical economics was. In that vision, which can already be found in Adam Smith, individuals are thought of as rational and self-interested, and as interacting only through voluntary exchanges. Smith and his intellectual descendents have sought to show how a systematic and beneficial organization of the economy results from such exchanges.

Fundamental models do not by themselves enable one to say much about the world. What makes the basic equilibrium model significant is that it forms the core of partial and general equilibrium analyses, of trivial exercises such as the simple consumption system mentioned before and of extremely sophisticated proofs of the existence or stability of general equilibrium. In both general and partial equilibrium models, the basic assumptions discussed above are supplemented with various simplifications and specifications concerning market and time structure, information, numbers of agents and commodities, and so forth. In partial equilibrium models such as the simple consumption model above, markets are assumed to be isolated from one another and there is often (largely implicit) aggregation, as in the assumption above that there are only two commodities. General equilibrium models avoid such isolating and aggregating assumptions and attempt to deal with the general interdependence of markets – although truly heroic assumptions are needed for the exercise. In any case, both partial and general equilibrium models are *augmentations* of the basic equilibrium model, which are designed to enable one to come to terms with specific practical or theoretical questions (Green 1981).

In locating the broader theoretical structure implicit in specific neoclassical theories and models, I am following a number of philosophers of science, who over the past two decades have come to appreciate the importance of general frameworks or "paradigms" or "research programmes" or "research traditions" in science (Kuhn 1970, Lakatos 1970, and Laudan 1977 are three well-known examples). In Thomas Kuhn's language, one might call equilibrium theory "the neoclassical paradigm." Or, if one prefers Imre Lakatos's way of putting things, one might consider equilibrium theory to be the "hard core" of the "neoclassical research programme."

But I do not think that it is helpful to rely on either Kuhn's or Lakatos's frameworks. Kuhn's notion of a paradigm is notoriously ambiguous and easily lends itself to an unreasonably irrationalist view of scientific development and change. Lakatos's account is not as ambiguous, but two interesting difficulties arise in attempting in assimilate my discussion of equilibrium theory to Lakatos's views. First, Lakatos sees theoretical development in science as a process of constructing (in accordance with the "positive heuristic" of a research programme) more precise and adequate specific theories which incorporate the same hard core (1978, pp. 50–51, 66–67). But after theorists master equilibrium theory, they devote their efforts to reformulating *it* and to applying it to particular problems, with various allowances or auxiliary assumptions (see Mill 1836, p. 327; Hausman 1981c, secs. 1, 2). Specific theories in economics tend to be direct and provisional applications of equilibrium theory.

The second reason why equilibrium theory ought not to be regarded as a Lakatosian hard core is that although it is the core of neoclassical economics, it is not hard. Its components have frequently been reformulated. Moreover, in particular studies neoclassical theorists may replace almost any constituent of equilibrium theory with sharply different alternatives. One finds, for example, neoclassical theories with satiation or with increasing returns to scale. Much more flexibility is permissible and, indeed, desirable, than Lakatos's talk of a hard core permits. In addition, the borderline between those claims that are fundamental to neoclassical theory and those that are not is neither sharp nor unchanging. Simplifications concerning information, market structure, etc., matter to the identity of neoclassical economics.

Let me now bring together my comments concerning models and theories and my comments concerning the fundamentals of neoclassical economics. In tackling particular problems, neoclassical economists begin with the basic "laws" of equilibrium theory. They may prefer to think of them merely as ubiquitous assumptions, but they are employed because economists believe that there is a good deal of truth to them. Combining those assumptions with various simplifications and specifications concerning the relevant circumstances, economists develop specific models. The process of model construction can be a challenging one, calling for considerable ingenuity and mathematical ability. But before one can make use of a model for specific explanatory or predictive purposes, one must have reason to believe that it applies to the relevant bit of the real world. And therein lie the tangled problems of theory assessment in economics.

It is entirely proper for theorists to be interested in model building, in constructing and investigating a conceptual apparatus to grasp economic reality. But in thus separating questions concerning their apparatus from questions concerning its applications, theorists neither answer nor ultimately avoid the problems of application and assessment. The worth of neoclassical economics depends on the adequacy of its fundamental laws and on the validity of the specific *theories* that incorporate them.

3

John Stuart Mill's philosophy of economics

John Stuart Mill regards economics as an inexact and separate science which employs a deductive method. This paper analyzes and restates Mill's views and considers whether they help one to understand philosophical peculiarities of contemporary microeconomic theory. The author concludes that it is philosophically enlightening to interpret microeconomics as an inexact and separate science, but that Mill's notion of a deductive method has only a little to contribute.

John Stuart Mill's reflections on the nature of economic theory and on the manner in which it is to be justified have not received the attention they deserve. Although Mill's views are problematic, they have much to contribute to current thinking about the methodology of economics. Mill offers philosophical interpretations of the nature and justification of economic theory in three main places: in Book VI of *A System of Logic,* in his earlier essay, "On the Definition of Political Economy and the Method of Investigation Proper to It," and, less explicitly, in scattered passages of his *Principles of Political Economy* and of his other essays on economics. The relationship of the actual economic theorizing Mill did in the *Principles* to his philosophical construal of the nature of economic theory is complicated and will not be discussed in this essay (see Keynes 1917, pp. 19–20). Mill's views on the nature of economics differ somewhat among and within these sources. These differences will be discussed briefly where relevant. My goal is not, however, to give a detailed reading of the texts. I hope rather to provide an interesting and accurate philosophical reconstruction of Mill's remarks – to translate and interpret his views that they may be of use in current discussions.

Mill's view, in a nutshell, is that economics is an inexact and separate science that employs a deductive method. Spelling out what this claim means brings one a long way in understanding the peculiarities of current microeconomics and equilibrium theories. In the claim are three different assertions – that economics is an inexact science, that it is a separate science, and that it employs a deductive method. In the following three sections I analyze these claims. In section 4 I

I have benefited greatly from discussing the issues considered in this paper with Margaret Atherton, Lindley Darden, Philip Ehrlich, Isaac Levi, Sidney Morgenbesser, Robert Schwartz, and Frederick Suppe. Conrad Johnson, Catherine Kautsky, Alexander Rosenberg, Dudley Shapere, Allen Stairs, and Paul Thagard read earlier drafts and offered helpful advice and criticism. Anonymous reviewers for this journal offered some useful criticism. The support of the National Science Foundation (Grant #SES 8007385) is gratefully acknowledged.

suggest that these claims are largely correct and insightful as interpretations of current equilibrium theories and that they have much to contribute to current debates about the justification of economic theory.

1. ECONOMICS AS AN INEXACT SCIENCE

After discussing difficulties concerning social science to which free will supposedly gives rise, Mill begins the argument of Book VI of his *Logic* by distinguishing between exact and inexact sciences. In an inexact science

the only laws as yet accurately ascertained are those of the causes which affect the phenomenon in all cases, and in considerable degree; while others which affect it in some cases only, or, if in all, only in a slight degree, have not been sufficiently ascertained and studied to enable us to lay down their laws, still less to deduce the completed law of the phenomenon, by compounding the effects of the greater with those of the minor causes. (6.3.1)[1]

The example Mill gives is the science of tides. Scientists know the laws of the greater causes, the gravitational pull of the sun and the moon, but are ignorant of the laws of the minor causes like the configuration of the shore and ocean bottom. One might suggest that there are no exact sciences,[2] although in some cases – for some purposes – the inexactness of a science may be negligible. Mill, however, believes that astronomy is an exact science,

because its phenomena have been brought under laws comprehending the whole of the causes by which the phenomena are influenced, whether in a great or only a trifling degree, whether in all or only in some cases, and assigning to each of those causes the share of the effect which really belongs to it. (6.3.1)

The model Mill has in mind when he speaks in the first quotation above of "compounding the effects" of causes is the vector addition of forces in mechanics. Mill draws an analogy between motives and forces and exploits it extensively. What are we to make of this notion of "compounding" the effects of causes (Cartwright 1980, pp. 78–80)? The answer, baldly stated (it will be discussed further in section 3), is that scientists so formulate laws that they are able to combine them in a theory from which precise consequences may be deduced.

Economics is not, however, an exact science. To provide a philosophical interpretation of economics, we need sensibly to construe the appealing idea that one may discover laws that state only how the "greater causes" operate. Possessing only such laws, scientists cannot infer invariably and precisely what actually

1 References in the form "(6.3.1)" will be to Mill's *Logic*. Read "6.3.1" for example, "Book VI, Chapter III, Section 1."

2 As Allen Stairs pointed out to me, fundamental theories like Newton's theory of motion or quantum mechanics raise different questions to which this paper may not supply any answers. Given Mill's definition, I do not believe that there could be any exact sciences.

occurs. There will be various "disturbing causes" (1836, pp. 330–32). The lawlike statements in an inexact science are thus themselves inexact or incomplete. Claims like "The preferences of consumers are transitive" are certainly (at best) inexact or incomplete. How are we to analyze them? How are we to make more precise the idea that scientists only know how some of the more important causes operate? How can we defend such knowledge claims?

When Mill talks about "an inexact science," he is not concerned with every science from which only inaccurate or imprecise implications may be drawn. It may happen that knowledge of the relevant causes is complete, yet one remains unable to make accurate predictions or to explain in detail because of difficulties in specifying the initial conditions or because of limitations in human mathematical powers. Despite the fact that the science of tides may, in fact, be a better example of inexactness due to such difficulties in specifying initial conditions or calculating their effects, Mill is concerned with inexactness *within laws*. I shall only be discussing sciences which are inexact because their laws are in some way not fully adequate.

I can think of five ways of analyzing the lawlike statements of inexact sciences. Most of these have some support in Mill's text. They are (i) that the generalizations in inexact sciences are approximate; (ii) that the generalizations are probabilistic or statistical; (iii) that the generalizations are "rough"; (iv) that the generalizations make modal or counterfactual assertions; and (v) that the generalizations of inexact sciences are qualified with implicit *ceteris paribus* clauses. The last interpretation is, I shall argue, most faithful to Mill's pronouncements in *A System of Logic*. The fourth interpretation better represents his views in "On the Definition of Political Economy. . . ." Mill's later view of laws in inexact sciences, as implicitly qualified with *ceteris paribus* clauses, seems to me a promising interpretation of current economic theory.

(i) Approximate generalizations

The first interpretation of inexactness as involving *approximation* is quite simple. Sometimes lawlike claims are made which are not true as stated, but which can be made true merely by specifying a margin of error in a certain domain. Kepler's Laws are in this sense approximate. Within a certain percentage of the calculated angular velocities or periods of revolution, these laws appear to be *true*.[3] By "smearing" what the laws assert, we achieve literally true propositions.

Mill, however, never interprets the laws of inexact sciences as true within a margin of error. Moreover, in fact only a small part of the inexactness of economic generalizations is a matter of approximation. Suppose in a recession it maximizes

3 There are also implicit *ceteris paribus* clauses involved. If a comet collided with Venus and changed its orbit, scientists would not regard Kepler's Laws as falsified.

profit for several companies each to lay off 1000 workers. If no company laid off fewer than 800 or more than 1200, then the evidence would confirm (within a margin of error of 20%) that firms attempt to maximize profits. Economic behavior is, however, more complicated. One can reduce the disconfirmations of economic generalizations by specifying a margin of error, but the bulk of the inexactness remains. Some firms feel responsible for their employees and might refuse to lay off any of them.

(ii) Probabilistic or statistical generalizations

Many economists have regarded the basic general statements of economics as probabilistic or statistical laws (see, for example, Hicks 1946, p. 11). There is, however, little support in Mill's writing for this construal and several considerations count against it. To regard economic laws (and indeed all empirical laws) as probabilistic, as Peter McClelland does (1975, ch. 1), is to confuse the results of testing with what laws assert. The fundamental general statements of economics do not appear to involve elements of chance or randomness. They are not stated statistically. They say nothing about the statistical distributions of properties. These generalizations merely appear to have counterexamples. To construe all generalizations that face counterexamples as probabilistic is merely to rechristen them. It may be that, unable to account for the inexactness of the basic laws of economics in any other way, one will eventually conclude that they are inadequately stated and understood statistical laws. Before coming to this negative conclusion one should, however, consider the other options.

(iii) Rough generalizations

Mill suggests on several occasion that some of the laws of inexact sciences are rough generalizations, reasonably, but not perfectly reliable (compare Rescher 1970, pp. 164–67). As I am using the term, a rough generalization is not a law, because it is not true. It is simply a generalization that faces some counterexamples, but not so many that one learns nothing from it. Mill believes that many of the "*empirical laws*" of the social sciences are merely rough generalizations. Indeed, he suggests that this is all we can hope for:

All propositions which can be framed respecting the actions of human beings as ordinarily classified, or as classified according to any kind of outward indications, are merely approximate. We can only say, most persons of a particular age, profession, country, or rank in society have such and such qualities; . . . (3.23.3)

Since rough generalizations are false, their explanatory power is dubious. Interpreting the laws of inexact sciences as merely for-the-most-part true leads one to question their adequacy. Mill recognizes this and should, I think, be interpreted as asserting *only* that the *empirical* laws of inexact sciences – those generalizations of inexact sciences which are in need of explanation – are rough generalizations. Mill believes, I think, that even in inexact sciences we can find causal laws, which are not thus "rough" (although informing us of "tendencies" only) to explain our (rough) empirical laws. Yet his claims are ambiguous:

This science of Ethology may be called the Exact Science of Human Nature; for its truths are not, like the empirical laws which depend on them, approximate generalizations but real laws. It is, however, (as in all cases of complex phenomena,) necessary to the exactness of the propositions that they should be hypothetical only, and affirm tendencies, not facts. (6.5.4)

This quotation apparently supports the view that in inexact sciences we have only rough generalizations. Yet Mill cannot believe that ethology (the science of formation of character) is an exact science. It is, as he concedes (6.5.6), hardly as yet a science at all. He would not maintain that social scientists know that laws of the minor as well as the greater causes and can compound them correctly. Nor can he mean that the truths of ethology can only be "real laws" when ethology becomes an exact science, since he goes on in the same passage to write:

It is a scientific proposition that bodily strength tends to make men courageous; not that it always makes them so: that an interest on one side of a question tends to bias the judgment; not that it invariably does so: that experience tends to give wisdom; not that such is always its effect. These propositions, being assertive only of tendencies, *are not the less universally true* because the tendencies may be frustrated. (6.5.4) [my emphasis]

What Mill means, I think, although he expresses himself badly, is that in inexact sciences one can come up with causal laws which "being assertive only of tendencies are not the less universally true." Inexact sciences need not consist of rough generalizations only. "Tendencies" are the genuine regularities which inexact laws express. The science of tides is an inexact science, although neither the law of gravitation nor the fundamental laws of tidology which are derived from it are rough. Mill writes:

. . . there is no reason that it [the science of human nature] should not be as much a science as Tidology is. . . .
. . . But in order to give a genuinely scientific character to the study, it is indispensable that these approximate generalisations, which in themselves would amount only to the lowest kind of empirical laws, should be connected deductively with the other laws of nature from which they result. . . . In other words, the science of Human Nature may be said to exist in proportion as the approximate truths which compose a practical knowledge of mankind can be exhibited as corollaries from the universal laws of human nature on which they rest, whereby the proper limits of those approximate truths would be shown,

37

and we should be enabled to deduce others for any new state of circumstances, in anticipation of specific experience. (6.3.2)

Mill begins here writing just what I take him to mean. The "science of Human Nature" is at present inexact and is likely to remain inexact for a long while. It is nevertheless a science insofar as its rough empirical laws can be connected deductively to genuine universal laws of human nature. Yet near the end he suggests that connecting the rough empirical laws of human nature with the genuine underlying laws would enable scientists "to deduce others for any new state of circumstances, in anticipation of specific experience." Notice, however, that if scientists can do this precisely and correctly, they have an exact, not an inexact science. Can Mill mean this? Surely one can show that certain rough generalizations are corollaries of "the universal laws of human nature" within an *inexact* science. Although much in Mill's text suggests that he takes the laws of inexact science to be rough generalizations, I doubt that he regards *the fundamental explanatory laws* of such sciences as merely such rough generalizations. The possibility of developing inexact sciences deductively, which Mill stresses, demands that the fundamental laws be more than rough generalizations. Mill does not locate the inexactness of sciences in the roughness of their laws.

(iv) Model or counterfactual laws

Like many others (Schumpeter 1954, pp. 1049–50n; Gibbard and Varian 1978, esp. pp. 673ff), Mill sometimes explains the inexactness of economic laws by arguing that these "laws" state how things *would be were* certain conditions met. They do not describe actual regularities. When one attempts to use them to discover how things are, one is sometimes led astray. When the hypothetical conditions implicit in the laws are not met, things are necessarily the way the laws say they would be. This counterfactual view of the inexact "laws" of economics is pronounced in Mill's, "On the Definition of Political Economy. . . ." He writes there:

The conclusions of Political Economy, consequently, like those of geometry, are only true as the common phrase is, *in the abstract;* that is, they are only true under certain suppositions in which none but general causes – causes common to the *whole class* of cases under consideration – are taken into the account.

. . . They would be true without qualification, only in a case which is purely imaginary. In proportion as the actual facts recede from the hypothesis, he [the economist] must allow a corresponding deviation from the strict letter of his conclusion; otherwise it will be true only of things such as he has arbitrarily supposed, not of such things as really exist. That which is true in the abstract, is always true in the concrete with proper *allowances*. When a certain cause really exists, and if left to itself would infallibly produce a certain

38

effect, that same effect, *modified* by all the other concurrent causes, will correctly correspond to the result really produced. (1836, pp. 326–27)

What are we to make of the claim (which Mill does not repeat in the *Logic*) that the conclusions of political economy are true "in the abstract"? What does he mean by claiming that the conclusions of the political economist will without qualification "be true only of things such as he has arbitrarily supposed, not of such things as really exist"? Mill can, I think, be read as suggesting that economic theories are "modal models" — that they are accounts of the relationships obtaining between certain possible entities in possible circumstances[4] (see Suppe 1974, 1976). They are thus not true, without allowances, of anything (real).

This position requires clarification. First, it should be carefully distinguished from the claim that economics contains *idealizations*. The proposition that L^* is ideal or contains idealizations is logically independent of the proposition that L^* is a modal or counterfactual claim. Roughly following Shapere (1969; see for example pp. 140–41), I regard an entity or property as ideal which scientists find useful to mention in stating or developing their theories, even though the existence of such entities or properties is conclusively ruled out by accepted knowledge. Ideal claims mention ideal entities or properties and are known to be false. Economics contains some ideal claims (*pace* Rosenberg 1976, p. 133). The assertion made in various general equilibrium theories that agents have perfect knowledge of the future is one example. This assertion may not conflict with any well-established scientific theory, but scientific theories are not, of course, the only source of knowledge. On the other hand, none of the purported *laws* of economics are ideal. Perhaps nobody's preferences are transitive, but that would be just chance. Given current knowledge, transitive preferences are perfectly possible.

Talk of idealizations thus does not contribute to understanding purported *laws* in economics. Indeed, even if some purported laws of economics were ideal, this fact would help little in understanding and rationalizing their inexactness. Whether a theory contains idealizations is a relatively superficial fact about it. When one finds that a theory contains idealizations, as many do, one has merely uncovered a problem requiring further analysis. Ideal statements are false. It is not clear how a theory which contains such false statements can still have explanatory power.

The modal interpretation of purported (inexact) laws is one attempt to explain how statements which are literally false (and in the case of idealizations necessarily so) can nevertheless be regarded as laws. In deriving the ideal gas law, physicists talk about volumeless point particles, which they know do not exist. This deriva-

---

4 I am construing the modal interpretation realistically. This paper is written from a realist perspective. Translating my points into the language of a noncognitive instrumentalist (see Morgenbesser 1969, p. 202) would change the discussion of the modal view considerably.

tion thus contains an idealization. The interesting question is what to make of it. The modal view asserts that the derivation shows how a collection of such non-existent point particles would behave. According to the modal view, the antecedent of the ideal gas law is not satisfied by any real gas.

It is also crucial to distinguish the substantial thesis that economic theories make modal claims from the obvious fact that economists work with *models* (see Suppes 1957, p. 254). Economists often take a set of axioms as defining a kind of system and investigate the logical implications of those axioms without considering whether the axioms are true (compare Giere 1979, ch. 5, esp. pp. 80–81). In his *Essays on Some Unsettled Questions of Political Economy* and again in the *Principles of Political Economy*, for example, Mill discusses the basic principles of international trade in the following way. First he employs a model of barter with no carrying costs between two nations (England and Germany) involving only two commodities (cloth and linen) (1844, pp. 232–61; 1871, pp. 584–96). These principles are then slightly modified by a consideration of some of the complexities initially assumed away. One can see what must be the case in the simple model and, from this, one can apparently understand what must, in essence, at least, be the case in messy actual economies. It might appear that economists are constantly developing modal models. But, in fact, there is no reason to infer from economists' incessant use of models like Mill's that they regard the axioms of such models as true of some possible economy. Perhaps they do, but they need not. In such models economists investigate the logical consequences of certain axioms or assumptions. If any way can be found to regard the axioms as inexactly true in real circumstances, the models can then be used to make inferences about those circumstances. The mere use of models does not imply that one is making modal claims.

Much of Mill's discussion is compatible with attributing to him the view that the laws of inexact sciences are modal claims. Consider the passage quoted at the beginning of this subsection or the way Mill writes in 6.9.2. R. P. Anschutz believes that this modal interpretation of inexact laws is Mill's settled view (1953, pp. 85–96, 118, 167). Yet, since Mill strongly endorses a Humean view of causation, he would be unhappy with an interpretation committing him to some sort of modal connective. Furthermore, Mill implicitly repudiates a modal interpretation of economic laws in the revisions of his views on the philosophy of economics for the *Logic*. In "On the Definition of Political Economy . . ." Mill is, as we have seen, willing to speak of "truth" in the abstract. In the *Logic*, Mill demands empirical verification for inexact laws.

(v) Implicitly qualified laws

On the last interpretation, the "laws" of inexact sciences carry with them implicit *ceteris paribus* clauses. This interpretation seems to me most (but not perfectly) consistent with Mill's general philosophical position and with what he writes about inexact sciences (see Keynes 1917, pp. 217–21). It is also sensible and persuasive. Mill does not himself mention *ceteris paribus* clauses. The only sort of provisos or implicit qualifications he discusses are precisely specified exceptions or limits which, when added to approximate claims, enable one to treat them as exact (3.23.7). The range of different sorts of qualifications one might find appended to scientific claims makes the mere assertion that the laws of inexact sciences are implicitly qualified rather unhelpful. Much more needs to be said about these *ceteris paribus* qualifications.

In fact, even exact sciences might contain *ceteris paribus* clauses, were they fully eliminable in favor of precise qualification. The *ceteris paribus* clauses which render laws inexact are, however, imprecise and ineliminable. Is it sensible to regard statements so vaguely qualified as laws (see Hutchison 1938, pp. 40ff)? It is certainly not the case that, *ceteris paribus,* we are all immortal or that ravens are pink. Not all appeals to *ceteris paribus* qualifications to explain away apparent disconfirmations are legitimate. One who regards the laws of inexact sciences as vaguely qualified claims must distinguish legitimate from illegitimate uses of ineliminable *ceteris paribus* clauses. When, if ever, can sentences with ineliminable *ceteris paribus* clauses be true? When is one justified in regarding them as laws?

Mill has little to say about truth conditions for sentences containing ineliminable *ceteris paribus* clauses. Such sentences state what happens when certain not-fully-specified conditions are satisfied. We can capture this aspect formally most simply by regarding the *ceteris paribus* clause as picking out different predicates in different contexts. When a sentence with the form, "*Ceteris paribus,* (x) $(Fx \rightarrow Gx)$" is truly a law, it expresses an assertion with the form (x) $(Fx \& Cx \rightarrow Gx)$, where "$C$" is a vague predicate picked out by the *ceteris paribus* clause in the given context.[5] In sketching this view I am going beyond anything that Mill ever worked out, although the following comments seem to point in this direction:

They [laws affirming tendencies only] must not assert that something will always or certainly happen, but only that such and such will be the effect of a given cause, so far as it operates uncounteracted. (6.5.4)

Implicitly qualified laws assert what will happen when the predicate the *ceteris paribus* clause picks out is not unsatisfied and the law thus not counteracted.

Mill provides a more substantial discussion of the conditions qualified sentences should satisfy before one is justified in regarding them as laws. The question, "When is one justified in regarding qualified (or, alternatively, counterfactual) assertions as laws?" is for many economists and philosophers the central philosophical question concerning economics. It is around this question that

5 I have benefited a great deal in this discussion from Levi and Morgenbesser (1964) and from conversations with the authors. They do not fully agree with my conclusions.

methodological controversy concerning economics has turned. Mill suggests that a sentence (S) can justifiably be regarded as a law only when the following three conditions are satisfied:

(i) S is lawlike.

(ii) When one removes the vague qualifications in S, S is in some "natural" class of cases often confirmed and seldom disconfirmed.

(iii) Scientists have some knowledge of the interfering factors that violate the *ceteris paribus* condition in S.

The restriction of *ceteris paribus* clauses to lawlike statements is suggested in Mill's concern with the operation of causes. Philosophers have found lawlikeness a difficult property to analyze (see, for example, Hempel and Oppenheim 1948, §6; Hempel 1965, pp. 338–47). I know of no good solution to the well-known philosophical difficulties here, but I do not believe that those difficulties should lead philosophers and scientists to abandon the notion of lawlikeness. The fact remains that scientists can discriminate lawlike from accidental generalizations.

Condition (ii) restates Mill's view that in an exact science scientists only understand the operation of the "greater" causes. It demands that each generalization be *reliable:* deleting its *ceteris paribus* clause and possibly adding some specific qualifications, the generalization is, within a certain class of cases, usually confirmed and seldom disconfirmed. The class of cases considered must be selected in some "natural" or independent way. The generalization that all rabbits are white is highly reliable in the class of white rabbits and quite reliable in the class of pet rabbits, but it does not satisfy condition (ii). I doubt whether much more in general can be said about how such classes are to be specified. Testing for reliability depends heavily on substantive (scientific) knowledge. Mill seems only to consider the case when the generalization is, without *any* qualifications, reliable – as, presumably, "greater" causes are. There is, however, no reason why scientists cannot seek or obtain knowledge of independently operating causes, even when these are not "greater."

Condition (iii) reformulates Mill's insistence that scientists have some knowledge of many causal factors operating, of which they do not yet know the laws, or to which they cannot assign any precise contribution to the net effect. This further knowledge would be empty if it were not possible to "refine" S and to "excuse" S. To refine S is to change or qualify S in such a way that it is reliable in a larger class of cases or more reliable in the same class. To excuse S is to explain away its apparent disconfirmations (compare Rescher 1970, p. 172). Mill is quite specific:

But if our deductions have led to the conclusion that from a particular combination of causes a given effect would result, . . . and where the effect has not followed, we must be able to show (or at least to make a probable surmise) what frustrated it: if we cannot, the theory is imperfect, and not yet to be relied upon. (3.11.3)

These justification conditions are, I believe, plausible and sensible. They seem a reasonable formulation of the implicit criteria by which scientists and laymen assess the legitimacy of invoking *ceteris paribus* clauses to explain away apparent disconfirmations. Unless a generalization meets these three conditions, one cannot reasonably regard it as a law.

Although Mill addresses the problem of justifying inexact laws most explicitly in the *Logic*, where he regards such laws as implicitly qualified, he is not unaware in his earlier essay, "On the Definition of Political Economy . . ." that such problems exist. In the earlier essay verification is needed to establish the applicability of the scientific conclusions, rather than their truth; but it is equally necessary. Are the problems of justification appreciably different when one adopts, as Mill does in his earlier essay, a counterfactual interpretation of inexact laws? I think not. Unless a generalization satisfies conditions very like the ones sketched above, one will not, *pace* the doctrine of "On the Definition of Political Economy . . . ," be justified in regarding it as a counterfactual law. The grounds for accepting a counterfactual law must be factual. Unless such a purported law possesses some reliability in this, the real world, and scientists are able to account for its apparent failures in this world, scientists are not justified in accepting the purported law as a law.

Is there then any important difference between interpreting inexact laws as qualified claims and regarding them as counterfactual assertions? There remain two differences. First, to regard inexact laws as implicitly qualified with *ceteris paribus* clauses is more modest metaphysically. It carries no explicit commitment to talk of possible worlds. Notice that if one is willing to talk of possible worlds, the qualified view entails the counterfactual view. If a generalization is true, with qualifications, in this world, it is true in that possible world in which those qualifications are always met.

The difference between the two interpretations of inexact laws is not exclusively metaphysical. Whether one regards inexact laws as qualified or counterfactual claims affects how one does science. The modal view creates an almost inevitable temptation to take characteristics of models seriously, even when one has no grounds to believe that the axioms are true (with qualifications) of anything real. Mill's discussion in "On the Definition of Political Economy . . ." is particularly instructive in this regard. He succumbs to this temptation, since he regards the theorems of economics as true "in the abstract" regardless of any observations of economic phenomena; yet he devotes a good part of "On the Definition . . ." to warning economists not to take such "abstract truth" (1836, p. 329) very seriously, unless it is verified! Consequently, the talk of "abstract truth" does not lead far. I am not denying that one can adopt a counterfactual interpretation of inexact laws, yet be entirely fastidious about the justification for such laws. Yet economists who interpret economic laws counterfactually too often console themselves unjustifiably in the face of unfavorable evidence with the conviction that they still possess the (counterfactual) truth. Confronted with apparent disconfirmations of their "laws," economists often comment that these "laws" are only guides to which concepts are central or accounts of how things *would* work out given perfect competition. Such claims require justification.[6] Insisting, as Mill does in the *Logic*,[7] that purported inexact laws are true only if they possess an unmysterious reliability is a good tonic for this carelessness.

Regarding the purported laws of economics as legitimately qualified in the above sense captures economists' conceptions of their own work. To assert that people's preferences are transitive or that the marginal utility of commodities is a diminishing function of the quantity possessed is to make a qualified claim. A change in tastes, for example, falsifies neither, since changes in tastes are ruled out by our implicit *ceteris paribus* clauses. Mill speaks of the "psychological law" "that a greater gain is preferred to a smaller." This "law" is relevant when the determining cause of action is the "desire of wealth." Mill is not claiming that people always prefer greater gains, but that this is one motivational "force" which often predominates in relevant circumstances. We should regard economists as telling us how real agents behave in the absence of various complications. The elaborate models which economists construct are intended to analyze the predominant factors that operate (although modified and sometimes counteracted by various complications) in real economic behavior.

Apparent failures of legitimately qualified lawlike claims are not falsifications, since one has the qualification to invoke as an excuse (see Rosenberg 1976, pp. 137–8). Yet this excuse must be deserved. In certain situations it must be invoked rarely, if at all. In others the excuse must be made specific. We can narrow the class of cases in which such an excuse is needed and make our excuse more specific by adding further predicates to the antecedents of our lawlike claims. This is one way in which we may "compound causes."[8]

The *ceteris paribus* clauses in our lawlike claims in economics remain ineliminable; not all of the operative causal factors are included. Economics is inexact. If

6   Weber's notion of an "ideal type" leads, in my opinion, to a similar carelessness. See Weber 1904, esp. p. 90.

7   I have not yet shown very adequately that Mill *does* insist in the *Logic* that inexact laws be verified before one can regard them as true. See the discussion of the deductive method in Section 3 below. In (6.9.1) Mill writes explicitly, "The ground of confidence in any concrete deductive science is not the *a priori* reasoning itself, but the accordance between its results and those of observation *a posteriori.*"

8   I am interpreting Mill's talk of "compounding causes" in two ways. One way that causes are compounded is by modifying a particular causal law, especially by adding to its antecedent. Another way is through deducing new causal relations from more than one law. The two interpretations of "compounding" are compatible with one another.

one managed to include all the lesser causes of economic phenomena, economics would merge with the other social sciences.

2. ECONOMICS AS A SEPARATE SCIENCE

According to Mill, economics is not only distinct from the other social sciences, but it is a "separate science." Mill writes:

Notwithstanding the universal *consensus* of the social phenomena, whereby nothing which takes place in any part of the operations of society is without its share of influence on every other part; . . . it is not the less true that different species of social facts are in the main dependent, immediately and in the first resort, on different kinds of causes; and therefore not only may with advantage, but must, be studied apart: . . . (6.9.3)

Mill is not asserting, trivially, that some social phenomena depend principally on a limited number of causal factors. Rather he is suggesting that a few causal factors are sufficient to account for at least the major features of a whole range of social phenomena. A full statement of Mill's view is the following:

There is, for example, one large class of social phenomena in which the immediately determining causes are principally those which act through the desire of wealth, and in which the psychological law mainly concerned is the familiar one that a greater gain is preferred to a smaller. I mean, of course, that portion of the phenomena of society which emanates from the industrial or productive operations of mankind, . . . By reasoning from that one law of human nature, and from the principal outward circumstances (whether universal or confined to particular states of society) which operate upon the human mind through that law, we may be enabled to explain and predict this portion of the phenomena of society, so far as they depend on that class of circumstances only, overlooking the influence of any other of the circumstances of society, . . .

It makes entire abstraction of every other human passion or motive, except those which may be regarded as perpetually antagonising principles to the desire of wealth, namely, aversion to labor, and desire of the present enjoyment of costly indulgences. (6.9.3)

Mill's vision of economics as a separate science consists of at least two assertions. First, since he believes that a single set of causal factors are "immediately determining" for "one large class of social phenomena," he believes that economics is a unified science. It would be extravagant to assert that a single theory serves *all* the explanatory and predictive purposes that economists have. Rather Mill means that a single theory accounts for all the major[9] economic phenomena and that much of economic theorizing consists in adding further auxiliary hypotheses

---

9 There is some circularity here, since the "major" economic phenomena are largely (but contra Stegmueller 1976, pp. 93, 176–77, *not* entirely) those which are central to the given theory. It is, of course, not obvious what counts as an "economic phenomenon." For more on these matters see Hausman 1981b, ch. 9, §2 and ch. 10, §2.

to that theory or making minor emendations in it, in order to account for more phenomena.

The second component of Mill's belief that economics is a separate science, is the conviction that economics is, within its own domain, complete. No explanatory or predictive purpose of economists would be served by fusing economics with any other science. Consider the following definition of economics, which is due to Mill's friend and disciple with respect to methodology, J. E. Cairnes. It suggests clearly the sense in which Mill believed economics to be complete. Political economy is defined by Cairnes "As the science which traces the phenomena of the production and distribution of wealth up to their causes, in the principles of human nature and the laws and events – physical, political, and social – of the external world" (1875, p. 71). According to this view, the explanatory task of economics is tracing economic phenomena to non-economic causal factors. What Mill and Cairnes have in mind, I think, is analogous to Mill's psychologism (see sec. 3 and footnote 12 below). The fundamental laws in economics cannot be explained within economics. They derive from psychological or natural scientific laws and specifications of economic circumstances. Unified and complete, economics is thus a separate science. The task of its practitioners is to apply the basic laws to particular problems.

The general idea that Mill is espousing is both appealing and relatively clear. If one can isolate the principal causal factors upon which production, distribution, and exchange depend, one can develop economics as an inexact science. One will then be able inexactly to explain and predict the principal economic phenomena. The results will not be exact, since Mill denies "that any political economist was ever so absurd as to suppose that mankind are really thus constituted" that they are only influenced by the desire for material gain (6.9.3). As a separate science, economics is necessarily inexact.

3. THE DEDUCTIVE METHOD

When an effect depends on a concurrence of causes, these causes must be studied one at a time, and their laws separately investigated, if we wish, through the causes, to obtain the power of either predicting or controlling the effect; since the law of the effect is compounded of the laws of all the causes which determine it. (6.9.3)

The talk of "compounding of the laws of all the causes" is crucial both to Mill's methodological views and to his actual economic theorizing. This compounding is, for Mill, largely a matter of deducing; and he argues that economics does and must follow a deductive method. Knowing that individuals seek wealth and that they tend to have many children, economists investigate deductively what follows from these tendencies in various situations given other plausible assumptions and simplifications. To some extent the deductive method is needed for all inexact sciences, since inexactness reveals a complexity of causal factors, which renders Mill's methods of induction inapplicable. [10] In inexact sciences the implications of theory will only agree with the results of experiment approximately for the most part. Inductive investigation will not be decisive. One will not have the sort of definite *proof*, which Mill believes that valid induction provides (3.2.4, 3.3.3, 3.9.6). Yet differences in degree here are significant. Unless we demand of induction the proof that Mill does, difficulties in theory construction and justification will only be acute in disciplines like economics where the correspondence between the data and the implications of theory is rough and complete failures are not infrequent. Since economic phenomena are the effects of numerous causes, many of which the theory does not deal with, we can expect nothing better. Yet, with only this sort of evidence, how could economists rationally come to construct their theories? What good reason do they have to accept them? Mill believes that we cannot answer these questions if we only consider how well the claims of economic theory are confirmed by observations of economic phenomena. Only the deductive method renders the construction of an economic theory reasonable and confidence in that theory justified.

By a deductive method Mill does not mean what others have meant by talking of a "hypothetico-deductive method." Mill calls the latter method the "hypothetical method" and is critical of it when it fails to prove its conclusions inductively (3.14.4–5). In insisting on the need for a deductive method, Mill is also not primarily concerned with how laws and theories are discovered. In discussing Whewell's views, Mill makes clear that his methods of induction, although they may serve the purposes of discovery, are most important for the justification of scientific claims (3.9.6). In discussing the need for a deductive method, Mill does sometimes sound as if he is criticizing induction as a method of discovery. He argues that theorists will lack solid inductive proof for economic generalizations and insists that the results of deductions be verified by empirical tests. Yet Mill is not maintaining that scientists create hypotheses rather than derive them from evidence. Quite the contrary – the deductive method is in part an account of how one can *derive* economic laws from evidence of a different kind. [11]

10 I doubt that Mill believes that inexact sciences demand that one employ the deductive method. His philosophical position implies this conclusion, since inexactness prevents inductive *proof*. Yet, if inexactness demands the deductive method, if follows that experimental sciences are all exact – which is surely an unacceptable implication. In the discussion below I shall challenge the claim that inexact sciences must employ a deductive method.

11 In one of the more confusing chapters in the *Logic* (6.8), Mill discusses what he calls the "geometric method" and contrasts it to the deductive, or "concrete" deductive method. Those who follow the geometric method do not allow for the "case of conflicting forces" (6.8.1). They suppose that each social phenomenon "results always from only one force, one single property of human nature" (6.8.1). Yet Mill concedes that the "Bentham School," against which the criticism is directed, applied their principles "with innumerable allowances. But it is not allowances

Mill's deductive method consists of three stages (3.11). In the first, one establishes certain laws by *induction*. Whether induction functions here as a method of discovery does not matter. First, for example, scientists induce the laws of mechanics and of gravitation. Second, they deduce the laws of tides from these fundamental laws and specifications of the relevant circumstances (which themselves may or may not be lawlike). Third, scientists must verify the deductive results. But notice that they are not testing the basic laws, just the validity of their inexact lawlike consequences concerning the tides. Since many causal factors are left out, one does not know without testing how accurate or reliable the theory of tides is. Mill concedes that the testing of inexact laws also to some extent tests the inductively established laws upon which they are based, but believes that the weight of such testing is generally slight (3.11.3). The more inexact the science, the less one can test its fundamental laws and the more one needs to develop it deductively on the basis of independently established laws borrowed from other disciplines. It is important to stress that for Mill induction and deduction are *not* contraries. What is opposed to deduction is experimentation (2.4.5). Deductive grounds for belief are all ultimately inductive. That evidence which supports (inductively) the premises of a deductive argument is the (inductive) basis for one's belief in the argument's conclusions (2.3.3).

In the case of economics, theorists first borrow basic lawlike assertions from the natural sciences or psychology (which Mill regards as an introspective experimental science). Then theorists develop economics deductively. Verification is important and unavoidable, but not in order to test the lawlike statements; borrowed from other sciences they are already established. In fact as I mentioned earlier, in his earlier essay, "On the Definition . . . ," Mill regarded resultant theorems concerning political economy also as true (in the abstract) regardless of what observation and experiment report (1836, pp. 325–26). The laws may turn out to be of no importance, but testing will never show that they are not laws, except by bringing to theorists' attention some mistake made either in the specific premises concerning the prevailing "outward" circumstances or in the deductions them-

that are wanted. There is little chance of making due amends in the superstructure of a theory for the want of sufficient breadth in its foundations" (6.8.3). Mill is trying to incorporate what he regards as the valid points in Macaulay's attack on James Mill's *Essay on Government* (see Mill 1873, pp. 121–22). Yet the philosophical point remains obscure to me. Mill is dissatisfied with the particular principles of the "Bentham School." I do not, however, see the methodological moral. R. P. Anschutz (1953, pp. 87–88), Alan Ryan (1974, pp. 89–91), and James Bonar (1893, pp. 243–44) assert that Mill holds that political economy employs the *geometrical* method. According to Ryan, Mill diagnoses the error his father and other Benthamites commit as applying the geometrical method to government, which, unlike political economy, cannot be studied separately. Ryan's interpretation make Mill's critique of the geometrical method sensible, but I cannot agree that Mill believes that political economy employs a geometrical method. Mill discusses the method of political economy in (6.9), entitled "Of the Physical, or Concrete Deductive Method" and shows, step by step, how the method of political economy matches the deductive method as outlined in (3.11).

selves. By the time he wrote the *Logic,* on the other hand, Mill is emphatic in insisting that deductively derived purported laws be verified in order to be counted as laws at all (3.9.3, 6.9.1).

Mill believes that the deductive method can be employed in economics because social phenomena are governed by "mechanical" laws. Mill distinguishes mechanical from chemical laws as follows:

> In the one [the case of mechanical laws], we can compute the effects of combinations of causes, whether real or hypothetical, from the laws which we know to govern those causes when acting separately, because they continue to observe the same laws when in combination which they observed when separate: whatever would have happened in consequence of each cause taken by itself, happens when they are together, and we have only to cast up the results. Not so in the phenomena which are the peculiar subject of the science of chemistry. (3.6.1)

The deductive method is applicable in economics, because theorists can "cast up the results" of the various causes when acting separately. Mill never justifies his claim that the phenomena of society are mechanical. In his view mechanical phenomena are the general rule in most domains (3.6.2). One can see how his own economic investigations would have made him confident that social phenomena are mechanical. In Chapter III of Book VI of the *Principles of Political Economy,* for one example ("Influence of the Progress of Industry and Population on Rents, Profits, and Wages"), he examines separately the effect on the development of an economy of an increase of capital (population and technology held constant), of an increase of population (capital and technology held constant), and a change in technology (capital and population held constant). He then, as it were, sums these three causal factors. The analogy to mechanics is palpable and persuasive. The conviction that social phenomena are mechanical is in essence what Karl Popper (1966, pp. 89–93) calls Mill's "psychologism."[12] Since laws governing social phenomena are mechanical, all fundamental laws in the social sciences must be psychological or, minimally, individualistic.

It should be stressed that the deductive development of economics (or of tidology) is not a matter of proving theorems with established laws as the only axioms. The premises of the deductions include as well a number of other stipulations or auxiliary hypotheses. Not only will these often be poorly established, but one will often know that some are great simplifications (and thus false). Furthermore, the existence of implicit *ceteris paribus* qualifications in the fundamental lawlike claims complicates matters. If one combines lawlike claims which are qualified with different *ceteris paribus* clauses, what sort of qualifications are the

---

12 Popper's critique of Mill's "psychologism" seems to me insensitive to Mill's thought and confused. Mill thought ethology (the science of the formation of character) to be the source of the fundamental causal laws of the social sciences. Popper's "situational logic" seems to me to treat social phenomena as, in Mill's sense, mechanical.

theorems supposed to carry? In the deductions, economists often simply ignore the implicit qualifications, which is tantamount to assuming that in the given case all things are in fact equal. But they seldom have much confidence in such an assumption.

The messiness of the "deduction" in the deductive method makes such a method of discovering and justifying scientific theories both more problematical and more interesting. One of the tasks of a logic of discovery (if there can be such a thing) is to lay bare the reasoning which makes plausible first attempts at scientific theories. The sort of wishy-washy deduction described above does make plausible what is deduced. If some economic claim can be shown to follow from more fundamental generalizations and auxiliary hypotheses which are reasonable approximations or simplifications, one has reason to take that claim seriously. Principles like Say's Law were embraced by economists on such grounds.

4. APPLICATION: JUSTIFYING CURRENT ECONOMIC THEORY

Much remains to be said about the adequacy of Mill's deductive method, but that discussion is best combined with an assessment of what Mill's views can contribute to current philosophical discussion concerning neoclassical economics. Mill's conception of economics as a separate science, although restrictive, is, I think, extremely helpful in interpreting the conceptual structure of the fundamental theory of current microeconomics and general equilibrium models and the strategy of neoclassical theorizing. This contention cannot, however, be well defended or even illustrated without extensive discussion of current economic theory, which I have provided elsewhere (Hausman 1981a) and which would be out of place here. Current equilibrium theory is intended to be both unified and complete in the senses discussed above in section 2. It is illuminating to regard it as a separate science (see Hausman 1981b, ch. 9, §2).

One need not, however, provide a detailed description of current economic theory in order to discuss whether it is helpful to regard economics, as Mill did, as an inexact science that employs (as it must) a deductive method. Philosophical discussion of economics has focused on one peculiarity of economic theory. The fundamental theory of microeconomics and of general equilibrium models seems simultaneously sophisticated, successful, bursting with explanatory power, and full of false statements. These false statements are not only simplifications or auxiliary hypotheses which enable economists to apply the fundamental "laws," but seem to include the fundamental "laws" themselves. We know full well not only that commodities are not infinitely divisible (which is only intended as a simplification), but that businessmen do not always attempt to maximize their profits and that the preferences of consumers are not always transitive. "Businessmen maximize profits" and "A consumer's preferences are transitive" are fundamental economic "laws." How can economists rationally accept a theory which is so full of falsehoods?

This is not the occasion to discuss the many answers which economists and philosophers have given to this last question. What I want to consider here is whether Mill's conceptions of inexact sciences and of the deductive method provide any solution to this problem of justification. I shall argue that Mill's conception of the laws of inexact sciences as implicitly qualified is a significant contribution. Mill's discussion of the deductive method, on the other hand, contributes only a little to understanding whether one is justified in regarding microeconomic theory as a good and well-confirmed scientific theory.

Many apparent difficulties with the "laws" of economics can be met by arguing that they contain legitimate implicit *ceteris paribus* clauses. Once we recognize that inexact sciences are perfectly respectable and, indeed, in my view, the best one can hope for in economics, some measure of apparent disconfirmation is only to be expected. Hedged, as they implicitly are, with *ceteris paribus* clauses, one can regard economic generalizations as laws despite apparent disconfirmations. No economist regards the generalization that consumer's preferences are transitive as falsified by a change in tastes. An entrepreneur who suddenly decides to give away the business and become a nun does not falsify the purported law that entrepreneurs attempt to maximize their profits. In each of these apparent disconfirmations, the *ceteris paribus* condition is violated.

Of course, not all uses of *ceteris paribus* clauses are intellectually defensible. We must go on to ask whether the "laws" of economics satisfy the justification conditions specified above. This question seems to me a difficult and unresolved empirical question. Except in restricted applications, I am dubious. If these conditions are not met, Mill's discussion of the legitimacy of inexact sciences may not contribute to the *defense* of microeconomics, although it may help us to understand its inadequacies.

Mill's discussion of the deductive method is not nearly as helpful. The deductive method is supposed to resolve difficulties in establishing the claims of inexact sciences. Yet, if the generalizations of an inexact science satisfy the justification conditions discussed above, the deductive method seems largely unnecessary. If one can come up with lawlike statements that are nearly always true in a certain natural class of circumstances and if one has some idea how to start filling in the implicit *ceteris paribus* qualifications, what need does one have of a deductive method? One does not have the sort of definitive inductive *proof* which Mill believes the science can achieve, but, in my view, one never has inductive evidence for any lawlike statement which is better in *kind* than this sort of evidence. To say this is not to deny that there are extremely important differences in *degree*. Nor is it to deny that deducing a given generalization from other statements which one has reason to accept provides additional confirmation for that generalization.

51

One might indeed argue that the deductive method can only be necessary when it cannot be applied. Crucial to Mill's notion of the deductive method is verification of the derived generalizations. But, if one can carry out this verification, what warrants the asymmetry between the claims of psychology, which Mill believes can be inductively established, and those of economics, which require the application of the deductive method?

Mill's deductive method thus has little to contribute to current philosophical discussions of the justification of microeconomic theory. Either the theory can meet the conditions for the legitimate use of *ceteris paribus* clauses, in which case Mill has provided a potent philosophical vehicle for defending current theory, or it cannot. The deductive method contributes little more. The inductively established "psychological laws" upon which theorists are supposed to base economic theory turn out to be unexciting platitudes about human beings (they do what they prefer) which, as is the common fate of platitudes, are not quite true anyway. At best, the deductive method points out that one can find further evidence for the claims of economics in everyday experience and casual introspection.

One should not, however, entirely discount the importance of Mill's deductive method in rationalizing the esteem in which current economic theory is held. Even if current microeconomics can pass the tests for the legitimate use of *ceteris paribus* clauses, it cannot pass them in all domains in which it is applied with the wide margin by which well-establisheed theories of physics pass. Apparent disconfirmations are frequent. Yet the explanatory power of the theory seems great. We could use further grounds for accepting such purported laws and further rationalizations for the confidence that we place in the explanations of the economist. Consider a generalization such as, "Other things being equal, when the price of a commodity C goes up, people will buy more of those commodities which are substitutes for C." My suggestion is that whether or not we believe that this generalization is a genuine law, we know from "psychology" (conceived introspectively as Mill conceived it) that there is a real causal connection between the increased price of C and the shift in consumption. Even if this connection cannot be captured (at least at present) in any unqualified universal generalization, we know that this is not merely an accidental correlation. Our ability to borrow this law from "psychology" or, more prosaically, to find support for it in our own experience, justifiably increases our confidence that this generalization is lawlike. The deductive method boosts in this way the explanatory power of inexact economic theory. Mill's deductive method thus has a modest contribution to make to current philosophical debate concerning microeconomic theory. It enables us to see how that theory can be explanatory, even if it only contains generalizations which, if true at all, require extensive qualifications.

Economists usually do not insist that their theories are as stated literally true.

Rather economic theories are supposed to be close to the truth — perhaps as close as their simplicity allows. Mill's conception of inexact sciences permits us to give a coherent philosophical construal of such a view. His notion of the deductive method helps rationalize the confidence economists place in their theories despite their empirical difficulties.

4

The deductive method

From the 1830s, when Nassau Senior (1836) and John Stuart Mill (1836) first wrote on economic methodology, until the 1930s, when positivist views become ascendent, there was a strong consensus among economists that economic methodology was in fact and ought to be deductive (see also, for example, Cairnes 1875 and Keynes 1917). The basic premises of economics – claims such as that people prefer more goods and services to fewer or the law of diminishing marginal utility – are established by introspection, casual experience, or direct test, and the rest of economics is then deduced from these established "laws" and descriptions of the particular material, institutional, and informational circumstances.

In the 1930s Lionel Robbins provided the following vivid statement of this view:

The propositions of economic theory, like all scientific theory, are obviously deductions from a series of postulates. . . . The main postulate of the theory of value is the fact that individuals can arrange their preferences in an order, and in fact do so. . . . These are not postulates the existence of whose counterpart in reality admits of extensive dispute once their nature is fully realized. We do not need controlled experiments to establish their validity: they are so much the stuff of our everyday experience that they have only to be stated to be recognized as obvious. (1935, 78–79)

J. J. Klant (1984, 56ff) aptly labels this view "empirical *a priorism*" (as opposed to the straight *a priorism* of von Mises [1981] and his followers). The basic "laws" are empirical, but they are so firmly established that the task of economics is merely to investigate their consequences.

1. THE INEXACT DEDUCTIVE METHOD

Let us look more carefully at this method of theory development and appraisal. John Stuart Mill provides the following general characterization and defense of the deductive method in science:

When an effect depends on a concurrence of causes, these causes must be studied one at a time, and their laws separately investigated, if we wish, through the causes, to obtain the

This paper is drawn from chapters 8 and 12 of my *The Inexact and Separate Science of Economics* 1992a. Many people have helped clarify my thinking on these issues. Neil de Marchi deserves special thanks. After writing this essay, I discovered two relevant discussions, Howson and Urbach 1989, 96–103, and Dorling 1979. I comment briefly on their views in my 1992a, p. 208.

power of either predicting or controlling the effect; since the law of the effect is compounded of the laws of all the causes which determine it. (1843, 6.9.3)

Note that "compounding of the laws of all the causes" is *deducing* the consequences of the concurrence of a plurality of causes.

By a deductive method Mill does *not* mean the hypothetico-deductive method, which he calls "hypothetical method" and which he criticizes, when it fails to prove its conclusions inductively (1843, 3.14.4–5). In insisting on the need for a deductive method, Mill is also not primarily concerned with how laws are *discovered*. Mill makes clear that his methods of induction are most important for the justification of scientific claims, although they may also serve the purposes of discovery (1843, 3.9.6). What distinguishes the deductive method is not that one creates hypotheses rather than derives them from evidence. Quite the contrary, the deductive method is in part an account of how one can *derive* economic laws from inductive evidence of a different kind.

Mill's deductive method consists of three stages (1843, 3.11). In the first, one establishes laws by *induction*. For example, scientists interested in tides induce the laws of mechanics and of gravitation, or borrow the results of the inductions of others. Good evidence for these laws comes from diverse sources, but little comes from complex phenomena such as tides. Second, scientists deduce the laws of tides from these fundamental laws and specifications of the relevant circumstances. Third, scientists must verify the deductive results. But notice that they are not testing the basic laws, just their (inexact) lawlike consequences concerning the tides. Mill argues that the verification of derived laws provides additional confirmation to the inductively established laws upon which they are based, but the possibility of disconfirmation is not even considered, and the evidential weight of such results is slight (1843, 3.11.3). The more complex the phenomena, the less one can study it directly and the more one needs to develop one's science deductively on the basis of laws that are independently established.

To make clearer the basic idea, let me give two further simple illustrations. Suppose *W* is sick, and we would like to know whether penicillin will help cure *W* (compare Mill 1843, 3.10.6). The empirical *a posteriori* method, or, as Mill calls it, the method of direct experience, would have us inquire whether others with symptoms resembling *W*'s recovered more often or more rapidly when given penicillin than when given nothing or a placebo. The deductive method or method *a priori* in contrast would have us draw upon our knowledge of the causes of *W*'s symptoms and on our knowledge of the operation of penicillin to decide whether penicillin will help cure *W*. Both methods are "empirical" and involve testing. The difference is that the former attempts to use experiment or observation to learn about the complex phenomenon directly, while the latter employs observation or experiment to study the relevant component causal factors. Similarly, one could determine empirically the range of an artillery piece directed at different angles with different wind conditions and atmospheric pressure. Or one could make use of the law of inertia, Galileo's law of falling bodies, and experimentally determined laws of air resistance to calculate the range. The latter deductive method is in Mill's view, the method of all advanced sciences, although, for practical applications, the method of direct experience is needed as a check on the deductive results.

Presented in conjunction with examples like those in the previous paragraph, the deductive method seems unobjectionable. One can get better evidence concerning the correctness of Galileo's law or the law of inertia from controlled experiments, in which the influence of other causal factors is almost absent, than from observations of the range of artillery pieces. So applications of these laws via the deductive method to complex phenomena test these laws only slightly. Notice that the laws clearly do not say what will inevitably happen, but only what *would* happen in the absence of other causal factors or what will happen *ceteris paribus*.

The application of the deductive method to economics is problematic, because, especially in contrast to the example of determining the range of the artillery piece, causal factors that are known to be significant are left out of the story. The inexactness is not negligible. Indeed Mill criticizes members of the "school of Bentham" (especially, by implication, his father, James Mill) for analogous "geometrical" theorizing about government. James Mill argued for representative government on the ground that individuals pursue their own interests and rulers in nonrepresentative governments will not have the same interests as those of the governed (1820). This account is, in the view of the younger Mill, not only empirically inadequate, but methodologically flawed, for it focuses on only one admittedly important causal factor and ignores many others. J. S. Mill writes:

They would have applied, and did apply, their principles with innumerable allowances. But it is not allowances that are wanted. . . . It is unphilosophical to construct a science out of a few of the agencies by which the phenomena are determined, and leave the rest to the routine of practice or the sagacity of conjecture. We either ought not to pretend to scientific forms, or we ought to study all the determining agencies equally, and endeavour, so far as it can be done, to include all of them within the pale of the science; else we shall infallibly bestow a disproportionate attention upon those which our theory takes into account, while we misestimate the rest, and probably underrate their importance. That the deductions should be from the whole and not from a part only of the laws of nature that are concerned, would be desirable even if those omitted were so insignificant in comparison with the others, that they might, for most purposes and on most occasions, be left out of the account. (1843, 6.8.3)

But when it comes to economics, John Stuart Mill apparently recommends just the methodological practice that he condemns in these remarks. For the correct method of including all of the "determining agencies" "within the pale of the science" is not feasible. Economists must set their sights lower and aim only at a *hypothetical* science of *tendencies* which is, in Mill's view, generally "insufficient for prediction" yet "most valuable for guidance" (1843, 6.9.3). Since in political economy "the immediate determining causes are principally those which act through the desire of wealth, . . ." (1843, 6.9.3), one can separate the subject matter of political economy from other social phenomena and theorize about political economy as if the desire for wealth were virtually the only relevant causal factor (see note 9 below).

Mill defends as follows this sort of partial deductive method, which so closely resembles the geometrical method of his father:

> The motive which suggests the separation of this portion of the social phenomena from the rest, and the creation of a distinct branch of science relating to them, is, that they do *mainly* depend, at least in the first resort, on one class of circumstances only; and that even when other circumstances interfere, the ascertainment of the effect due to the one class of circumstances alone is a sufficiently intricate and difficult business to make it expedient to perform it once for all, and then allow for the effect of the modifying circumstances; especially as certain fixed combinations of the former are apt to recur often, in conjunction with ever-varying circumstances in the latter class. (1843, 6.9.3)

The defenses Mill offers for employing this partial or inexact deductive method thus seem to be (1) practical, that there is no alternative, (2) metaphysical, that, although the results are only hypothetical the same causal influences persist even when there are other disturbing causes, and (3) pragmatic, that this is an efficient way of theorizing and that more order can be found this way than in any other.[1]

In the case of economics, theorists first borrow basic "laws" from the natural sciences or psychology (which Mill regards as an introspective experimental science). One tests the fundamental laws upon which economics is constructed on *other* phenomena where there are fewer disturbances or interferences. Then theorists develop economics deductively. Verification is essential, but not in order to test the basic laws; they are already established and could hardly be cast in doubt by the empirical vicissitudes of a deduction from a partial set of causes.

It should be stressed that the deductive development of economics is not a matter of proving theorems with nothing but established laws and true descriptions of the relevant circumstances as premises. The premises of the deductions include as well a number of other stipulations or auxiliary hypotheses, such as assertions that agents have perfect knowledge or that there are only two commodities in the economy. These often are poorly established, even known to be false.

The messiness of the "deduction" in the inexact deductive method as it is applied in economics makes such a method of discovering and justifying scientific

---

1 Surely much the same argument could have been given by Mill's father in his own defense. There is an irony here in the fact that recent extensions of neoclassical economic models to political phenomena recapitulate (although more subtly) the account of political behavior presented by James Mill. See, for example, Buchanan (1975; 1979).

theories both problematic and interesting. One task of a weak logic of discovery is to lay bare the reasoning which makes plausible first attempts at scientific theories, and deduction from somewhat plausible premises does make what is deduced plausible (Nooteboom 1986). If an economic claim can be shown to follow from more fundamental generalizations and auxiliary hypotheses, which are reasonable approximations or simplifications, one has reason to take that claim seriously. Principles such as Say's Law have been embraced by economists on such grounds.

It might be argued that the partial deductive method can do no more than help make economic hypotheses initially plausible. For, as Mill stresses (because of the *ceteris paribus* clauses in the basic laws and the other simplifications), the deduced implications must themselves be confirmed, and it might be contended that whether or not they are confirmed, the fact that they were deduced from inductively established laws (and various simplifications) seems irrelevant. Either way our confidence in the implications would depend on the extent to which they were confirmed.[2]

But this dismissal of the inexact or partial deductive method would be unjustified. There are degrees of confirmation and degrees of belief. Our confidence in generalizations such as those concerning market demand and supply may be rationally increased by showing that they can be derived from the inexact fundamental laws of the theory of consumer choice and various specifications of relevant circumstances. The general strategy of developing models that incorporate independently credible laws provides the implications of those models with a certain credibility in advance of and apart from any testing of them.

To sharpen the discussion, let us then formulate a schema, Table 1, expressing the broad outlines of the deductive, or *a priori* method, as it may have been conceived by Mill to apply to economics. Qualifications will be needed later, but at this point a bold formulation will provide a useful focus.

I have added the parenthetical "inexact" in order to stress the fact that the deductive method need not leave out significant causal factors, as it inevitably will in economics. Indeed Mill regards this method as something of a cheat. The true deductive method will rely only on facts and causes, not on simplifications. I have left out the "proving" of the laws concerning relevant causal factors, which Mill takes to be the first step of the deductive method, because I want to focus on the tasks of economists, who are concerned with applying psychological and technical laws, not with establishing them. Formulating the deductive method in this way also helps to make clear how this method differs from the hypothetico-deductive method. The differences are in step 1, where one begins with proven (but inexact) laws rather than mere hypotheses to be tested, and in step 4. Since

---

2   I suggested this in a confused discussion of these points (1981c, 383) [this volume, p. 52]. I did not make clear that one employs the deductive method to justify the implications of the inductively derived fundamental laws, not to justify those laws themselves.

Table 1. *The (inexact) deductive method*

1. *Borrow* proven (*ceteris paribus*) laws concerning the operation of relevant causal factors.
2. *Deduce* from these laws and statements of initial conditions, simplifications, etc., predictions concerning relevant phenomena.
3. *Test* the predictions.
4. *Judge* (a) whether there is any mistake in the nonlaw premises in the deduction, (b) what sort of interferences occurred, (c) how central the borrowed laws are (how major the causal factors they identify are), and whether the set of borrowed laws should be expanded or contracted.

the laws are already established, they are not open to question in this judgment step. Apart from discovering the logical errors in the deduction, all that is open to assessment are the sufficiency and accuracy of the other premises and the extent of the "coverage" provided by the borrowed laws.

Knowing that individuals seek wealth and that they tend to have many children, economists in Mill's day investigated deductively what follows from these tendencies in various circumstances. The deductive method is needed for all sciences, whether exact or inexact, in which the complexity of causal factors renders inductive methods such as Mill's inapplicable. In inexact sciences the implications of theory will, moreover, only agree with the results of experiment approximately for the most part.

2. QUALMS

During the past half century, most of those concerned with economic methodology have found something fishy or fraudulent in Mill's and Robbins's tolerant attitude toward inexact fundamental laws and their frequently disconfirmed consequences. For it seems that, on Mill's and Robbins's view, evidence can only confirm theory or show that there is some interference. There seems to be no real possibility of empirical criticism and, thus, no real empirical justification for the theory. In the judgment step, no judgment of the laws themselves is permitted.

Mill's inexact deductive method has been subject to logical, methodological, and practical criticisms. The logical criticism maintains that statements that are vaguely qualified with *ceteris paribus* clauses are scientifically illegitimate because they cannot be conclusively refuted by empirical testing (Hutchison 1938, ch. 2). As I have argued at length elsewhere (1992a, chs. 8 and 9), this criticism is misconceived. Not only is the methodological demand that scientific claims be conclusively verifiable or falsifiable untenable, but one can give truth conditions for inexact claims qualified with *ceteris paribus* clauses, and one can defend conditions for distinguishing when one is justified in accepting such generalizations (Hausman 1981b, pp. 120–33 and 1992a, ch. 8; Kincaid 1989).

The methodological criticism maintains that the rules implicit in the deductive method are unacceptably dogmatic (de Marchi 1970; 1986). In particular it may plausibly be argued that one ought not to regard the basic laws as proven or to refuse ever to regard unfavorable test results as disconfirming them. Adhering to the deductive method thus, it is alleged, impedes the progress of economics and leads to the sort of *ad hoc* response to apparent disconfirmation characteristic of a degenerating research program.

Furthermore, methodological vice is alleged to lead to practical impotence. The practical criticism maintains that by regarding apparent disconfirmations as inevitably the result of some disturbing cause, the inexact deductive method winds up justifying theories that cannot be of any practical use (Friedman 1953c). For policy purposes we need to know what *will* happen, not what *would* happen in the absence of disturbing causes.

These are serious criticisms, and indeed, since the early 1940s, the only extended defenses of the traditional view of justification in economics have been I. M. W. Stewart's (1979), mine, and (usually on the basis of an anti-empiricist epistemology) that of the Austrian school (Dolan 1976). There has been a dramatic revolution in theorizing about economic methodology, which has led to a repudiation of the inexact deductive method in precept, although, interestingly, not in practice.[3] Perhaps methodological practice in economics is overdue for a major overhaul, but first let us look again at that practice to see whether it is as mistaken as has been asserted.

Can the methodological and practical objections be answered? Can something like the inexact deductive method and the existing methodological practice in microeconomics be defended? Can the apparent dogmatism be tempered or justified? Do economists disregard apparent disconfirmations? Must they fail to learn from experience? Can the method of discovery and appraisal employed by economists make it rational to rely on economic theories for policy purposes?

3. APPARENT DOGMATISM AND THE THEORY OF CONSUMER CHOICE

Although I shall argue that the methodological rules of the inexact deductive method as presented in Table 1 cannot be defended, I shall nevertheless defend

---

3 I have no systematic argument in support of this assertion, and I am not claiming that all branches of economics display the same methodology. In a decade of presenting this view to a large, but scarcely random sample of economists, I have found little disagreement with the contention that the practice of microeconomics still *appears to* conform closely to Mill's deductive method.

the existing practices of theory assessment among economists. These practices appear to be consistent with the inexact deductive method, but they are, I shall contend, also consistent with the recommendations of standard methods of theory appraisal given the particular circumstances with which economists have to cope. Although apparent Millians in practice, economists can be good Bayesians or hypothetico-deductivists in principle.[4] Given the task economists face, Bayesian and hypothetico-deductivist confirmation theories recommend confirmational practice that is almost indistinguishable from what Mill's inexact deductive method recommends. The methodological practice of economists may be defensible, even though the inexact deductive method is indefensible, and economists appear to conform to it.

To make this discussion concrete, let us focus on the standard theory of consumer choice, for its basic generalizations or behavioral postulates are both simple and revealing. Consumer choice theory is made up of the following five "laws":

(1) (Completeness or comparability) Given any agent A and options x and y, either A prefers x to y or A prefers y to x or A is indifferent between x and y.

(2) (Transitivity) Given any agent A and options x, y, and z, if A prefers x to y and y to z, then A prefers x to z.

(3) (Utility maximization) Among the feasible or attainable options, an agent A chooses x if and only if A does not prefer any other option y to x.

(4) (Nonsatiation) For all agents A and all commodity bundles b and c, A prefers b to c if and only if b is larger than c.

(5) (Diminishing marginal utility) For all agents A, the amount by which an additional unit of a commodity or service t increases A's utility is a decreasing function of the amount of t that A possesses.

This characterization is rough and oversimplified in many ways. The notion of "larger" with respect to bundles or vectors of commodities or services needs spelling out. Contemporary economics is committed to diminishing marginal rates of substitution rather than diminishing marginal utility. Standard economic presentations do not distinguish sharply, as I have, between preference and choice. Weaker claims (such as acyclicity in place of transitivity) are sufficient in certain contexts. These claims must be supplemented by a continuity or closure axiom in order to entail the existence of a continuous utility function for individuals (where utility is simply an ordinal index of preference ranking: Debreu 1959, 54–59; Harsanyi 1977, ch. 3). But these and many other questions are not for

---

4 Mill might agree with my critique of what I have formulated as the inexact deductive method. It is, in my view, more consistent with the text to attribute to Mill the view that the invulnerability of the laws is due to the difficulties of disentangling the effects of different causes, not to any methodological rule.

this occasion. This rough characterization should provide a sufficient grasp of what the generalizations of consumer choice theory assert.

The most important feature of the "laws" of consumer choice theory for our purposes is that there is, obviously, a good deal of truth to each of them, but, equally obviously, they are not all true exceptionless universal generalizations. It is unquestionably sensible to regard them, at least in some qualified or hedged form, as possessing considerable initial credibility. Although the generalizations of consumer choice theory are hardly as well established as Newton's laws of motion (not that economists ever believed otherwise), it may still be reasonable to maintain that one has captured in these inexact generalizations significant causes of human behavior.

The credibility attributed to the generalizations of consumer choice theory thus falls short of the sort of proven or obvious truth that Mill and Robbins believe economists can begin with. Only some fancy philosophical footwork permits one to regard these generalizations as true at all, and it is questionable whether these axioms can be regarded as exactly well established.

One can thus defend one part of the inexact deductive method, although in a highly attenuated form: it may be intellectually legitimate to regard one's basic laws as possessing a high credibility apart from the successes or failures of the particular theory. In the particular case of economics, this initial credibility is only moderate, for the generalizations of consumer choice theory are problematic. They are plausible approximations, and they also have important pragmatic vindications.

The other main methodological recommendation of the inexact deductive method, that one *never* attribute apparent disconfirmations to shortcomings in one's laws, is defensible only as a rule of thumb that is appropriate for particular circumstances. It is unacceptable as a general methodological rule. To follow it would truly prevent one from ever discovering inadequacies in those laws. Except in the happy circumstances in which those laws possessed no inadequacies, it would hinder theoretical and empirical progress. Such a rule is unacceptably dogmatic.

Yet it is not unacceptably dogmatic not to find appreciable disconfirmation of economic "laws" in the welter of empirical failures to which economic theories are subject. Whether the correct response to empirical anomaly is to question the generalizations of consumer choice theory or to cite interferences depends on the particular circumstances. When the anomalies are those cast up by largely uncontrolled observation of complicated market phenomena, then it may be most rational to pin the blame on some of the many disturbing causes, which are always present. Since one's confidence in the simplifications and *ceteris paribus* assumptions necessary to apply economic theory to actual market phenomena will gener-

62

ally be much lower than one's confidence in the basic laws, the more likely explanation for the apparent disconfirmation will always be a failure of the simplifications rather than the laws. In consequence little can be learned about the purported laws from observation, but the failure will issue from the difficulties of the task not from methodological mistake. The possibility of discovering errors in the "laws" of equilibrium theory will be foreclosed by inadequate data and limited knowledge, not by unjustifiable methodological fiat.

Let me document this claim with respect to a simple Bayesian account of confirmation (see for example Eells 1982; Hesse 1974; Horwich 1983; Jeffrey 1983; or Rosenkranz 1977). Let H be either a "law" of consumer choice theory or a conjunction of such laws and A be the conjunction of all the other statements needed to derive a prediction, e from H. The prior probability of H, prob(H) is much larger than the prior probability of A, prob(A). (The probability of the conjunction, A, will, of course, be much smaller than that of the separate conjuncts, which are themselves improbable.) To keep things simple, although at the cost of unreality, let us suppose that H and A are probabilistically independent of each other, so that prob($H \cdot A$) = prob(H) $\cdot$ prob(A). Personalist Bayesians typically suppose that relevant probabilities are known, and I shall partially join them, although the assumption is fantastic (see M. Kaplan 1983; 1989).

Suppose now that H&A entail e, so that prob($e/H \cdot A$) = 1. Given this fact, the independence of H and A, and Bayes's theorem, we know that

$$\text{prob}(H \cdot A/e) = \text{prob}(H) \cdot \text{prob}(A)/\text{prob}(e); \tag{1}$$

and, of course,

$$\text{prob}(H \cdot A/ \sim e) = 0, \text{ where} \sim e \text{ is the negation of } e. \tag{2}$$

If e is borne out by observation, the (1) tells us that the ratio of the prior probability of H&A to the posterior probability of H&A is prob(e). Since

$$\text{prob}(H/e) = \text{prob}(H \cdot A/e) + \text{prob}(H \cdot \sim A/e), \tag{3}$$

we know by Bayes's theorem that

$$\text{prob}(H/e) = \text{prob}(H) \cdot \text{prob}(A)/\text{prob}(e) + $$
$$\text{prob}(H) \cdot \text{prob}(\sim A) \cdot \text{prob}(e/H \cdot \sim A)/\text{prob}(e) \text{ or} \tag{4}$$

$$\text{prob}(H/e) = [\text{prob}(H)/\text{prob}(e)] \cdot [\text{prob}(A) + \text{prob}(\sim A) \cdot \text{prob}(e/H \cdot \sim A)]. \tag{5}$$

Since prob(A) is small, and there is no reason in general to expect that prob($e/H \cdot \sim A$) will be close to one, H will be appreciably less well confirmed by e than is the conjunction H&A. Since

$$\text{prob}(H/\sim e) = \text{prob}(H \cdot A/\sim e) + \text{prob}(H \cdot \sim A/\sim e), \tag{6}$$

and the first term on the right hand side of (6) is zero, we can see that the posterior probability of H given unfavorable evidence $\sim e$ will be larger as prob(A) is smaller. Expanding the second term by means of Bayes's theorem we find,

$$\text{prob}(H/\sim e) = \text{prob}(H) \cdot \text{prob}(\sim A) \cdot \text{prob}(\sim e/H \cdot \sim A)/\text{prob}(\sim e). \tag{7}$$

Since there is no reason to expect that prob($\sim e/H \cdot \sim A$) will be smaller than prob($\sim e$) and prob($\sim A$) is also large, the observation of $\sim e$ only weakly disconfirms H. Given how weakly evidence will bear on H (and the indeterminacies in our probability judgments, which are assumed away in this discussion), pragmatic factors may justifiably come into their own in influencing one's reactions to apparent disconfirmations.[5] So in nonexperimental circumstances the credible "laws" with which economists begin will be *de facto* nonfalsifiable.

If one never had any better data than casual experience and market statistics, then there would be no way to tell whether economists employed the unjustifiably dogmatic inexact deductive method presented in Table 1 or whether they were good Bayesians or hypothetico-deductivists hampered by lack of knowledge and evidence. But experiments are only difficult in economics, not impossible; and there is by now a good deal of experimental evidence bearing on consumer choice theory. Economists and decision theorists are thus in the interesting situation of possessing considerable experimental evidence that apparently disconfirms consumer choice theory.[6] In experimental circumstances, it is possible to become justifiably confident that the predictive failure is not due to errors in the other statements needed to derive predictions from the generalizations of consumer choice theory. Consequently, in such a setting, one must take seriously the possibility of disconfirming the generalizations of consumer choice theory. Only the unjustifiable Millian method *a priori* would permit one to discount this possibility altogether. Since a willingness to take the possibility of disconfirmation seriously in experimental circumstances is consistent with a general inclination to treat apparent disconfirmations as due to interferences, that general inclination is no proof of unjustifiable dogmatism.

4. PRAGMATIC CONSIDERATIONS

One important effect of taking seriously experiments that mitigate the empirical difficulties that stand in the way of testing inexact claims is to make the concep-

5 Since (from a Bayesian perspective) theory choice, like all choice, depends on both probabilities and utilities, one might go on to attempt a systematic account of the importance of the pragmatic virtues of the standard theory.

6 I have in mind, for example, the experimental results concerning "preference reversal." See Chapter 15. For a useful overview, see Roth (1988). See also Lichtenstein and Slovic (1971), Grether and Plott (1979), Slovic and Lichtenstein (1983), Berg et al. (1985), Karni and Safra (1987), and Cox and Epstein (1989).

tual difficulties clearer. To explain away an apparent disconfirmation by changing an auxiliary hypothesis or citing a disturbing cause is to change one's applied theory in response to apparent disconfirmation. The new applied theory has, of necessity, different empirical consequence than the old. Hence it is wrong to say that those who always cite some interference to explain away unfavorable evidence *ignore* disconfirmations. Perhaps they do not react correctly, but they do react.

Disturbing causes, like all causes, have their (inexact) laws, and to explain away a disconfirmation by citing an interference thus may not be purely *ad hoc*. For the disturbing cause cited is to be expected in similar circumstances, and the modification has some nonvacuous empirical content – although the complexity of the phenomena may make testing impossible. The more general the disturbing cause, the more contentful and less *ad hoc* is the hypothesis that cites it.

The right question in a well-controlled experimental context is not "Is the theory disconfirmed or is there an interference?" but "What should one do about this disconfirmation? Should one add a qualification to the theory (which might in many contexts harmlessly be ignored), or should one revise the theory in a more fundamental way?" One cannot draw any sharp line between qualifications and modifications, but one does not need to do so. In both cases empirical evidence exerts real control over theory change. *The difference is pragmatic: qualifications can often be ignored, while modifications leave a permanent mark.* The significant question is whether one can fruitfully and frequently employ the unqualified theory; and the answer to this question depends both on the evidence and on one's purposes (see Mill 1843, 6.9.3).

Another way of grasping the issue here would be to ask how one is supposed to know, in Mill's terminology, that economic theory has captured the *"greater"* causes of economic phenomena.[7] Introspection and thoughts about rationality can provide evidence that transitivity is a significant causal factor affecting choice behavior, but neither could give one solid reason to believe that transitivity is more important than, for example, attitudes toward risk.

How then can one decide whether a disturbing cause is major or minor and whether one may justifiably regard consumer choice theory as capturing the "greater causes" of consumer behavior? Do experimental anomalies demand fundamental revisions or merely qualifications that for many purposes need not even be noted? The decision depends on both pragmatic and empirical factors. In its pragmatic aspect this question demands that one be clear about both practical and theoretical *employments* and *aspirations* for the theory. What does one want the theory for and what sort of theoretical grasp of the subject matter does one think possible?[8]

---

7   I am indebted for this way of thinking about this question to Joseph Stiglitz.
8   "[T]he critics of the simplified psychology used by economic theorists have made little headway in bringing forth substitute principles. I do not believe they ever will. Their strictures are valid as *limitations* on the familiar reasoning, not as negations. The principles of the established economics

But the decision also hinges on the empirical scope, frequency, and distribution of the disconfirmations experimenters have uncovered. If, for example, the disconfirmations are slight in the range of phenomena that are of the greatest theoretical and practical importance, and one does not believe that a much better theory is likely to be found (which, obviously will depend on what alternatives have been suggested), then it would be reasonable to account for the disconfirmations in terms of "interferences." If, on the other hand, the qualifications need to be invoked often, and one believes that considerably more exactness is possible, then it would be more reasonable to seek to modify the theory decisively.

Notice how significantly the reasoning here differs from the deductive method. What drives economists to regard interferences as minor disturbing causes is not the manifest truth of the basic axioms nor any methodological rule prohibiting revisions of them, but the nature of the disconfirmations coupled with the pragmatic attractions of consumer choice theory.

The presence and promise of alternatives would and should also strongly influence one's decisions here. Indeed, it is fair to say (following to some extent Lakatos's view [1970]), that what converts experimental results from anomalies or difficulties for consumer choice theory into disconfirming evidence demanding fundamental theory modification is the formulation of alternatives to consumer choice theory, which accommodate these anomalies within a theory that can do at least some of the work done by consumer choice theory. For some of these alternatives see Levi (1986), Machina (1987), and McClennen (1990).

5. THE ECONOMISTS' DEDUCTIVE METHOD

We are now in a position to formulate a schema (Table 2) sketching a deductive method that is justifiable and consistent with existing theoretical practice. This schema is as much a repudiation of the inexact deductive method as it is a revision of it, for it is consistent with standard views of confirmation such as the hypothetico-deductive method or those espoused by Bayesians.

What justifies continuing to call it a deductive method, despite its concessions that the inexact laws with which one begins are not proven and that they can be refuted by economic evidence? First (in contrast especially to Popperian methodological views), independent confirmation of the basic inexact laws plays a crucial role. Second, refutation is still largely proscribed, albeit by the circumstances, not by methodological rule. Since economists are typically dealing with complex phenomena in which many simplifications are required and in which interferences are to be expected, the evidential weight of a predictive failure will be very small.

are partial statements, but sound as far as they go, and they go about as far as general principles can be carried" (Knight 1921, 145). This response supposes that the limitations are unsystematic errors.

66

Table 2: *Economists' deductive method*

---

1. *Formulate* highly credible (*ceteris paribus*) and pragmatically convenient laws concerning the operation of causal factors that are relevant to the complex phenomena of concern.
2. *Deduce* from these laws and statements of initial conditions, simplifications, etc., predictions concerning relevant phenomena.
3. *Test* the predictions.
4. If the predictions are correct, then regard the whole amalgam as confirmed. If the predictions are not correct, then *compare* alternative accounts of the failure on the basis of empirical progress and pragmatic usefulness.

It will rarely be rational to surrender a credible hypothesis because of a predictive failure in circumstances such as these.

The economists' deductive method suggests two grounds for judging how much disconfirmation results from unsuccessful prediction. The first derives from Lakatos and directs one to consider what sort of theory modifications or qualifications will most increase the confirmed empirical content of the theory. Given the acute *practical* Quine–Duhem problem here, which is a consequence of how dubious are the various auxiliary hypotheses necessary in order to perform any tests, it will be extremely difficult to judge theory modifications on empirical grounds. The second, pragmatic ground, may consequently play a justifiably large role. For if one cannot tell which theory modification is empirically better, it is sensible to choose the one that has greater pragmatic virtues – that is, the one that it is easier to use, gives sharper advice, lends itself to cleaner mathematical expression and development, and so forth.

The inexact deductive method, as formulated in Table 1, is indefensibly dogmatic, for evidence, even the weak evidence of uncontrolled observation, can occasionally force one to rethink basic laws, and, in any case, the basic "laws" of economics are a motley crew. One cannot rule out employing unfavorable evidence to argue against the "laws" themselves rather than the simplifications or the *ceteris paribus* assumption that interferences were not present. But the complexity and messiness of economic observations will largely nullify this possibility.

It is still thus perfectly rational to behave in very much the manner in which Mill recommended. (Hence one can see why Mill's views seemed so plausible, were so easily refuted, yet methodological practice continues apparently to conform to them.) The "laws" of consumer choice theory can be regarded as reasonable approximations that have a good deal of truth to them and great pragmatic convenience. One can, in this way, behave in an empirically responsive and rationally justifiable way and yet largely conform to the deductive method.

Indeed, with respect to phenomena such as those of economies, one has no other good choice. Powerful tests require either experimentation with its possibilities of intervention and control, a great deal of knowledge, or fabulous good fortune, and without such tests (or superior alternatives) it would be irrational to surrender credible hypotheses with great pragmatic attractions in the face of apparent disconfirmation.

As formulated in Table 2 above, the economists' deductive method does not forbid fundamental theory revision. But given the circumstances in which economists find themselves, it is unlikely that market data will ever be taken to disconfirm the basic laws or behavioral postulates of consumer choice theory. The relevant features of those circumstances are: (1) the initial credibility of relevant, but highly inexact laws; (2) the difficulty of performing experiments; (3) the complexity of the phenomena (the significant influence of many different causes of many different kinds); and (4) the limitations of knowledge of economic phenomena. If economists can do experiments, they can control for various disturbances and avoid the complexity of the phenomena with which they are presented nonexperimentally. If they knew enough, they could exert much the same control even if experiments were not possible. If, on the other hand, they were blessed with a comparatively simple set of phenomena such as those of celestial motion, then neither the inability to experiment nor the paucity of our knowledge would be crippling. But the combination of (2)–(4) makes knowledge of economic phenomena hard to garner.

When experiments are possible and when alternatives are available that have some of the initial credibility of the accepted theory and offer similar pragmatic advantages, then theory change is possible, according to the economist's deductive method. And if one studies how economists respond to experimental anomalies, one can, I think, see that they are not necessarily committed to a dogmatic view, such as the inexact deductive method. Although one finds, not surprisingly, some dogmatism in these responses, it is not the shared methodological rule and it is more the consequence of a commitment to a particular image of economics than to a dogmatic theory of confirmation.[9] Many modifications are in fact proposed, discussed, and tested.

6. THE DEDUCTIVE METHOD AND THE DEMANDS OF POLICY

Although I have discussed at length the methodological criticisms of the inexact deductive method and have, depending on how one conceives of matters, either

---

9 This image of economics also goes back to Mill. It sees economists as focusing on only a small number of causal factors and developing a single systematic theory that, apart from various interferences or disturbing causes, is sufficient to account for all important economic phenomena. See chapters 8 and 12 of my 1992a.

answered them or have shown them not necessarily to apply to the methodological practice of economists, I have not yet directly addressed the practical criticism that in following a deductive method, economists condemn their work to practical futility.

But having clarified the varieties of the deductive method, one can easily see that this criticism is specious. The economists' deductive method does not rule out theory changes when doing so will increase the empirical content of the theory – on the contrary it mandates them. Nor does it – or any other variety of the deductive method – condemn empirical generalization. Mill is explicit in endorsing obvious common sense on this point: if something works, use it (though with due caution). Moreover, the development of empirical generalizations for which no deductive derivation is currently possible is also of great *theoretical* importance, for such generalizations constitute the most important *data* for which theories need to account.

The point of the deductive method is not to condemn useful empirical generalizations or to abandon accurate predictive devices. It is instead to condemn naive reliance on unreliable empirical generalizations and to provide an *additional* means of getting a predictive grasp on the phenomena. Whether the best way to aim an artillery piece is by firing it in various circumstances and fitting a curve to the data points or by calculating from fundamental laws is an empirical question. Rather than forbidding the first procedure, the deductive method offers a way of improving and correcting the results one gets by it.

If the standard neoclassical theory of the firm had all the empirical virtues claimed for it by economists such as Milton Friedman (1953c), then one should make use of it for relevant practical purposes. The economist's deductive method does not recommend the sort of theoretical purism that spurns useful tools that are not in perfect condition and perfectly understood. But by considering the realism of the theory's assumptions – the constituent causal processes and their laws – one may be able to get some guidance concerning when the predictions of the theory are likely to break down and concerning how to modify the theory in the face of apparent disconfirmation.

5

Why look under the hood?

Methodologists have had few kind words for Milton Friedman's "The Methodology of Positive Economics" (1953c) yet its influence persists. Why? One answer is that methodologists have missed an important argument, which economists have found persuasive. Unlike Hirsch and de Marchi (1990), I am concerned here with the argument, not with "what Friedman really meant."

Friedman declares, "The ultimate goal of a positive science is the development of a "theory" or "hypothesis" that yields valid and meaningful (i.e., not truistic) predictions about phenomena not yet observed" (p. 7). This is the central thesis of instrumentalism. But from a standard instrumentalist perspective, in which *all* the observable consequences of a theory are significant, it is impossible to defend Friedman's central claim that the realism of assumptions is irrelevant to the assessment of a scientific theory. For the assumptions of economics are testable, and a standard instrumentalist would not dismiss apparent disconfirmations. Indeed, the distinction between assumptions and implications is superficial. The survey results reported by Richard Lester and others, which Friedman finds irrelevant and wrong-headed (pp. 15, 31f), are as much predictions of neoclassical theory as are claims about market phenomena.

But, like Lawrence Boland (1979), I contend that Friedman is *not* a standard instrumentalist. Consider the following passages:

Viewed as a body of substantive hypotheses, theory is to be judged by its predictive power for the class of phenomena which it is intended to "explain." (pp. 8–9)

For this test [of predictions] to be relevant, the deduced facts must be about the class of phenomena the hypothesis is designed to explain; . . . (pp. 12–13)

The decisive test is whether the hypothesis works for the phenomena it purports to explain. (p. 30)[1]

Friedman *rejects* a standard instrumentalist concern with *all* the predictions of a theory. A good tool need not be an all-purpose tool. Friedman holds that the goal of economics is "narrow predictive success" – correct prediction only for "the class of phenomena the hypothesis is designed to explain." Lester's surveys are irrele-

I would like to thank John Dreher, Martin Finkler, Daniel Hammond, Erkki Koskela, Michael McPherson, and Herbert Simon for useful criticisms and suggestions.
1   See also pp. 15, 20, and 41.

vant because their results are not among the phenomena that the theory of the firm was designed to explain. On just these grounds, many economists dismiss any inquiry into whether the claims of the theory of consumer choice are true of individuals.

I suggest that Friedman uses this view that science aims at narrow predictive success as a premise in the following implicit argument:

(1) A good hypothesis provides valid and meaningful predictions concerning the class of phenomena it is intended to explain. (premise)

(2) The only test of whether an hypothesis is a good hypothesis is whether it provides valid and meaningful predictions concerning the class of phenomena it is intended to explain.[2] (invalidly from 1)

(3) Any other facts about an hypothesis, including whether its assumptions are realistic, are irrelevant to its scientific assessment. (trivially from 2)

If (1) the criterion of a good theory is narrow predictive success, then surely (2) the test of a good theory is narrow predictive success, and Friedman's claim that the realism of assumptions is irrelevant follows trivially. This is a tempting and persuasive argument.

But it is fallacious. (2) is not true and does not follow from (1). To see why, consider the following analogous argument:

(1') A good used car drives safely, economically, and comfortably. (oversimplified premise)

(2') The only test of whether a used car is a good used car is whether it drives safely, economically, and comfortably. (invalidly from 1')

(3') Anything one discovers by opening the hood and checking the separate components of a used car is irrelevant to its assessment. (trivially from 2')

---

2   Notice that (2) does not say that the only test of a hypothesis is whether its predictions are valid. It says that the only test is the validity of only *some* of its predictions, namely those concerning "the class of phenomena the hypothesis is intended to explain." This is overstated, and (I repeat) I am not concerned to provide the best interpretation of Friedman's whole methodology. In his essay Friedman concedes a role for assumptions in facilitating an "indirect" test of a theory: "Yet, in the absence of other evidence, the success of the hypothesis for one purpose – in explaining one class of phenomena – will give us greater confidence than we would otherwise have that it may succeed for another purpose – in explaining another class of phenomena. It is much harder to say how much greater confidence it justifies. For this depends on how closely related we judge the two classes of phenomena to be . . ." (p. 28). The last sentence still limits the relevance of the correctness of predictions concerning phenomena that are remote from those that the theory is designed to explain, and Friedman clearly believes that the evidential force of indirect tests is much less than that of tests concerning the range of phenomena that the theory is intended to "explain." Daniel Hammond (unpublished) has argued that these qualifications were not part of the original draft of the essay.

Presumably nobody believes 3'.[3] What is wrong with the argument? It assumes that a road test is a conclusive test of a car's future performance. If this assumption were true, if it were possible (and cheap) to do a total check of the performance of a used car for the whole of its future, then there would indeed be no point in looking under the hood. For we would know everything about its performance, which is all we care about. But a road test only provides a small sample of this performance. Thus a mechanic who examines the engine can provide relevant and useful information. The mechanic's input is particularly important when one wants to use the car under new circumstances and when the car breaks down. Obviously one wants a sensible mechanic who notes not just that the components are used and imperfect, but who can judge how well the components are likely to serve their separate purposes.

Similarly, given Friedman's view of the goal of science, there would be no point in examining the assumptions of a theory if it were possible to do a "total" assessment of its performance with respect to the phenomena it was designed to explain. But one cannot make such an assessment. Indeed, the point of a theory is to guide us in circumstances where we do not already know whether the predictions are correct.[4] There is thus much that may be learned by examining the components (assumptions) of a theory and its "irrelevant" predictions. Such consideration of the "realism" of assumptions is particularly important when extending the theory to new circumstances or when revising it in the face of predictive failure.[5] Again what is relevant is not whether the assumptions are perfectly true, but whether they are adequate approximations and whether their falsehood is likely to matter for particular purposes. Saying this is not conceding Friedman's case. Wide, not narrow predictive success constitutes the grounds for judging whether a theory's assumptions are adequate approximations. The fact that a computer program works in a few instances does not render study of its algorithm and code superfluous or irrelevant.

There is a grain of truth in Friedman's defense of theories containing unrealistic assumptions. For *some* failures of assumptions may be irrelevant. Just as a malfunc-

3 Those who do should get in touch. I've got some fine old cars for you at bargain prices.
4 Friedman partially recognizes this point when he writes (according to Hammond, echoing criticisms George Stigler and Arthur Burns offered of an earlier draft), "The decisive test is whether the hypothesis works for the phenomena it purports to explain. But a judgment may be required before any satisfactory test of this kind has been made, and, perhaps, when it cannot be made in the near future, in which case, the judgment will have to be based on the inadequate evidence available." (1953c, p. 30)
5 With what seems to me inconsistent good sense, Friedman again partly recognizes the point, "I do not mean to imply that questionnaire studies of businessmen's or other's motives or beliefs about the forces affecting their behavior are useless for all purposes in economics. They may be extremely valuable in suggesting leads to follow in accounting for divergences between predicted and observed results; that is, in constructing new hypotheses or revising old ones. Whatever their suggestive value in this respect, they seem to me almost entirely useless as a means of *testing* the validity of economic hypotheses " (1953c, p. 31n).

tioning air-conditioner is insignificant to a car's performance in Alaska, so is the falsity of the assumption of infinite divisibility unimportant in hypotheses concerning markets for basic grains. Given Friedman's narrow view of the goals of science (which I am conceding for the purposes of argument, but would otherwise contest), the realism of assumptions may thus sometimes be irrelevant. But this bit of practical wisdom does not support Friedman's strong conclusion that only narrow predictive success is relevant to the assessment of an hypothesis.

One should note three qualifications. First, we sometimes have a wealth of information concerning the track record of both theories and of used cars. I may know that my friend's old Mustang has been running without trouble for the past seven years. The more information we have about performance, the less important is separate examination of components. But it remains sensible to assess assumptions or components, particularly in circumstances of breakdown and when considering a new use. Second, intellectual tools, unlike mechanical tools, do not wear out. But if one has not yet grasped the fundamental laws governing a subject matter and does not fully know the scope of the laws and the boundary conditions on their validity, then generalizations are as likely to break down as are physical implements. Third (as Erkki Koskela reminded me), it is easier to interpret a road test than an econometric study. The difficulties of testing in economics make it all the more mandatory to look under the hood.

When either theories or used cars work, it makes sense to use them – although caution is in order if their parts have not been examined or appear to be faulty. But known performance in some sample of their given tasks is not the only information relevant to an accurate assessment of either. Economists must (and do) look under the hoods of their theoretical vehicles. When they find embarrassing things there, they must not avert their eyes and claim that what they have found cannot matter. *Even if all one cares about is predictive success in some limited domain, one should still be concerned about the realism of the assumptions of an hypothesis and the truth of its irrelevant or unimportant predictions.*

6

An appraisal of Popperian methodology

Professor Klant, in his masterful overview of economic methodology, *The Rules of the Game*, relies heavily on Karl Popper's writings on the philosophy of science. For, like Popper, Professor Klant is concerned about whether theories are genuinely testable and whether they are truly supported by empirical evidence. I respect these concerns and share them, yet I have serious objections to Popper's philosophy of science. Indeed, I shall argue in this chapter that nontrivial questions about the testability of economics cannot be asked within the confines of Popper's falsificationism. A reasoned concern with falsifiability demands the repudiation of Popper's philosophy of science. Moreover, there is no way to amend his views without eviscerating them and making Popper's central theses little more than truisms accepted no less by anti-Popperians than by Popperians.[1] Much of the appeal of Popper's philosophy of science depends upon ambiguities and equivocations concerning the notion of falsifiability. I shall argue that the notion of falsification as a purely logical relation between theories and basic statements or observation reports, which Popper has stressed again and again throughout his long career, is irrelevant to any important questions concerning science. On the other hand, Popper's relevant views concerning falsificationism as a methodology or a policy are unfounded and unacceptable.

1. LOGICAL FALSIFIABILITY

Popper argues that what distinguishes scientific theories, such as Newton's or Einstein's, from unscientific theories, such as Freud's or those endorsed by astrologers, is that scientific theories are *falsifiable*. Intuitively speaking, a theory is falsifiable if it is not guaranteed that it will pass all tests. There must be some

1 Many of the points made in this chapter are not new. The critique of Popper's views on induction follows, to a considerable extent, criticisms made by Levison (1974), Lieberson (1982a, 1982b), Putnam (1974), Grünbaum (1976), and Salmon (1981), although only Lieberson was a major influence. Isaac Levi's work (1967, 1980) has also influenced me, and in my argument for the possibility of verifications, I was assisted by Nisbett and Thagard's (1982) discussion of induction. Lakatos's critique and his plea for a "whiff of inductivism" is much weaker, since his own treatment of induction differs so little from Popper's (Lakatos 1974, pp. 241–73). David Miller's defense of Popper's account of induction (1982) does not touch the simple and, in my view, decisive arguments given in this chapter. I would like to thank Ernie Alleva, Clark Glymour, Wade Hands, Kevin Kelly, Jonathan Lieberson, Michael McPherson, Jonathan Pressler, Teddy Seidenfeld, and Wilfrid Sieg for comments on earlier versions of this chapter.

possible tests or observations that, if the results are unfavorable, would be evidence that the theory is false. "All swans are white" is the sort of statement that is appropriate in science, because the observation of a nonwhite swan would establish its falsity (Popper's own example, 1968, p. 27).

Popper refines this intuitive notion as follows: First, he distinguishes a class of "basic statements" upon whose truth agreement is easily obtained. Basic statements are true or false reports of observations that are of an "*unquestioned empirical character*" (1969a, p. 386; see also 1968, secs. 28, 29). Accepted basic statements are not certain, infallible, or incorrigible. We are not *forced* by the facts to accept them. But we do (albeit tentatively) *decide* to do so, and we rather easily reach lasting agreement on which basic statements to accept. Basic statements have a special importance because of this agreement, since they are particularly easy to test, and since, as empiricists, we take test reports to be particularly important in the acceptance or rejection of scientific theories.[2]

Given the notion of a basic statement, Popper can then give a precise construal of falsifiability. A theory is falsifiable if and only if it is logically inconsistent with some finite set of basic statements. A theory that is, in fact, true would not, of course, be inconsistent with any set of *true* basic statements, but the definition does not say that the basic statements whose negation is entailed by a scientific theory are true.

It is, unfortunately, impossible to tell how important logical falsifiability is to Popper, since he contradicts himself on the question.[3] In an introduction to the *Postscript to the Logic of Scientific Discovery* written in the early 1980s, he states:

It is of great importance to current discussion to notice that falsifiability in the sense of my demarcation criterion is a purely logical affair. It has to do only with the logical structure of statements and of classes of statements. . . .

A statement or theory is, according to my criterion, falsifiable if and only if there exists at least one potential falsifier – at least one possible basic statement that conflicts with it logically. (1983, p. xx)

Yet in *The Logic of Scientific Discovery* itself, Popper writes:

Indeed, it is impossible to decide, by analysing its logical form, whether a system of statements is a conventional system of irrefutable implicit definitions, or whether it is a system which is empirical in my sense; that is, a refutable system. . . . *Only with reference to*

---

2 Although Popper takes basic statements in *The Logic of Scientific Discovery* to be existential statements, I shall cautiously simplify, as Popper also does (1972, p. 7), and take them to be singular statements.

3 Partly as the result of reading Lakatos's "Falsification and the Methodology of Scientific Research Programmes" (1970), I had been inclined, out of what I took to be charity, to ignore logical falsificationism. Although Popper (1983, pp. xxii–xxiii) is correct to distinguish it from what Lakatos calls "dogmatic falsificationism" (pp. 95–103), its vices are, as I shall argue subsequently, just as serious.

the methods applied to a theoretical system is it at all possible to ask whether we are dealing with a conventionalist or an empirical theory. (1968, p. 82)

If we take the first quotation as representing Popper's current views, then logical falsifiability is supposed to be the criterion that demarcates science from everything else. But throughout his career, Popper has stressed the importance of methodological decisions in distinguishing science from other activities.

As a corollary of the precise notion of logical falsifiability, Popper repeatedly emphasizes a trivial "asymmetry between verifiability and falsifiability; an asymmetry which results from the logical form of universal statements" (1968, p. 41; see also 1983, pp. 181–9). A universal statement concerning an infinite or unbounded domain may be falsifiable – that is, it may be inconsistent with some basic statements. But it will not be verifiable – it will not be deducible from any finite set of basic statements (its negation will not be inconsistent with any finite set of basic statements). For example, "This swan is black" falsifies "All swans are white." It is not possible to verify any truly universal statement, but we can, of course, verify its negation.

Popper argues that this asymmetry between falsifiability and verifiability leads to a solution to the problem of induction. In more or less the formulation Popper prefers (1972, p. 7), Hume's problem of induction is the problem of finding a good argument with only basic statements as premises and some universal statement as a conclusion.[4] If by "good argument" one means "valid deductive argument" (and I shall not discuss any alternative interpretations here), then there are no good arguments with only basic statements as premises and universal statements as conclusions. But one can provide valid deductive arguments *against* universal statements. One can thus (albeit fallibly, since basic statements are not themselves infallible) find out that theories are wrong. By the elimination of error our knowledge can, in this Pickwickian sense, grow.

Notice that even if Popper's insistence that scientific theories be logically falsifiable were not plagued by the difficulties to be discussed soon, this so-called solution to the problem of induction would be profoundly unsatisfactory. Only the fallacy of elimination enables one to find theory T meritorious merely because

---

4 But, as is obvious from the subsequent argument, I do not concur in Popper's sharp separation of what he calls the "logical" from the "pragmatic" problem of induction. Although I do not know precisely what the identity criteria for problems are, it seems to me that there is basically only one problem here. Thus Popper manages to be extremely misleading when he makes the entirely correct (within his set of definitions) claim, "For anybody who adopts an instrumentalist view, *the* [logical] *problem of induction* [as formulated by Popper] *disappears*" (1983, p. 117). But, as Popper himself notes (1983, p. 120), the point is an entirely trivial one, since the instrumentalist faces an entirely analogous problem of deciding which statements to rely on. The point would hardly be worth making but for the fact that Popper's formulation has perhaps misled Lawrence Boland, who argues mistakenly that instrumentalism is a response to the problem of induction (1979, p. 508).

an alternative theory, T', has been refuted. The logical conclusion, although clothed in soothing words about how rational the procedure is (for example, 1972, pp. 22, 27, 58, 81, 95), is a skepticism that is as extreme as Hume's, for Popper explicitly denies that there is any room for argument in support of any theory or law. He writes, for example, "that in spite of the 'rationality' of choosing the best-tested theory as a basis of action, this choice is *not* 'rational' in the sense that it is based upon *good reasons* for expecting that it will in practice be a successful choice; *there can be no good reasons* in this sense, and this is precisely Hume's result" (1972, p. 22). We have no better reason to expect that the predictions of well-tested theories will be correct than to expect that completely untested theories will predict correctly.

But this purported solution to the problem of induction falsely presupposes that individual scientific statements, or at least individual scientific *theories*, are falsifiable. Statistical and probabilistic claims are obviously not logically falsifiable. Even flipping a million heads in a row does not logically falsify the claim that a particular coin is unbiased. Even more seriously, all claims that cannot be tested *individually* are not logically falsifiable. For if a sentence is not, *by itself*, inconsistent with some finite set of basic statements, then it is not logically falsifiable. And the fact is that virtually no scientific claims of any interest are *by themselves* inconsistent with basic statements. To falsify even an utterly simple scientific claim, such as Galileo's law of falling bodies, requires not only basic statements, but also some nonbasic statements concerning whether nongravitational forces are present. If individual statements can be regarded as scientific only if they are logically falsifiable, it will turn out that almost all interesting science is not science after all.

Although Popper talks constantly of the falsifiability of scientific theories, he nevertheless knows all this; and he has discussed at length not only the role of background knowledge in testing, but also the sort of "conventionalist stratagems" one might employ to shield theories from falsification. Sometimes he seems to forget what he knows, as, for example, when he mistakenly argues against Lakatos that the observation of a dancing tea cup would, by itself, falsify Newton's theory of motion and gravitation (1974, p. 1005).[5] But he does have an answer to this criticism. His answer is that *logical falsifiability is not a criterion that scientific statements or even whole scientific theories have to satisfy individually.* What distinguishes scientific theories from nonscientific theories is that the whole systems of scientific theories, auxiliary assumptions, and statements of initial conditions created to derive predictions are falsifiable (1983, p. 187). Logical

---

5 Watkins (1984, p. 326) also notices Popper's blunder here. Popper says that the observation report would falsify the theory if we ignore the possibility of immunizing stratagems. But it is not just the observation report that falsifies the theory. We also need the knowledge that the other explanations of the predictive failure are in fact merely immunizing stratagems.

falsifiability enters when one concludes that the experimental results conflict with what was predicted on the basis of a conglomerate, including the particular theory under test. Let us call such conglomerates, which will often be mammoth, "test systems." Galileo's law of falling bodies is not itself logically falsifiable, but conjoined with claims about resistance and friction, it forms a falsifiable test system.

Although there is no mistake in demanding logical falsifiability of test systems, there are nevertheless three things wrong with the proposal that to be scientific, a theory need only be incorporated or incorporable into logically falsifiable test systems. First, logical falsifiability turns out to play only a minute role in the actual process of theory rejection or revision.[6] The fact that a theory is part of a logically falsifiable test system enables the further methodological rules that guide the scientist to get some grip, but logical falsifiability itself becomes merely an uninteresting necessary condition. Furthermore, although this necessary condition that theories be part of logically falsifiable test systems may have escaped the crude, early attempts of the logical positivists to capture the logic of science, it is an undisputed truism.

The second thing wrong with Popper's restriction of the requirement of logical falsifiability to test systems is that it no longer functions as a plausible criterion of demarcation. Freud's psychological theories are not unfalsifiable in this sense. On the contrary, analysts and amateurs alike are constantly deriving predictions about how people will talk and act from Freudian theory and a wealth of other assumptions. The problem is not that these predictions (and thus the test systems from which they are derived) are never inconsistent with sets of basic statements. The problem with Freud's theories (if there is one) is rather (as Popper himself notes)[7] that the logical falsifications are not taken by analysts as evidence against the theories. The mistake is always taken to lie elsewhere. Astrologers, similarly, constantly make predictions that can conflict with basic statements. Since astrological theory is best interpreted as a statistical theory, these predictions are not deductive consequences of astrological theory and the various other premises. But, as Popper himself points out (1968, pp. 198–205), by adding methodological rules specifying the permissible range of disagreement betweeen measured values and probabilistic predictions, one can

---

6 Zahar's proposed phenomenological reconstrual of basic statements (1983, pp. 156–61) and of logical falsifiability would only underscore how small a role logical falsification plays in the process of theory revision. Popper disputes this claim, which was emphasized by Duhem (1954, p. 187), by arguing that $H2$ might entail $\sim P$, whereas $H1$ entails P when $H1$ and $H2$ are conjoined to a common set of additional premises, S. But even in such a case, $\sim H2$ does not, of course, follow deductively from our acceptance of P as a true basic statement. We still need to decide (for whatever reasons) to regard the members of S as true. See Grünbaum (1976, pp. 248–50) and footnote 15.

7 "But what kind of clinical responses would refute to the satisfaction of the analyst not merely a particular analytic diagnosis but psycho-analysis itself?" (1969a, p. 38n)

deduce predictions that can be inconsistent with sets of basic statements. The problem, once again, is not that there are no logically falsifiable astrological test systems. The problem is rather that astrologers refuse to take failures of their predictions as casting doubt on astrology. As a criterion of demarcation, logical falsifiability applied to whole systems of theories is far too weak; little, if anything, will fail to count as science.

The third difficulty with the claim that only whole conglomerates need be logically falsifiable is that its negation is presupposed by Popper's purported solution to the problem of induction. Since individual scientific theories need not be falsifiable, Popper must concede that there is no logical asymmetry between the verifiability and falsifiability of particular scientific *theories:* They are *neither* (logically) verifiable *nor* (logically) falsifiable. And thus, there is no longer any semblance of a solution to the problem of induction. Accepted basic statements and deductive logic can get one to the falsity of whole test systems and no further. There is never a shred of evidence for *or against* any particular statements or theories. As we shall see later, Popper explicitly allows that we can also make use of what he calls "background knowledge" to achieve falsifications, but in this section I have been concerned exclusively with logical falsifiability.

Whether taken as a condition on individual scientific claims or as a condition that applies only to test systems, logical falsifiability and the logical asymmetry between falsification and verification should be of little interest to philosophers of science or economic methodologists. Few theoretical claims in economics are, by themselves, logically falsifiable, but the same goes for science as a whole. And I know of no economic theories that cannot enter into logically falsifiable test systems (which would, of course, include specifications of statistical techniques and *ceteris paribus* clauses in addition to theories from economics and from other domains). Popper's claims about the asymmetry of logical falsifiability and logical verifiability (of whole test systems) are as correct as they are irrelevant. They provide no solution to the problem of induction.

2. FALSIFICATIONISM AS A METHODOLOGY – A SET OF NORMS THAT SHOULD GOVERN THE BEHAVIOR OF SCIENTISTS

So, let us move on to a notion of falsification that is of interest and importance to philosophers of science and economic methodologists. Popper has always recognized and stressed that methodology is concerned with rules, not simply with logic. Indeed, as previously documented, he sometimes maintains that what distinguishes sciences from nonsciences is not logical falsifiability, but the norms and behavior of scientists.

Conceived of as a methodology, Popper's falsificationism consists in outline of three simple rules addressed to the scientist: (1) Propose and consider only testable or falsifiable theories; (2) seek only to falsify scientific theories; (3) accept theories that withstand attempts to falsify them as worthy of further critical discussion, never as certain or even as probably true or close to the truth.

In somewhat more detail these rules can be restated as follows:

(1)   Although untestable theories may be suggestive and useful for theory generation, consider as candidates for scientific knowledge only theories that may be subjected to hard tests. A hard test is a test that a theory not only could fail but, moreover, a test that, given background knowledge or the alternatives, one should expect the theory to fail. Prefer theories with much content and many possibilities for falsification.

(2)   Scientists should, at least collectively, have a critical attitude; they should try to falsify existing theories, not to support or confirm them. This attitude requires, in particular, three things: First, scientists must look for harsh tests of existing scientific theories. In order to do so, they must, second, accept both some basic and nonbasic statements as true, at least for the purposes of testing. Otherwise there would be no way to falsify anything apart from whole test systems. In other inquiries, they can (and should) test their presuppositions, although these further tests will have their own further presuppositions. Finally, when a theory fails a test and scientists cannot find a reasonable excuse, they must reject the theory and look for an alternative. A reasonable excuse is at least an excuse that can itself be readily tested. A scientist might, for example, question whether a particular instrument was operating properly. There is no simple algorithm stating when it is unreasonable to make further reasonable excuses, but provided that one is seeking to falsify rather than to hold on to theories, no algorithm is needed.[8]

(3)   If a theory has not yet been falsified, scientists should accept it tentatively. Theories that have survived harsh testing are not better supported or more worthy of belief than are theories that have not been tested at all. They are merely particularly difficult to falsify and worth testing further. "The theoretician's choice," in Popper's view, "is the hypothesis most worthy of *further critical discussion* (rather than *acceptance*)" (1969a, p. 218n). Although Popper argues that there may be evidence that one theory has more true and fewer false consequences than another (1972, pp. 58, 81–2; 265), there is never, in his view, any good evidence that a law or a theory is correct or even close to correct.

8   This requirement, like the last, is not so much a requirement of each individual scientist as it is of the institution of science as a whole (1969b, p. 112; but see 1972, p. 266). Provided that there is open and free communication, the institution as a whole may be critical, even though each individual scientist attempts to protect his on her own theory from criticism.

What we do – or should do – is to *hold on, for the time being, to the most improbable of the surviving theories* or, more precisely, to the one that can be most severely tested. We tentatively *"accept"* this theory – but only in the sense that we select it as worthy to be subjected to further criticism, and to the severest tests we can design.[9] (1968, p. 419)

Are these good rules of procedure for scientists to follow? The answer presumably depends on what the objectives of scientists would be. And therein lies a long and tangled story, which we had better avoid here. In order to keep this chapter short and focused on Popper's views, I shall not argue that these are in fact bad rules. Instead I shall merely show that Popper has not provided any good arguments in their defense. Given their implausibility, this demonstration of their lack of justification should be a sufficient criticism.

One can, at least in outline, grant the first rule, that proposed scientific theories be testable, that science seeks theories with much content and theories that can be tested harshly and in many ways. But apart from the important insistence on content, there is no news in any of these methodological rules. Inductivists have been saying these things since at least the seventeenth century (Grünbaum 1976, pp. 217ff).

The second and third rules are less plausible. To claim that scientists should seek only to falsify theories, never to support them, and that they should never regard theories as anything more than conjectures that may be worthy of criticism is to make two apparently outrageous suggestions.[10] Why should anyone accept them? Popper offers four reasons. First, he maintains that confirming evidence is worthless, since "it is easy to obtain confirmations, or verifications, for nearly every theory – if we look for confirmations" (1969a, p. 36). So it is a mistake to look for confirmations or to regard what one finds as really supporting or establishing any theory. But Popper is mistaken. Cheap confirmation is readily available; merely locating another instance of a generalization may be as easy as it is worthless. Good supporting evidence is, on the other hand, hard to obtain. Much of it comes from just the sort of harsh testing that Popper insists on (see Grünbaum 1976, pp. 215–29).

9 Popper chides Lakatos (1974, p. 1003) for, in effect, ignoring the sentence that follows: "On the positive side, we may be entitled to add that the surviving theory is the best theory – and the best tested theory – of which we know." But this last sentence changes nothing concerning what Popper takes corroboration and "acceptance" of scientific theories to be. Popper has, of course, a theory of verisimilitude that met with an unfortunate formal demise (Tichy 1974). But regardless of formal vicissitudes, Popper has insisted that corroboration is no evidence of verisimilitude. In very special and limited circumstances we can justifiably maintain that one theory has greater verisimilitude than another, but there is never any justification for maintaining that a theory has high verisimilitude (1972, pp. 47ff).

10 And indeed, Popper is unable to follow his own advice consistently, for he writes: "What we believe (rightly or wrongly) is not that Newton's theory of Einstein's theory is true, but that they are *good approximations* to the truth, though capable of being superseded by a better one. But this belief, I assert, *is* rational" (1983, p. 57).

Second, Popper argues that to seek confirmation or to believe that one has found quite a lot is to show a dogmatic attitude rather than the sort of open and critical attitude shown by those who seek falsifications (1969a, pp. 49ff). But this is just name calling. Even someone devoted to giving evidence in support of a favorite theory need not be credulous, closed-minded, or dogmatic in doing so. And it is certainly not the case that a person seeking the solution to a problem, who is thus concerned *both* with confirming *and* with disconfirming evidence, automatically qualifies as a dogmatic, unscientific sort.

Third, Popper suggests that to seek supporting evidence or to regard scientific theories as sometimes well established rests on a view of scientific knowledge as infallible. Popper argues that the overthrow of Newtonian physics renders such a view completely untenable. But one can, of course, concede that human knowledge is fallible without denying that particular knowledge claims may be well supported.[11]

Popper's fourth argument for the injunction to seek to falsify theories and never to seek to support them rests on the thesis that it is impossible for evidence to support scientific theories. Scientific theories simply *cannot* be confirmed, so it is obviously a mistake to attempt to do so. Popper says bluntly, "there *are* no such things as good positive reasons; nor do we need such things" (1974, p. 1043). There is no such thing as supporting evidence.[12] This argument may appear to be inconsistent with the claim that supporting evidence is easy to obtain. But there is no real contradiction here. In Popper's view, evidence that *truly provides* a positive reason for accepting a scientific claim cannot be had, whereas evidence that inductivists *mistakenly take to support* scientific theories is easy to obtain.

It would be foolish to attempt to find evidence in support of scientific theories if such evidence were completely unattainable. But why believe that one *never* has good reason to accept any scientific claims or that one *never* has good reason to believe that some claims are more likely to pass future tests than others? Popper makes just these assertions.

What convinces Popper that we can never have evidence in support of scientific claims is the problem of induction. There are no good arguments with only basic statements as premises and scientific laws and theories as conclusions. So there is no supporting evidence, no sense in seeking it, and no sense in believing that one has found it. In Popper's view, it remains rational to seek to falsify and to criticize

11 And Isaac Levi (1980) has even argued that one can regard one's knowledge as *in*fallible, without regarding it as incorrigible.
12 There are, however, some verbal difficulties here, since Popper offers an explicit analysis of what it is for evidence to support a theory (see esp. 1983, pp. 236ff). This is not a contradiction, however, for in the Popperian sense in which evidence "supports" or "corroborates" theories, it gives one no reason to believe that the theory is true or close to the truth and no reason to believe that the theory will pass any future tests. Evidence that supports or corroborates theories in Popper's sense does not support theories.

scientific theories, because such theories are falsifiable: There are good arguments against them.

But this argument restates Popper's solution to the problem of induction, which in turn depends on the mistaken view, explicitly denied by Popper, that individual laws and theories in science are falsifiable. So this argument derives its specious plausibility from Popper playing fast and loose with what it is that is supposed to be falsifiable. If the problem of induction gave one good reason not to seek confirming evidence, it would also give one good reason not to seek falsifying evidence.

But Popper introduces a complication that needs to be examined with care. For he stresses that for the purpose of testing, it is entirely legitimate to make further decisions to take nonbasic statements as unproblematic background knowledge. Given these further decisions, it becomes possible to falsify specific scientific theories.

To avoid possible confusion let us call falsifications that not only depend on basic statements and deductive logic but that require decisions to regard portions of a test system as background knowledge "conventional falsifications," as opposed to logical falsifications that depend only on logic and basic statements. [13] Perhaps Popper's solution to the problem of induction (and the methodological injunctions that depend on this purported solution) can be saved if we interpret Popper as arguing that there is an asymmetry of conventional falsification that enables us to provide good arguments against scientific theories even though no good arguments can be provided for them. The premises in such arguments would not, of course, be restricted to basic statements. Background knowledge must be allowed in as well.

But there is no asymmetry of *conventional* falsification and verification. There are two ways to establish this claim. Others have argued that if we cannot verify statements, we do not have enough premises to get beyond more logical falsification of whole test system conglomerates – if we can get even that far (Lieberson 1982b). In answer to this criticism, Popperians maintain that decisions will do in place of verifications (Watkins 1984). In response, one can point out (correctly, in my view) that arbitrary decisions will not do. We need to consider how well confirmed different statements are. Popperians implausibly (in my view) dispute this claim. [14] But I shall not pursue this line of argument. Regardless of the basis

13 These labels may be somewhat misleading. Remember that our tentative acceptance of some basic statements as true is just as conventional as our decision to regard nonbasic statements as background knowledge.

14 In actual scientific practice, the bulk of the premises needed to derive the refuted implication are regardless as well established and either true or good approximations to the truth. This judgment may change, of course, but it is crucial to the interpretation of experimental failures. If, for example, someone reports experimental results showing that particular objects fell toward the earth with decreasing acceleration, physicists would, of course, conclude that there was some

upon which the decisions are made, only decisions to take other statements as premises in refuting arguments make it possible to falsify particular scientific theories and claims.[15]

What I shall argue instead is that if it is permissible to enlarge the set of permissible premises to include background knowledge in order to make conventional falsifications possible, one also makes conventional verifications possible. Given the background knowledge that scientists employ, there may be no more difficulty in verifying universal statements than there is in falsifying them.

experimental error or that other forces besides gravity were involved. This conclusion, obviously (unless one is a Popperian), is based on the judgment that Galileo's law of falling bodies is a good approximation to the truth. If this judgment is unsupportable, as Popper alleges, science proceeds irrationally and should be replaced by a rational Popperian science.

It is, perhaps, possible to describe a completely noninductive enterprise (see Watkins, 1984). In deciding what to do in light of the failure of a prediction of a whole theoretical system, one might be guided entirely by consideration of which revisions are maximally content increasing, least ad hoc, etc. Questions about how well-supported the various constituents of the system are might conceivably play no role. But such an enterprise is radically unlike science, and, indeed, Popper is hesitant in presenting it. Zahar (1983, p. 168) quotes the following passages from Popper (1979) (written in 1930–31), which illustrate vividly Popper's early hesitance.

We unquestionably believe in the probability of hypotheses. And what is more significant: our belief that many a hypothesis is more probable than others is motivated by reasons which undeniably possess an objective character (*Grunde, denen ein objecktiver Zug nicht abgesprochen werden kann*). (1979, p. 145)

The subjective belief in the probability [of hypothesis] can be based on their corroboration, but it goes beyond what corroboration can effectively do. This belief assumes that a corroborated hypothesis will be corroborated again. It is clear that without this belief we could not act and hence that we could not live either. There is in this belief nothing further which should intrigue us. Its objective motives are clarified by the notion of corroboration to such an extent that this belief should not give rise to the deployment of any further epistemological questions. (Ibid., p. 155)

In his better-known discussions in English, Popper states that in the course of testing, scientists do and should take various propositions to be unproblematic background knowledge, although this background knowledge may itself be regarded as problematic in other inquiries. "There is first the layered structure of our theories – the layers of depth, of universality, and of precision. This structure allows us to distinguish between more risky or exposed parts of our theory, and other parts which we may – *comparatively speaking* – take for granted in testing an exposed hypothesis" (1983, p. 188). There is perhaps no formal contradiction here, since Popper could maintain that decisions to take propositions as part of background knowledge are unaffected by any judgment of how well-supported the propositions are. But without an illegitimate whiff or inductivism, this is an odd way to talk.

15 Popper (1957, p. 132) and some of his followers (e.g., Zahar 1983, pp. 155ff) suggest a method for making such decisions, which might appear to do away with the need for such decisions after all. Suppose the conjunction (S and U) has been logically falsified. The problem is to determine which is the culprit. If (S and U'), (S and U''), (S and U'''), etc., are all not logically falsified, whereas at least one of (S' and U), (S'' and U), (S''' and U), etc. is, we may conclude that U is the culprit, not S. As Glymour (1980, pp. 34–5) has pointed out, this suggestion faces serious formal difficulties. But the crucial point for my purposes is that this suggestion in no way obviates the need to rely on background knowledge. Indeed, what is happening here is that the failure to falsify (S and U'), (S and U''), (S and U'''), etc., is being used to provide an unacknowledged inductive justification for S, so that we can take the logical falsification of (S and U) as a falsification of U.

84

Consider, for example, a scientist attempting to determine the spectrum of a newly discovered metallic element (Nisbett and Thagard 1982). The scientist already knows that the spectrum of an element is invariant in particular ways from pure sample to sample. Given (1) this background knowledge, (2) the report of a particular Bunsen burner's flame turning orange, and (3) the claim that the particular sample was pure, the scientist can *deduce* that all pure samples of the element will turn a Bunsen burner's flame orange. So conventional verifications are no more impossible than are conventional falsifications. Straightforward probabilistic arguments can, of course, also be made. Given background knowledge in addition to basic statements, one can thus provide good arguments for as well as against universal statements. There is, of course, no claim to incorrigibility in pointing to such possibilities of verification, and one need be no more dogmatic in offering such arguments than one is when one relies on basic statements and background knowledge to falsify scientific claims. Notice that the possibility of providing such arguments is entirely independent of the question of whether there exists any sort of inductive logic, in the sense of a rational procedure according to which the acceptance of basic statements might justify the acceptance of nonbasic statements.

So Popper has provided no good arguments for his implausible second and third methodological rules. He has not shown that one should not seek evidence in support of scientific theories, and he has not shown that one should never regard scientific theories as well established. And, indeed, there are no good arguments for these injunctions, for they are mistaken. It is sensible to regard theories that have been extremely well tested and have passed those tests as close to the truth, and as admissible into the background knowledge that we rely upon in developing and testing new theories — just as it is sensible to regard such theories as a reliable basis for engineering purposes. In learning more, we are stuck on Neurath's boat, and as it becomes more seaworthy, we can repair it better.

3. FURTHER COMMENTS ON INDUCTION, FALSIFICATION, AND VERIFICATION

Popper believes he solved the problem of induction almost sixty years ago, and he is not reticent about saying so (1969a, p. 55; 1972, pp. 1–2). In a 1980 Addendum to the *Postscript to the Logic of Scientific Discovery* he writes:

> When I first wrote this section, I did not lay much stress upon the refutation of the historical myth that Newton's theory is the result of induction, because I thought that I had destroyed the theory of induction twenty years earlier; and I was enough of an optimist to believe that all the resistance still emanating from the defenders of induction would soon disappear. . . .
>
> Since then, inductivists have taken some heart; partly because I have no longer replied

to their arguments, which were all clearly refuted in various parts of my earlier writings. I no longer replied to them because I thought, and still think, that the issue was long settled and therefore boring. (1983, p. 147)

At the risk of boring Popper further, let me return to the problem of induction. For the issues are central not only in Popper's philosophy of science but in most accounts of the nature of science.

Hume's problem of induction follows from the combination of (1) his *empiricism,* which limits the evidence that can support or disconfirm statements to reports of sensory experiences and which treats reports of sensory experiences as self-justified, justified somehow by the experiences themselves, or as not needing justification and of (2) his *foundationalism,* which stipulates that a statement is justified only if it is self-justified or follows from self-justified statements by means of a good argument. It seems to me that, put together, empiricism and foundationalism create an insoluble problem of induction. But the proper reaction is not to conclude that all generalizations are equally unsupported. The proper reaction, rather, is to recognize that the piecemeal, nonfoundational justification of generalizations relative to what one regards as unproblematic background knowledge differs drastically from generalization to generalization and that this piecemeal "internal" justification is what matters in both science and practice. As Isaac Levi has rightly stressed, justification plays its part in responding to specific challenges to parts of our body of knowledge and in changing our body of knowledge (1980; compare Williams 1977, and Popper 1969a, p. 228).

Popper almost grants the point. For he recognizes and stresses that human knowledge does not rest on any epistemically privileged foundations. Even basic statements are not certain. We decide to accept them, even though such decisions may lead us astray. And our decisions do not stop there. The way that we advance beyond the uninformative logical falsification of a whole test system is to *decide* to take a large portion of the system as background knowledge and to attribute the failure or error to the remaining part. In doing so, one may err, but without doing so, one cannot learn anything.

We must go beyond merely logical falsification, and if we want science to grow rationally, we need a rational basis for deciding what statements to take to be true in order to test others. Popper denies that the extent to which a hypothesis is "corroborated" by the data ever provides such a basis. We may take various claims to be part of background knowledge, but we never have any good reason to believe that they are true. But as we have seen, either this claim is part of a complete skepticism about empirical knowledge, or it is unjustifiable.

This question of whether we can rely on what we think we have established in learning more about the world goes to the heart of traditional discussions of economic methodology, which have been dominated by what Professor Klant calls "empirical a priorism." Nassau Senior, John Stuart Mill, John Neville Keynes, and Lionel Robbins all emphasize that basic axioms of economic theory – claims such as "Agents prefer more commodities to fewer"[16] – are well established by everyday experience, including introspection. In using them in economic theorizing, one employs what Mill called the "deductive method" (see this volume, Chapter 3). The economist takes the axioms as already well established and explores their implications deductively. In doing so, he or she provides positive reasons to accept the derived conclusions. Testing the deductive conclusions is important to determine whether one has left out some relevant factor, not to determine whether the axioms or their deductive implications are correct.

So, for example, the strongest argument for the hypothesis of rational expectations is surely not that it survives hard tests, but that it seems to follow from the axioms of neoclassical theory, once one accepts the claim that knowledge is, from an economic perspective, a commodity like any other. Consider the famous argument that John Muth offered:

. . . I should like to suggest that expectations, since they are informed predictions of future events, are essentially the same as the predictions of the relevant economic theory. . . .

If the prediction of the theory were substantially better than the expectations of the firms, then there would be opportunities for the "insider" to profit from the knowledge – by inventory speculation if possible, by operating a firm, or by selling a price forecasting service to the firms. The profit opportunities would no longer exist if the aggregate expectation of the firms is the same as the prediction of the theory. (1961, pp. 316, 318)

This argument can be reformulated as deductively valid – that is, as an argument whose conclusion must be true if its premises all are true (see this volume, Chapter 13). The conclusion here is the generalization that, *ceteris paribus*, the expectations of firms "are essentially the same as the predictions of the relevant economic theory." Some of the largely implicit premises, such as that few firms run by economists make extraordinary profits or that the expectations of some firms are informed by and coincide with the predictions of economic theory, are roughly reports of observations. But also involved in the argument are premises concerning the advantages of accurate expectations and the accuracy of the predictions of economic theory, which are very far from being reports of observations. Some of these premises are questionable and have been questioned; and I do not maintain that the premises are all true and that the argument is thus sound. But whether or not the argument is sound, it is still valid, and the premises are largely contained within the background knowledge of a neoclassical economist. If one permits scientists to make use of background knowledge – as one must if there is to be

16   The example would, of course, have to be changed for the classical economists.

any science at all – then there are some valid arguments with acceptable premises for the truth of general scientific conclusions.[17]

If one surrenders foundationalism and regards conventional falsifications and verifications as acceptable arguments, one has immediately a partial non-Popperian solution to the problem of induction. Note that this solution turns crucially on its reformulation and on changing what one takes justification to be, as well as what one expects of a justification. For Hume would not, of course, permit us to help ourselves to the premises in the preceding argument that are not reports of perceptions. But without a foundationalist epistemology, there is no good reason even for an empiricist to insist that the premises can only be basic statements or, more stringently still, reports of sensory experiences. Popper correctly notes that epistemology should be concerned with *changes* in our body of knowledge. But his proposed solution to the problem of induction is a step backward toward the foundationalism that he rejects. Falsifications in the significant conventional sense depend not only on results of observations, but on many other statements that scientists take to be true. And the same expanded set of premises permits verifications as well.

4. CONCLUSION AND APPLICATIONS TO ECONOMIC METHODOLOGY

Even if Popper's rules for scientific procedure were free of the difficulties discussed previously, they would be of little or no value to economists. For within Popper's philosophy of science, there are no interesting questions to be asked concerning the falsifiability of economic theory (or of any other theory). Are economic theories logically falsifiable by themselves? No, of course not, but neither are any interesting theories in science. Can economic theories be incorporated into logically falsifiable test systems? Yes, of course they can, but the same goes for theories of practically all disciplines, no matter how patently unscientific they may appear to be. Can one take the other statements in such test systems to be background knowledge and regard economic theories as conventionally falsifiable? It all depends on whether the other statements have been falsified and thus, ultimately, on whether one can decide to take other statements to be background knowledge. Such decisions are, in Popper's view, more or less arbitrary. If one wants to, there is little difficulty in taking any statement to be conventionally falsifiable.

So, if one is concerned about whether economic theory is falsifiable, as many economists have been, what question is one asking? Once one leaves Popper's

17 McCloskey's 1985 interesting discussion of the sense in which it is metaphorical to claim that knowledge is a commodity may thus contribute little to understanding why many economists accept the hypothesis of rational expectations without waiting for experimental confirmation.

frame of reference, the answer is simple. Economists have wanted to know whether one could come, as the result of experiment or observation, to have *good reason* to believe that economic theories are false and mistaken. A necessary condition is that it be possible to incorporate such theories into logically falsifiable test systems. What is needed, in addition, is that one have good reason to believe that the other statements in such test statements are true or close to the truth. But, according to Popper, one never has such good reason. One can never justify the decision to regard a claim as a part of background knowledge on the grounds of its confirmation or corroboration (Lieberson 1982b). Consequently, within Popper's philosophy of science, there is no way to capture the questions economists ask concerning the falsifiability of their theories.

I should note parenthetically that although it might be reasonable to demand such a non-Popperian falsifiability of scientific theories, it is still not reasonable to seek falsifications only and unflinchingly to discard falsified theories. As I argue [in Chapter 7, this volume], virtually all of the fundamental "laws" and theories of economics have been falsified. For, as commonly stated, claims such as "All firms attempt to maximize profits" or "The preferences of individuals are transitive" are false (Hausman 1981b, chs. 6, 7). If one insisted that science consists only of falsifiable but unfalsified claims, either one would have to regard economic theory as a simple empirical failure or one could give it a conventionalist twist and regard it as an unfalsifiable metaphysical theory that might be of use in the development of empirical theories.[18] Although Popper does not explicitly say so, in his discussion of "the logic of the situation" he seems inclined to the latter view (Hands 1985a). Even though one might still find economics of value as useful metaphysics, the costs of such an interpretation are considerable. For on such a view, there are no empirical discriminations to be drawn between neoclassical economics and other approaches (unless, unlike neoclassical economics, some of the other approaches actually qualify as scientific), nor can one discriminate among propositions of neoclassical theory in terms of the extent to which they are supported by the evidence.

The most prominent economic methodologists who have defended parts of the Popperian gospel – and these are major figures such as Klant, Blaug (1980), and Hutchison (1977, 1978) – have been unwilling to draw such drastic conclusions, for they are too sensible and too knowledgeable about economics. Rather than defending extreme and indefensible views, they have simply argued for the importance of criticism and of empirical testing. In doing so, they have certainly not done the profession harm. Indeed, in their emphasis on the importance of testing in science, they may have done some significant good.

18 It might be suggested that economic theory remains of normative importance even though of no positive merit. But norms concerning what one ought to do must be based in part on positive theories of what will happen if. . . .

But to base one's advice on a mistaken philosophical doctrine, even when that doctrine has some true and uplifting things to say, is a dangerous practice that should stop. Some of Popper's general slogans can be retained, for they are consistent with the reasoned consensus within the philosophy of science. Empirical criticism is important to science, and scientific theories must, however indirectly, be open to criticism that uses the results of observations and experiments. The most important evidence in support of scientific theories comes from hard tests and analogous remarkable explanatory achievements, not from adding up unimportant favorable instances. Scientific knowledge is corrigible, and we may be led to surrender even the most important and best established theories. All of these Popperian (and equally, non-Popperian) theses may be retained and used to criticize quacks and irresponsible proponents of ill-founded and unsupported theories. But once nonphilosophers tie themselves to a philosophical system such as Popper's, they will be trapped with the unhelpful and even absurd consequences of such a system. A greater measure of philosophical agnosticism among economic methodologists would be more sensible.

If one takes Popper's methodology for science seriously, its flaws both from the perspective of knowledge acquisition and from the perspective of error avoidance are dramatic. Decisions about what to regard as unproblematic background knowledge must depend on the evidence. Just as we want theories to be well supported when we rely on them to build bridges or to manage inflation, so we want the theories we use to test other theories to be well supported. Without knowledge of the degree to which various claims about the world are supported by the evidence, scientists are as unable to engage in intelligent testing as engineers are unable to make practical use of the results of science. We need confirmations in order to decide which theories to use in practice and to decide which theories to rely on when testing others. And, as I have shown, we can have confirmations, too, although I do not pretend to understand all their complexities.

But one might object that this critique of Popper is really just semantics. It all comes down to the same thing. Are not the decisions Popper would have us make to take some things as true in order to test others motivated in fact by just the considerations of confirmation, whose necessity I have been stressing? Popper prefers his language because he wants to stress the absence of foundations and the consequent necessity of choice, with its complexities and uncertainties. But perhaps the disagreement is only one of language. He writes, for example, "the decision to ascribe the refutation of a theory to any particular part of it amounts, indeed, to the adoption of a hypothesis; and the risk involved is precisely the same" (1983, p. 189). Perhaps Popper is only denying that we can have foundational justifications for our claims.

I wish there were such an easy reconciliation, but there is not. We not only cannot have foundational justifications; we cannot have foundational falsifications either, both because basic statements are not foundational and because they do not suffice to falsify significant individual claims in science. The relevant notion of falsification is conventional falsification, and at this level there is no sharp asymmetry between verification and falsification. To make his philosophy of science acceptable, Popper would have to start by conceding that both in theory and in practice we need to consider how well supported theories are by the evidence. But to make such a concession, Popper would have to surrender most of his characteristic theses. He would have to consider what induction is and how it is justified, rather than denying that it exists. He would have to reject falsificationism as an apt label for his views, for science would sensibly be devoted to seeking verifications as well as falsifications, although, of course, neither is incorrigible. Essential to Popper's life's work has been not just the bland message that scientists should be critical and should seek and take seriously disconfirming evidence, but the striking and mistaken message that there is nothing to scientific rationality except conjecture, evidentially unsupportable methodological decision making, and consequent refutation. I doubt that an enterprise that functioned according to Popper's methodology could exist. It would be a poor tool for acquiring knowledge and of no use in practice. I should also note that despite Lakatos's plea for a "whiff of inductivism," his so-called methodology of scientific research programs is also vulnerable to the criticisms presented in the preceding discussion of induction.

One should not use a philosopher's theory as the criterion to judge/assess a particular set of eco knowledge

7

Is falsificationism unpractised or unpractisable?

Bruce Caldwell has recently argued that falsificationism is just too hard to practice in economics. He takes falsificationism to demand that theories be put to tests which are such that if the results are unfavorable, the theory under test must be given up or substantially modified. But it would obviously be silly to permit the results of any test, no matter how faulty it might be, to lead to such a drastic action. Thus,

> . . . for falsificationism to be viable, straightforward empirical tests must be possible. This requires that general laws be present; that initial conditions be relatively few in number, known, not subject to change, and easily checkable, that a test be a test of a theory, not a model; that data be trustworthy, complete, and accurately representative of analogous constructs in the theory. It is now perhaps understandable why falsificationism, though dominant in the methodological literature, seems to have been little practiced by working economists. (1984, p. 494)

Indeed, but if falsificationism really demands all this, it is not understandable why falsificationism is dominant in the methodological literature nor why anybody would stop to consider such an implausible doctrine. For remember that falsifiability is not supposed to be merely some nice trait of theories such as linearity or avoidance of imaginary numbers. In Popper's view falsifiability is the mark of science. And whether something is science or not is not a mere taxonomic question, but a question of whether the claims are genuinely empirically supported or corroborated or not.[1]

Popper himself must shoulder some of the blame for such misunderstanding, since in his popular presentations, he sometimes makes falsificationism sound something like this.[2] Straightforward empirical tests are required, but what makes for a straightforward empirical test is as much the behavior and the decisions of those carrying out the test as any peculiarities of the subject matter under test. Decisions are needed to defeat the obstacles presented by the subject matter. Otherwise one would have to require purely universal laws – and one would have to regard all statistical claims as incapable of empirical test and thus unscientific. Without methodological decisions, initial conditions would have to

---

1 "But it [any theory which is not scientific] cannot claim to be backed by empirical evidence in the scientific sense. . ." (1969a, p. 38).
2 Compare Lakatos's "dogmatic falsificationist" Popper (1968, 1978, pp. 12–19).

satisfy all of Caldwell's conditions – and one would then have to throw away the rest of science, too. For example, an observation of the return of a comet to its perihelion could not count as a test of gravitational theory, since initial conditions, such as its interactions with bodies very distant from the earth cannot be clearly observed.[3] The requirement that tests be tests of theories rather than models would be just as destructive. And however trustworthy, complete and accurately representative of analogous constructs in the theory the data may be, we are virtually never going to be in the position in any domain to be sure that our data are this good.

Popper recognized all this more than fifty years ago and stressed that the possibility of falsification rests on methodological decisions not to complain about the unreliability of the data, the interference of unspecified disturbing factors, or the inadequacy of the particular mathematical sharpening and refining of the theory from which the test prediction is derived.[4] Of course such decisions are not completely arbitrary, and when a well-corroborated theory is at stake it is sensible to double check before one takes the big step of regarding the theory as falsified. But neither are such decisions merely a ratification of given "facts."

Let us examine in more detail how methodological decisions overcome the obstacles of falsification that Caldwell discusses. He points out the following five complications of testing in economics that, he argues, should lead us to regard falsificationism as inapplicable:

(*a*) The initial conditions that one needs to derive predictions from economic theories are numerous and unstable, and it is impossible to specify more than a small number of them.

(*b*) Some of the initial conditions, such as those concerning individual preferences and expectations cannot be tested.

(*c*) Economics has no falsifiable general laws.

(*d*) Economic theories are not themselves tested. Instead models are tested, and models not only incorporate and sharpen claims of economic theories, but they also contain additional assertions and simplifications.

(*e*) The connection between the variables in economic theory and the data which are supposed to tell us what the values of the variable are is complex and ambiguous.

First a couple of remarks are in order concerning the truth of these claims: a, d, and e are true, b as stated is false, but can be salvaged, while c as stated is true, but not at all in the way that Caldwell intends. My objection to b may be in part a quibble about terms. There are, as far as I can see, no insuperable obstacles to determining (fallibly, of course, but with adequate assurance) the relevant prefer-

3 See Giere's lucid introductory discussion of the logic of testing (1982, chap. 6).
4 See Popper's *Logic of Scientific Discovery* (1934, rev. ed. 1968, esp. secs.9, 20, 29, and 30).

ences and beliefs of individuals, although there are lots of serious practical problems in so determining. Certainly Caldwell provides no argument to the contrary. But what really is bothering Caldwell, I think, is something different. In order to draw conclusions concerning market behavior from stylized claims about individual preferences, economists make a whole raft of simplifying assumptions: that tastes do not change, that new information does not become available or, more commonly, that information about the relevant past, present and future is perfect all along, that commodities are infinitely divisible, that individuals cannot directly influence the prices at which they buy and sell, and so forth. The problem with these claims is not that they are untestable, but that they are false, and when the predictions derived with their help go astray, there is no way to know for sure whether the failure is not due to such simplifications. This claim which is expressed in a slightly different way in d is correct.

But although c may be, strictly speaking, true, the point that Caldwell wishes to make cannot be sustained. Caldwell is heavily influenced by the fact that economists do not like to talk and think in terms of laws. They are more comfortable talking about the assumptions upon which their models are built. But some of the assumptions that they use to construct their models are not merely simplifications (such as infinite divisibility of commodities), but are assertions about people which are believed to capture (imperfectly) truths with important implications for how economies work. Whether economists use this language or not, whether they prefer to call these assertions "analytical devices" (p. 492) or to think of themselves as purveyors of models only, as soon as they draw inferences from their models and express some confidence in the conclusions inferred, they show such statements to be "laws" in economics. Examples are "The preferences of individuals are transitive and complete." "Individuals choose that option which they most prefer." "Entrepreneurs or firms attempt to maximize their net returns." The problem with such claims and the reason why "laws" last occurred in scare quotes is that not all of these general statements are true.[5] In the usage of most philosophers, to call a statement a law is of course to imply that it is true. Thus Caldwell may well be right in maintaining that there are no general laws in economics. He may also be verbally vindicated by the possibly narrow scope of these "laws." But falsifiability does not require unrestricted scope, and it obviously does not require that the statements to be tested be (true) *laws*, only that they be lawlike general statements. Economics has some of these.

Of course, if Caldwell is correct in his claim that there are insuperable obstacles to falsifying the claims of economics, then my assertions in the last two paragraphs are insupportable. For I maintained that statements of initial conditions are testable and often known to be false and that central generalizations of

5   See Hausman 1981b, chap. 6, sec. 2.

economics are testable and can also in many cases be shown to be false. So let us consider how falsificationism overcomes Caldwell's obstacles.

The answer is straightforward and in outline has already been given: decisions. Caldwell is right when he claims *a* that not all of the relevant variables have been measured or even considered. Should one then be unwilling to carry out tests of one's theory or unwilling to regard any tests as falsifications? No. One decides that the variables left out of account are of much less importance than those considered, forswears the easy excuses "disturbances" always provide, subjects one's theory to test and is willing to regard it as falsified when it fails the test. Suppose, for example, one tests whether a person's preferences are transitive by giving people long lists of pairs of descriptions of options and asks them to circle the description of the option they prefer in each pair.[6] When intransitivities arise, there are always excuses to be made – but the whole point of falsificationism is not to make such excuses unless a good testable case can be made for them. The tactic for dealing with the other obstacles is just the same. Of course there is lots of distance between the claims of an economic theory and the data one relies on in testing the theory of *d, e* and it may well be that the discrepancy between observation and prediction is due to mistakes made in squeezing a prediction out of the theory. But Popper's falsificationism rules out making such excuses unless the excuse is a precise and testable one. For every obstacle, there is a decision that overcomes it. This is the essence of Popper's message.

Just consider the following argument that Caldwell makes against the testability of initial conditions (although it is in fact an argument against the testability of economic "laws"):

Say the rationality postulate (transitivity in choice over a well-ordered preference function) is tested using the revealed preference approach. Transitive choice is taken to mean the consumer is rational, but if his preference function was not well-ordered (because tastes changed or information was imperfect), transitivity in choice reveals the consumer as irrational. Similarly, if intransitivities are revealed, is the consumer irrational, or do we assume that there was a change in one of the initial conditions? (p. 492n.)

Such problems are ubiquitous in all scientific testing, and Popper's falsificationism is designed specifically to overcome them. Provided that our results are consistently replicable, the answer to the last question is that in the absence of specific evidence that tastes changed or that information was particularly imperfect, we must regard the consumer as irrational (or, more accurately, we should regard the "rationality postulate" as falsified).[7]

6 The well-established phenomenon of "preference reversal" shows regular apparent intransitivities in preferences over amounts of money and specific gambles. See Grether and Plott 1979.
7 Economists often take the basic postulates of utility theory as defining rationality rather than taking them to be generalizations concerning human behavior. But when they apply their models to explain and predict economic phenomena, they necessarily assume that people are more or less

In fact, an honest falsificationist *must* regard virtually the whole of economic theory as false or unscientific.[8] The main obstacle to employing falsificationism in economics is not that it is too hard to falsify economic theories, but that it is too easy – with few, if any exceptions, anyone with a critical attitude would quickly falsify all of economics.

One might argue that this result is not as counterintuitive as it might appear – that the options falsificationism leaves open are not as unattractive as they might seem. If one adopts the first alternative and concedes that economic theory has been falsified and should be regarded as false, one can still emphasize its practical importance. Falsifiability is inapplicable because it has already done its work. What one is after in economics is not science, but rules of thumb that will help in the design and assessment of policies. One possible way to read Milton Friedman's influential "The Methodology of Positive Economics" (1953c) is as such a rejection of scientific ambitions. Note that such a tactic should *not* be confused with the sort of instrumentalism defended by the pragmatists or the early logical positivists nor with contemporary antirealist views of science.[9] Apparent disconfirmations are just as important to instrumentalists and antirealists as they are to realists, although, of course, they will be described differently.

The second alternative is not to regard economic theories as false, but as untestable metaphysical frameworks. Such frameworks may be useful in generating scientific theories and generalizations, but one does not treat them as scientific theories themselves, and one does not subject them to harsh empirical criticism. In his discussions of "situational logic" as the best method of social inquiry, Popper seems implicitly to take just this view of neoclassical economics.[10]

But both of these alternatives start from the denial that standard economic theories may be regarded as respectable well-corroborated scientific theories. Perhaps a better option still is to question the falsificationism which forces one to this conclusion. And, indeed, I think that a good case can be made that Popper's falsificationism is much too demanding. It is efficient at eliminating error, but if all we wanted was to avoid error, we could just refuse to assert anything at all. Whether instrumentalists, realists, conventionalists, or simply people, we also want some information; and given how hard it is to think up theories that are plausible and remotely consistent with the data, it seems sensible to look for a

---

rational, at least on average. So one must eventually face the question of what to think about claims such as "the rationality postulate" as generalizations about human behavior. See my 1981b, chap. 3, secs. 3, 4; chap. 6, chap. 2, or this volume, Chapter 3.

8 This point is argued at length in chap. 7 of my 1981b.

9 For an example of the sort of confusion I am warning against see Boland 1979. Caldwell also mistakenly supposes that instrumentalists can be cavalier about failures of their instruments (p. 492).

10 See Popper 1957, pp. 149ff, and D. Wade Hands 1985a.

methodology that lets more information through than does Popper's, but does not let so many errors slip in that the information is valueless.[11]

Indeed it seems to me that one might capture the spirit of Caldwell's comment by objecting that it does not seem sensible to cast away the best economic theories available — however imperfect they may be — on the strength of the methodological decisions that make testing possible. Caldwell's essay can then be interpreted as a demonstration of just how extensive and dubious such methodological decisions have to be. Perhaps a critical attitude is then not in order. Might there not be a more sensible way to react to falsifying instances of claims such as that the preferences of all consumers are complete and transitive? Given how much there is to be said *for* the claim that preferences are complete and transitive as a plausible exaggeration of a much more complicated reality and given the absence of superior alternatives, might it not be sensible to hang on to orthodox utility theory? Of course such a defense of orthodox utility theory requires that one make sense of there being evidence *for* propositions[12] and it also requires that one do a great deal of detailed work exposing the virtues and vices of utility theory. But the only alternative to such daunting tasks is to rule the bulk of economics out of science and, on similar grounds, to rule most of the rest of science out, too.

Caldwell concludes by arguing that ". . . it still seems to make sense for economic methodologists to start with the practice of economists, rather than with the writings of prescriptivist philosophers of science, in coming to terms with the methodology of their discipline."

Although I think that the point is perhaps a bit misleadingly made, I want to conclude by defending its spirit. What is at issue, I think, is not whether one ought to read prescriptivist philosophers of science at all, nor when one should do

---

11 My perspective here is heavily influenced by Isaac Levi. See his 1967, 1980.

12 Popper frequently comes close to flatly denying that it is possible to give evidence for theories. According to Popper, the best corroborated theory is only more worthy of test than is a testable, but as yet completely untested conjecture. It is, in his view, not one bit more credible. "What we do – or should do – is to *hold on, for the time being, to the most improbable of the surviving theories*, or more precisely, to the one that can be most severely tested. We tentatively *"accept"* this theory – but only in the sense that we select it as worthy to be subject to further criticism, and to the severest tests we can design."

He then concludes with the baffling and possibly contradictory remark, "On the positive side, we may be entitled to add that the surviving theory is the best theory – and the best tested theory – of which we know" (1968, p. 419). Not only does this view condemn scientists to a Sisyphusian task of pursuing a goal (truth) toward which they can never have reason to believe they are advancing, but this view can hardly be taken seriously in practical life. If somebody is about to try out some drug on my child, I don't care how severely tested the theories concerning this drug's effects *can be*. I care about how severely tested they have been and how well supported they are by the results of those tests. Among the tasks of the philosopher of science should be the elucidation of how it is that evidence supports theories, not the denial that they do. Indeed Popper himself reports that his original reason for becoming interested in the problem of demarcation was to distinguish theories which are genuinely "backed" by empirical evidence from those which aren't (1969a, p. 38).

so. What Caldwell is counseling rather is hesitation about taking philosophical pronouncements as established truth, ready for incisive, if not devastating application. Even if falsificationism were the best methodology for economics, one would have little solid ground for this conclusion until one paid a great deal of attention to how exactly falsificationism would work in economics. This sensible caution is based on Caldwell's just appreciation of the weaknesses in existing normative philosophical theories, not on any general proof that philosophers cannot reach conclusions that are well established and generally applicable. [13]

But even if philosophers make poor authorities, they still may make thought-provoking reading. Caldwell's caution about taking them to be authorities does not liberate writers on economic methodology from taking seriously prescriptive philosophy of science and considering just where it breaks down. Caldwell himself makes just such an effort in his *Beyond Positivism* (1982) and in the discussion note I have been reacting to, and although I have faulted him for his interpretation of Popper and for some of the details of his claims about testing in economics, I do not fault him at all for the nature of his task and the tenor of his comments. I agree, moreover, that falsificationism is not a good methodology for economics. But this shared conclusion will never be well established and its moral properly drawn, unless falsificationism is fairly presented and its central flaws (which have relatively little to do with any peculiarities of economics) clearly understood.

13 For an extensive discussion of these metamethodological issues, see the Postscript to my 1981b or this volume, Chapter 16.

8

The limits of economic science

When beset with fundamental doubts about the value of their achievements, economists look longingly to philosophy for help. No doubt scientists in other disciplines fiddle with the philosophy of science, too. They oversimplify it in introductory lectures and in introductory chapters of textbooks. They throw it in one another's teeth in the heat of polemical battles. They think seriously about it when they confront new problems that seem peculiar or confusing. But the self-doubts of economists are exceptional. They are only equalled by those that torment the practitioners of other, even less-developed social sciences.

When times are hard for economic theory – as they are now – (see Bell and Kristol, 1981), economists start boning up their philosophy of science, because they hope that they will be able to trace their difficulties to some simple, but definite methodological error or errors. Economists would, ironically, like nothing better than to discover that they have been methodological boneheads! In that case their ailments would have a definite cure.

By praising the methodological practices of economists, one crushes their hopes for such a philosophical "quick-fix." One also shows that scientific methods have their limits. Such praise for economists should not be exaggerated. One can, if one wishes, compile a hair-raising catalogue of stupendous methodological stupidities endorsed by and committed by economists. But economists have no monopoly on such gaffs. Einstein and Bohr could revolutionize physics while expounding (but probably not putting into practice) untenable methodological views. I shall argue that the inadequacies of economics are not mainly due to the methodological blunders of its practitioners, but to the recalcitrance of its subject matter. Scientific method has simply not served economists well.

On first glance this assertion might appear to be a variety of "anti-social scientific naturalism" (see Morgenbesser 1970, p. 20). Hundreds of authors have argued that social phenomena like those studied by economists lie beyond the limits of scientific method – or at least beyond the method of the natural sciences. Such antinaturalists have maintained that the methods of the natural sciences *cannot* apply to the study of societies and that various aspects of social life demand different methods of investigation. This paper contends, on the contrary, only that scientific methods have not worked very well for economists and that

I would like to thank Paul Thagard for comments on an earlier draft of this paper.

they are unlikely to work well. It does not assert that the inefficacy of scientific methods in economics is absolute or that it follows from anything special about human beings. Furthermore, I shall not argue, and I do not believe that there are any better ways to study economic phenomena than to employ scientific methods. I am instead making the more pessimistic claim that these, the best methods of knowledge acquisition, nevertheless have their limits and that one should not expect much of economics.

It is difficult to articulate and defend the thesis that scientific methods have not worked well and are unlikely to work well in economics, since nobody has established any detailed and explicit account of what "scientific method" is. It is thus hard to judge definitely whether economists have in fact followed scientific methods and have, to a considerable extent, failed *nevertheless*. Instead of making any futile attempt to say what scientific method is, I shall focus on the main lines of methodological *criticism* to which economic theory has been subject and shall point out that: (1) those methodological features of economics which have been criticized often differ little from actual characteristics of various natural sciences; (2) that the few real methodological differences between economics and some of the natural sciences can be explained as reasonable responses by economists to specific difficulties posed by the subject matter of economics; and (3) that there is no reason to believe that all the failures of economics can be attributed to methodological blunders of economists.

Since its first formulation, standard microeconomic theory has been subject to numerous methodological criticisms. The most important and pervasive of these runs as follows:

The fundamental theory of neoclassical economics is too "unrealistic." If taken literally and without qualifications, the basic "laws" of economics are simply false. It is not true that all businessmen always attempt to maximize profits or that individuals are never satisfied. If qualified with *ceteris paribus* clauses, such claims are insulated from any possible experimental refutation – of which there is not much danger anyway, since economists pay so little attention to testing. Economists instead devote their energies to mathematical efforts to discover what various formulations of their basic "laws" coupled with diverse auxiliary assumptions imply. Demonstrations of the existence and stability of "equilibrium" under a variety of simplified circumstances and comparisons of the properties of different equilibria make up the bulk of standard economics. If one leafs through almost any economics journal, one will find an assortment of models developed with an almost blithe disregard for questions of application or testing.

This general methodological complaint is repeated again and again not only by critics of mainstream economics, like the American institutionalists (Veblen 1898), but also by orthodox economists themselves when they turn to methodological musings in presidential addresses or in essays on how to do economics (Leontief 1971; Blaug 1980, esp. ch. 7).

The above criticism points out four features of mainstream economics and argues that these are in fact four methodological *errors:*

(1) Economists rely on generalizations that, if taken literally and without qualifications, are false.

(2) Economists hedge their generalization with *ceteris paribus* clauses which render them unfalsifiable.

(3) Economists devote little effort to testing their basic theory and are largely unperturbed by apparent refutations.

(4) Economists devote an undue amount of effort to developing abstact and inapplicable mathematical models.

Each of these characteristics of economics calls for detailed discussion, which I have undertaken elsewhere (Hausman 1981b, esp. ch. 7) and cannot provide in this short paper. But I think that one can show that (1)–(4) are not *errors* at all.

First, the basic "laws" of economics are, if taken literally and without qualifications, false. But so are the laws of virtually all sciences. There will always be possible disturbances and interferences of which theories take no explicit account. To adopt Galileo's strategy and to abstract from the complexities of real-world circumstances is not, in itself, to commit any methodological error. Other tactics *might,* of course, work better in economics. I have, in fact, argued elsewhere that the abstractions and idealizations of orthodox economics are probably too extreme (Hausman 1981a; 1981b, ch. 7). The orthodox approach may well not be optimal, but it is not unscientific.

But are the results of employing a Galilean strategy in economics usable and testable? The second criticism asserts that the *ceteris paribus* qualifications implicitly attached to the basic "laws" of economics make them unfalsifiable (Hutchison 1938, pp. 40–46). If "falsifiability" is supposed to be some sort of conclusive affair that employs only deductive logic, then it is quite true that *ceteris paribus* qualifications render generalizations unfalsifiable. But this sort of falsifiability exists, of course, nowhere except in careless formulations of Popper's views. The possibility of making allowances for "disturbances" or "interferences" does not always render generalizations untestable. Otherwise one would never be able to test any scientific laws (Rosenberg 1976, p. 137). So the problem must lie with the specific *ceteris paribus* qualifications that economists make. But few critics have realized that they need to point out some *special* vice of *ceteris paribus* clauses in economics (Blaug 1980, pp. 67–69, is a notable exception), and none have succeeded in doing so (Hausman 1981b, ch. 7).

The claims of economics are particularly difficult to test, and economists have been particularly loathe to test them. As the third criticism above alleges, testing plays a comparatively smaller role in economics than it does in many of the natural sciences. Herein lies a real methodological *difference.* Is it also a methodological *error?* Is orthodox microeconomics in reality a "dogmatic" "metaphysics" (fueled no doubt by ideological pressures) masquerading as science? Some economists who wear Popperian spectacles have made virtually this charge (see for example Hutchison 1938; or, less pejoratively, Bray 1977).

Economists do little testing for three reasons. First, even though the basic generalizations of economics are certainly not universal laws, economists already know that there is some truth to them (Robbins 1935, pp. 15, 77; Mill 1843, Bk. VI, ch. ix). Very little reflection on one's own behavior shows that there is certainly *something* to the claim that individuals have transitive preferences. With only a little further reflection (and there is some experimental evidence as well), it is equally obvious that people's preferences are not always entirely transitive. No test will ever show that the generalization that people's preferences are transitive is universally valid or entirely worthless. Second, economists are generally unable to do controlled experiments. Since it is generally impossible to escape the disturbances and the mess of real economic circumstances, it is extremely difficult to get informative results (Mill 1843, Bk. VI, ch. vii). Third, even if one were able to get reliable test results, they might well be of little comfort and assistance because of the extent to which economic circumstances are changing (Hicks 1979, pp. x–xi). Suppose one develops some model, ventures to apply it, and makes a "risky" prediction. The prediction is, let us suppose, borne out, and the economist feels that she is on the scent of something true and useful. But by the next time one attempts to apply the model, the relative importance of the various causal factors involved may have changed dramatically. Those factors which are left out of the theory and regarded as merely interferences may have become predominant.

So what should economists do? Spend more time testing their basic theory? For what purpose? How much effort should one expend to generate some largely ephemeral demarcation between those circumstances to which the theory reliably applies and those to which it does not? Perhaps with more testing economists might find out that their basic theory works even more miserably than is now recognized. The result might motivate more economists to look for alternative theories or to seek only relatively superficial generalizations. But such results will never and (if philosophers of science like Kuhn [1970, p. 77], Lakatos [1970, p. 12] and Laudan [1977, pp. 27–30] are to be believed at all) ought never to lead economists to give up a theory with the heuristic and classificational powers of standard microeconomics.

There is, moreover, no compelling reason why economists should attempt to formulate more superficial and directly testable generalizations. Those who have tried to do so, like the nineteenth-century German historical school or the twentieth-century American institutionalists, have had little success. There was nothing unscientific about their efforts; they just did not succeed. Given the constantly changing importance of the different causal factors that affect economic phenomena, there is certainly no conclusive reason to believe that more "realistic" generalizations will be valuable and informative. There is nothing unscientific about pursuing an abstract economic theory which is hard to test.

But, finally, one might still question whether economists do not devote unjustifiably great attention to abstract and completely inapplicable mathematical models. Again, I see no methodological *mistake*. In investigating and elaborating the implications of the basic laws they have discovered, physicists have explored various models, even when they knew that the basic claims of the models could not possibly be true of nature. Mainstream orthodox economists have attempted to follow exactly this strategy.

The strategy has not worked very well. Galilean abstraction thrives on the possibility of doing controlled experiments (or on the good fortune of being able to study a virtually closed system like the solar system). Unable to perform controlled experiments and cursed with a nasty messy subject matter, economists have not gotten very far. They have not been entirely in the dark, though, since casual experience and even introspection given one good reason to believe that the basic "laws" of economics, although problematic, are not entirely worthless. Economists have hoped, through the articulation of ever more complicated models, eventually to achieve a theory with enough scope and structure that its predictions will be clearly (although probably only intermittently) visible through the incessant interferences and complications of economic phenomena.

So I see nothing unscientific in the overall strategy of mainstream theorizing. At least in regard to its reliance on "unrealistic generalizations," economics is not greatly different from the natural sciences methodologically. Its limited success does not result from any fundamental methodological *error*. There are some real methodological *differences* — especially the relative unimportance of testing in economics. But these differences, as well as the failures of economics, result from difficulties inherent in the particular subject matter of economics. We have referred to three such difficulties: (i) economists are generally unable to perform controlled experiments; (ii) the subject matter of economics is "complex" — a large number of different *kinds* of causal factors influence economic phenomena; and (iii) the subject matter of economics is changing — the relative importance of different kinds of causal factors differs at different times.

A much more popular explanation for the limited success of scientific method in economics relies on the fact that economics concerns human behavior. In a sense I agree: the fact economics concerns human behavior contributes to the complexity and changeability of the subject matter and to the difficulties of performing experiments in economics. Moreover, as we shall shortly see, the fact that economists are concerned with the nature and consequences of human actions makes these difficulties particularly hard to avoid. Yet to claim that

103

scientific methods do not succeed in economics because economics is concerned with people is quite misleading. It suggests that there is something peculiar about people – free will, perhaps – which is beyond scientific study. Scientific methods are unlikely to work well on any complex and changeable subject matter on which experiments cannot be performed – regardless of whether human actions are involved.

In pointing to these peculiarities of the subject matter of economics to explain why scientific method has not served economists very well, I am not claiming that those who study the natural sciences never face similar difficulties. Astronomers, geologists, meteorologists and oceanographers are also unable to perform many controlled experiments; yet astronomers and geologists have far more solid achievements to their credit than do economists. Some biologists must confront problems concerning complexity and change which are similar to those faced by economists. Confronted by all these difficulties simultaneously, economists merely find the cards badly stacked against them.

There remains, however, a fundamental philosophical objection to my entire line of reasoning, which needs to be discussed. As philosophers and economists have often stressed, the complexity or the changeability of a subject matter depends on the means of classification that one possesses and thus on the theories one accepts. The gross motion of the planets appeared much more complicated before Kepler and Newton than they did afterward. In the same way, it is possible that in ten years, having developed a much better theory, theorists will find that economies are affected by few variables and that the relative importance of these influences changes very little. So there is no argument here against the *possibility* that scientific methods will succeed.

But this argument is weaker than it may appear. One is still entitled, given what one currently knows, to make estimates of how likely it is that economics and its subject matter will be thus transformed, and one may still reasonably maintain that the specific difficulties posed by the subject matter of economics (as that subject matter is currently conceptualized and understood) explain why economists have had so little success. Such explanations are not empty. Of course every unsuccessful science can complain about the complexity of its subject matter. But not every unsuccessful scientist can, like the economist, point to such a large number of different *kinds* of relevant causal factors nor to such evident and gross changes in the importance of different causal factors over time as those that economists have observed. These features of economic phenomena may evaporate with the development of better economic theory, but they do not merely indicate theoretical failure.

There are, in fact, two further reasons why it is particularly unlikely that scientific methods will work any better in the future for economists than they have in the past. First, the enormous pressure economists encounter to produce

immediately usable results militates against unfamiliar or "revolutionary" concep-
tualizations of economic phenomena. An esoteric theory that divided up the
phenomena which theorists now regard as "economic" in an entirely different way
would be unlikely to have any immediate predictive pay-offs. Second, economists
face in practice a serious restriction on the sort of explanations they can offer.
Since economic phenomena result from or are constituted by ordinary human
actions under various constraints, one expects those actions to be described and
explained in relatively familiar and recognizable ways (Machlup 1955, pp. 16–
17). An economist does not, of course, make any methodological *mistake* if he or
she depicts human action in some novel way (just as a theorist in cognitive
psychology makes no methodological mistake if he or she boldly suggests that
there are no such things as beliefs – see, for example, Churchland 1981). But to
break with our ordinary way of conceiving of human action is extraordinarily
difficult. There are thus strong sanctions which lead economists to continue to
talk about familiar and important phenomena in familiar terms.

Provided that economists do not abandon the attempt to explain and to predict
things like unemployment or inflation and to do so in terms of human actions
within institutional contraints, they cannot escape the familiar ways of classifying
economic phenomena. And until economic phenomena are radically reconceived,
their complexity and unsteadiness will remain. That complexity and unsteadiness
along with the inability to perform controlled experiments explain why economists have had such limited success. In principle there is no reason why scientific
methods might not triumph in economics. In practice, given the nature of the
subject matter of economics, they are unlikely to. In confronting a subject matter
like economies, scientific method has been impotent.

PART II

Causality in economics

As the essays in this part all argue, when economists make claims about influences and dependencies they are almost always asserting that various factors stand in causal, rather than merely mathematical, relations. Economics is unavoidably full of generalizations about the causes of phenomena, and there is no reason to lament this fact, for there is nothing objectionably metaphysical about causal claims. Moreover, as argued in Chapter 9, clarity about the causal character of economics helps avoid confusions about the relations between models and reality. Furthermore, as the Chapters 10 and 11 argue, recognition that economic generalizations are causal generalizations is crucial to understanding their *ceteris paribus* conditions and to employing sensibly the methods of comparative statics. These essays are not concerned with issues of theory assessment, but the methodological issues they discuss are nevertheless of importance both to philosophers and to economists.

9

Are there causal relations among dependent variables?

This paper makes explicit and takes issue with the bizarre view, which is unfortunately prevalent among social scientists, that causal relations are features of models only. There are some good reasons to represent causal factors with independent variables. But the association between causes and independent variables is only a desideratum model construction. It is not a criterion for judging which things are causes and which are effects.

INTRODUCTION

We would like to have answers to many causal questions about our economy and our society. Do large budget deficits cause higher interest rates or increased inflation? Will controlling the money supply control inflation? What other effects will controlling the money supply have? Will a particular policy of preferential hiring lead to a change in the status of disadvantaged groups?

Economists and social scientists often employ mathematical models, especially linear equation systems, in attempting to answer questions like these. But these tools are imperfect and have often been misunderstood even by their makers. Causal relations are only weakly represented by mathematical functions, because it is difficult to represent the effectiveness or asymmetry of causality. Functional relations do not unambiguously imply the existence of causal relations. Tests which establish the correctness of various functional relations do not automatically establish the truth of any causal claims. The mathematical relations between the growth in the supply of money in a given period and the rate of inflation in another period can, for example, be just the same whether the growth in the money supply affects the rate of inflation, the rate of inflation affects the money supply, they are mutually dependent, or they are both effects of some common cause.

This gap between mathematical and causal claims is particularly evident in those cases in which the mathematical relation is not supposed to capture any single causal relation. To give a simple example from the natural sciences, the ideal gas law, $PV = kT$ does not pick out some variables as causes and some as

The research for this paper was generously supported by the National Science Foundation (Grant # SES 8007385). Douglas Ehring provided invaluable assistance in thinking through related problems concerning causal asymmetry. Raymond Martin, Martin Osborne, Herbert Simon, and Paul Thagard made helpful criticisms. Susan Byers provided expert research assistance.

effects. On a particular occasion a change in temperature may cause a change in pressure. On another occasion a change in pressure may cause a change in temperature or a change in volume. $PV = kT$ continues, of course, to hold; but to know what will happen in the various circumstances, additional causal generalizations are needed.

One possible response to these difficulties might be to give up talking about causality. But this response has found few proponents. We need answers to causal questions like those in the first paragraph. To know whether one can do something about the status of Afro-Americans by means of preferential hiring, one needs causal knowledge. Policy decisions depend on causal generalizations. As econometricians have stressed, "Historical correlations may indeed be an easy way to forecast correctly so long as nothing happens to disturb the observed associations. . . . When something happens to alter the situation, however, structural information is indispensable" (Fisher 1966, p. 3. See also Marschak 1950, pp. 13, 16; 1953, pp. 4–8, 16–17, 23–24; and Koopmans 1949, pp. 46–47). Philosophers (like Cartwright 1979) have argued that knowledge of functional relations can never by itself be sufficient to guide policy. In any case, given the current state of the social sciences and even of most of physics, one needs causal knowledge to design policies rationally.

If theorists hope that their mathematical models can guide policy making, they must find some way to use them to make causal claims. Unfortunately, there has been considerable unclarity and confusion about how to relate mathematical equations and causal claims. My goal in this paper is to help make the connections precise and transparent. In particular, I hope to clarify the relationship between a cause and an independent variable and to show that there is no good reason to deny, as some social scientists have, that one can learn about objectively real causal relations obtaining among events or states of affairs.

In large part, this paper is in fact a defense of the platitude that causal generalizations are true or false assertions concerning real events or states of affairs. In order to show why such an obvious claim requires discussion and defense, I shall devote considerable space to illustrate some of the odd things that social scientists say about causality. In particular, in the next four sections, I shall examine a number of possible interpretations of the claim (made by Don Patinkin, a prominent economist) that dependent variables cannot depend on one another. One way of interpreting this claim, which some social scientists have endorsed explicitly, involves denying that one can ever offer generalizations concerning the causal relations obtaining among real events or states. In section 5 I shall examine and criticize the grounds for such a denial. In the course of presenting and criticizing interpretations of the claim that only independent variables may be causes, I shall be progressively clarifying the relations between causes and

110

independent variables, or, in other words, between the mathematical structure of models and equation systems and the causal structure of reality.

1. CAN DEPENDENT VARIABLES DEPEND ON ONE ANOTHER?

In his important book, *Money, Interest and Prices*, Don Patinkin writes the following:

> It is tempting to replace these complicated distinctions with the simple statement that . . . the equilibrium rate of interest depends on the *real* quantity of money. . . . Tempting — but, strictly speaking, meaningless. For both the rate of interest and the real quantity of money in the economy are dependent variables of the analysis; hence their equilibrium values cannot be dependent on each other, but only on the independent variables. (1956, p. 183)

This peculiar quotation is taken from an important book by a distinguished economist. Patinkin relies on the puzzling thesis that dependent variables or equilibrium values of dependent variables cannot depend on one another. In fact he claims that it is *meaningless* to assert that the equilibrium value of one dependent variable depends on the value of another. Patinkin also does not distinguish the relations that may obtain among economic phenomena (like the rate of interest) from relations that may obtain among variables (like "*r*").

The last observation may appear mere philosophical pedantry. In elementary logic one learns to distinguish use and mention, names and things that are named, properties and predicates, and so forth. As soon as one works with logic and mathematics in scientific investigations, one discovers the virtues of sloppiness about these matters. Economists almost never put quotation marks around variables like "*r*" when they are talking about the term, not about a rate of interest. The term "variable" is by now at least thoroughly ambiguous. In some contexts variables are syntactic objects, in others they are things in the world. Such looseness is usually innocuous. Patinkin obviously knows that the real quantity of money, M/p, bears a different relation to the rate of interest r, than the symbol "M/p" bears to "r," but he has better things to do than to bother with such details. As we shall see, however, this looseness is not entirely harmless, since it reflects and contributes to an inchoate and often relativistic causal instrumentalism, which is common among social scientists. I shall, however, indulge to some extent in the vice I decry. It would be tedious to avoid completely the ambiguities of the term "variable."

Patinkin maintains that equilibrium values of dependent variables cannot depend on one another. But it is obviously false to say that there can be no functional or mathematical dependence among dependent variables or among their values. Suppose one is given the size of one angle of a right triangle and the length of the hypotenuse. The lengths of the two legs of the triangle and the size of the other angle are all dependent variables, yet there are well-known functional relations among them.

Patinkin is not, I think, maintaining that there are no functional relations among dependent variables. Instead he is denying that dependent variables may *causally* depend on one another. The principle he relies on should be restated: Only (those things denoted by) independent variables may be causes. Notice that Patinkin, like all theorists, is primarily concerned with causal generalizations, not with singular causal claims.

Patinkin's principle, that only independent variables may be causes, is strikingly implausible. In general equilibrium models of economies, virtually all economically significant features are dependent variables. Accepting such a general equilibrium model, as many mainstream economists do, and given Patinkin's principle, one could never truly say things like "The Jones family eats a great deal of potatoes because they are poor," or "The shoe factory closed because it was inefficient." Neither the poverty of the Jones family nor the inefficiency of the shoe factory is an independent variable in general equilibrium theories.

Unlike some who espouse similar views of causality (see, for example, Jaffé 1954, pp. 512–13; or Bliss 1975, pp. 29, 34, 120), Patinkin might attempt to escape these implausible consequences by disavowing the general equilibrium model that generates them. The difficulty lies, however, with his causal principle, not with any particular model. Any simple general economic model will treat factors as endogenous or dependent which economists and laymen on various occasions reasonably regard as causes.

Why, then, does Patinkin believe that dependent variables cannot be causes? In a mathematical appendix to the work from which I have already quoted, Patinkin gives the following example (1956, p. 277):

$$q^D = f(p,t)$$

$$q^S = g(p)$$

$$q^D = q^S \tag{1.7}$$

(1.7) is Patinkin's numbering. The first equation says that the quantity demanded of a certain commodity, q^D is a function of its price, p, and a parameter, t "assumed to be uninfluenced by the economic forces of our market" (1956, p. 277). "t" might, for example, denote population size. By assumption, t does not depend on p, p^S, or q^D. The second equation (Patinkin's 1.10) says that q^S, the quantity supplied, is a function of the commodity's price, p. The third equation says that the quantity supplied equals the quantity demanded. These three equations with the three unknowns can be solved to give p, q^S, and q^D as functions of the parameter t (1956, p. 278):

$$p = J(t)$$

$$q^D = q^S = q = K(t) \tag{1.10}$$

p, q^S, and q^D are dependent variables and, given Patinkin's principle, there can be no causal relations among them.

The following appears to be an argument for the principle (the footnote is Patinkin's):

> From system (1.10) we can immediately see that as long as t remains constant there can be no change in either p or q. Hence in system (1.7) as a whole, . . . it remains meaningless[‡] to inquire as to the effect of a change in p or q, or vice versa. For p and q are the dependent variables of the system: they cannot change unless the independent variable, t, changes first. All that we can meaningfully ask for is the effects of a change in t on p or on q.

> [‡]Meaningless, that is, as long as the dependent and independent variables are defined as they are above. . . . (Patinkin 1956, p. 278)

Patinkin may believe that it is "meaningless" to inquire as to the effect of a change in one dependent variable, because there is no way to test one's conclusions (see also 1956, p. 15). Since one can only change p or q by changing t, how can one know what part of the change in q was due to the change in p and what part was due directly to t? With positivism in decline, few would now go so far as to say that it is *meaningless* "to inquire as to the effect of a change in p on q," but if the results of such inquiries are untestable, such inquiries are at least problematic – if not obviously unscientific.

The premise of this argument is, however, false. A simultaneous equation system like (1.7) is at best an approximate account of what is in reality a complicated causal process.[1] "The usual terminology is to regard such endogenous [dependent] variables as 'jointly determined' by the other variables in the model, but while this fairly describes the arithmetic involved, it is not a fair description of the underlying causal structure" (Fisher 1969, p. 492. See also Bentzel and Hansen 1954, p. 161). As soon as one ceases to regard the given model as sacrosanct, one can see that there are a variety of possible experiments that can provide evidence concerning the effect of a change in price on quantity demanded or quantity supplied. Prices could, for example, be set by fiat and the effects observed (see Fisher 1969, p. 494).

The general principle that only independent variables may be causes is thus unsupported, implausible and, at least from the pedantic perspective of an ana-

---

1 Herman Wold has been a persistent advocate of recursive models (which will be discussed later) in which, instead of mutual determination, one finds causal relations among the variables (1954; 1969, esp. p. 459). Wold does not, however, deny that nonrecursive models are legitimate for some purposes (Strotz and Wold 1960, p. 421). See also Strotz (1960), Basmann (1963, pp. 439–42), and Garb (1964, pp. 604ff).

lytic philosopher, ambiguous or incoherent. Yet this is no silly aberration. Patinkin is an important economist. The general principle is at least implicit in the work of many other economists and social scientists and is an explicit part of the method of comparative statics. Something more must be involved.

2. CAUSAL ORDERING AND RELATIVE INDEPENDENCE

Some qualifications make Patinkin's principle more reasonable. In a "causally-ordered" model, as Herbert Simon explains (1953), variables may be as it were "relatively independent." Consider the following general linear model:

$$s_1 q^S + d_1 q^D + w_1 p = a_1 t$$

$$s_2 q^S + d_2 q^D + w_2 p = a_2 t$$

$$s_3 q^S + d_3 q^D + w_3 p = a_3 t$$

"t" is an independent parameter. Its value is taken as a given and assumed not to depend on q^S, q^D, or p. If $s_1 = d_2 = a_2 = w_3 = a_3 = 0$ and $d_3 = -s_3$ (Case 1), one has a linear version of Patinkin's (1.7). In Case 1 the system is, in Simon's terminology, "fully integrated" (1953, p. 60). To solve for any of the unknowns, all three equations are needed. Another possibility is that $d_1 = s_1 = w_2 = w_3 = 0$ (Case 2). In Case 2, Simon calls the system "unintegrated" (1953, p. 60). It can be divided into two "subsystems." In the subsystem consisting of the first equation, one can solve for the value of "p." In the subsystem consisting of the second and third equations, one can solve independently for the values of "q^S" and "q^D." A "subsystem" is any set of equations in which one can solve for all the variables in the set either independently or given values calculated in other subsystems. All this is very briefly and casually said. The "subsystem" terminology is mine. For a rigorous and elegant presentation, see Simon's original article (1953).

There is a more interesting possibility. Suppose $d_1 = s_1 = d_2 = a_3 = 0$ (Case 3). In Case 3 the model is "causally ordered" (1953, p. 60). Each equation is a separate subsystem (which need not be the case in every causally ordered system – the model would still be causally ordered if d_2, for example, were not zero). Systems like Case 3 are called "recursive" or "triangular" (since the nonzero coefficients form a triangular array; "block triangular" systems are also causally ordered, although their subsystems are not). In subsystem one, the value of "p" may be calculated. Substituting that value into the second equation, one can solve for "q^S." Substituting for "p" and "q^S" in the third equation, one may solve for "q^D." In Simon's terminology, "p" is "directly causally dependent on "t," and "q^D" is directly causally dependent on "q^S" and "p" (1953, p. 61). Variables are causes of those that directly depend on them and of those that directly depend on those that directly depend on them and so forth (1953, p. 66). "t" is thus a cause of "q^D" even though "q^D" does not *directly* depend on "t." A variable is "exogenous" in any particular subsystem if its value is a given in that subsystem. A variable is "endogenous" in a subsystem if its value is calculated in that subsystem (1953, p. 61). In Case 3, for example, "t" is exogenous in subsystems one and two, "p" is endogenous in subsystem one and exogenous in subsystems two and three and so forth. Exogenity is the "relative independence" I referred to before. Only variables that are exogenous in some subsystem (even though they may be dependent in the system as a whole) are causes. Simon does not, by the way, play on any ambiguities of the term, "variable." The notion of causal ordering he defines is a metalanguage notion concerning the structure of an equation system.

To maintain that only variables that are exogenous in some subsystem may be causes is much more plausible than insisting that only independent variables may be causes.[2] If one takes Patinkin literally, the fact that a factory's inefficiency depends on the production possibilities is a sufficient reason to deny that the factory's inefficiency is a cause of its closing. In the spirit of Patinkin's principle, one could endorse the weaker thesis that only variables that are exogenous in some subsystem represent causes.

This seemingly plausible modification is not without its difficulties. For any linear model with any causal structure, one can always derive other models with every possible alternative causal structure, all of which have the same solution. In particular, it is possible to derive "reduced form" equations (like Patinkin's 1.10) in which each variable is a function of the independent parameters only, yet has the same solution or equilibrium value. Why then should one attach any significance to what Simon calls the "causal ordering" of equation systems?[3] How is one's choice of a particular structure supposed to be controlled by empirical evidence? One also wants to know what the "causal order" of a model has to do with the causal structure of the world.

There is a simple answer to the first two questions, while the third query will be discussed below in sections 3 and 5. There are other factors that influence prices and quantities supplied and demanded than are included in the model. Some of these may occur spontaneously; others may be brought into play by (experimental) intervention. The possibility of intervening is of great practical importance, but is not necessary in principle. Suppose one finds that whenever prices differ (whether as a result of intervention or "spontaneously"), the quantity supplied and the quantity demanded differ (but population remains fixed), while quantities supplied and demanded sometimes differ when prices and population remain fixed. Such data would be fallible evidence against Cases 1 and 2 and for the assertion that price is a cause of quantity supplied and demanded. One tests a

---

2 Wold argues (1954, pp. 172, 176 and 1955, p. 196) against the converse; not all equations state causal relations. See also Puu (1969, pp. 121–23).

3 Wolfson (1970, esp. pp. 255–56) argues that causal ordering is, in fact, of no significance.

check

causal ordering in which in some subsystem "x" is exogenous while "y" is endogenous by finding out whether whatever affects x affects y, while something affects y but not x (which is precisely how one tests whether events or states of affairs denoted by "x" are causes of events or states of affairs denoted by "y") (Hausman 1984a, Simon 1953, pp. 69–70; Simon 1974; Blalock 1964; Bunzl 1984). Note that causality is primarily a relation among individual events. Yet I shall talk (as is common) of x, an event type or a property of individual events, causing y, another event type. This way of talking can give rise to needless problems. Recall the ideal gas example in the introduction. There is no sense in asserting that changes in pressure, for example, cause changes in temperature unless one specifies the circumstances. Talk of x causing y should always be understood as asserting that instances of x cause instances of y in specified circumstances.

The revised principle, "x is a direct cause of y if and only if in some subsystem "x" is exogenous and "y" is endogenous" is much more plausible than Patinkin's own thesis; but a fundamental objection remains. *This principle,* like Patinkin's, *is a principle of model construction, not a criterion for deciding whether x causes y.* It is not as if "p," "q^S" and "q^D" are given as independent or dependent and on that basis one decides whether prices are causes of supply or demand. Instead one decides whether "p" should be an independent variable by deciding whether it is causally dependent on other phenomena being studied (Ando 1963, p. 1; Wold 1969, p. 443). When one finds in Patinkin's model that both "r" and "M/p" are dependent variables (and not causally ordered), one can infer that Patinkin believes that the rate of interest is not a cause or an effect of the real quantity of money; but the fact that "r" and "M/p" are both dependent variables is not *grounds* to deny that r and M/p are causally related.

3. INDIRECT TESTING OF CAUSAL GENERALIZATIONS

To leave the issue at this point would be to accuse Patinkin and others (Bliss 1975, ch. 25; Marshall 1930, p. 538; Schumpeter 1954, p. 943) of a silly mistake. Their denial that x can cause y on the grounds that "x" and "y" are dependent variables would be no better than denying that the earth revolves around the sun on the grounds that in Aristotle's cosmology it is *said to be* stationary in the center of the universe. The analogy suggests, however, a fairer construal of the position. Although one denotes by independent variables only those factors that one believes to be independent of or causally prior to the other states and events mentioned, one cannot judge whether changes in the supply of money cause inflation merely by looking and seeing. When one tests a model, it might be argued that one thereby gets evidence for the correctness of its causal structure. On this construal, Patinkin is thus arguing that the rate of interest is neither cause nor effect of the real quantity of money, because only models in which both "r" and "M/p" are dependent variables are well-confirmed. "As an assumption of the model, it [the causal dependence of one variable on another] is tested, along with all of the assumptions incorporated into the model, by the correspondence between the model and the data" (Blalock and Costner 1972, p. 836). The image here is that one compares the predictions of two models with different causal structures and accepts the causal order of well-confirmed models.

Let us examine this reconstruction of Patinkin's views carefully. Although it fits Patinkin's exposition badly (he does not argue that his model is well-confirmed, and he has little to say about the evidence), it raises important questions. As we have seen, models with different causal structures do *not* necessarily predict different equilibrium values of the variables. To test the causal ordering of a model, one must have recourse to the experimental or statistical manipulations mentioned previously. It thus seems awkward to talk of testing causal claims indirectly by means of testing models in which they are embedded. Tests of causality do not rely on all the functional relations within the model, but focus fairly directly on its causal structure. It seems that one tests the causal ordering of "x" and "y" by testing to see whether x causes y. One apparently confirms (in part) a model, M, in which "y" is causally dependent on "x" by confirming the generalization that (in the specified circumstances) x causes y. One does not confirm the latter indirectly when assessing M's overall adequacy. To argue that x does not cause y because in M "y" does not causally depend on "x" is to put the cart before the horse. One's acceptance of M rests on one's causal judgments, not *vice versa.*

But the relations between the testing of a causal generalization and the testing of a model in which it is contained are more intricate. Consider more carefully what is involved in experimental interventions. Let X and Y be instances of kinds of events x and y or possess properties x and y. In general the experimenter assumes that X's cause Y's if and only if Y's are affected whenever one acts on X's, but X's sometimes stay put when Y's are "wiggled." Regardless of how one analyzes causality, this asymmetry remains a crucial and an enormously useful fact. Whenever experimental intervention is possible, one tests a causal ordering by finding out whether whatever affects X's affect Y's but not *vice versa.*

Why is our ability to act and to intervene of such importance in testing causal generalizations? Although some philosophers (for example, von Wright, 1975) have seen a deeper significance here, I suggest that the reason is that we can be reasonably sure that our actions are not themselves caused by the changes in the phenomena we are investigating or by causes of those changes. If our apparent direct influence on Y were in fact caused by the change in X (or by some other cause of X's change), we could mistakenly jump to the conclusion that whatever affects Y's affects X's and get the causal ordering wrong. Investigation of causal relations by experimental (and statistical) means always depends on prior knowledge or assumptions about what causal factors may be involved and how they may

117

be related. To the extent that the model in which the causal generalization is embedded specifies such things, our "direct" testing of causal ordering presupposes the correctness of other parts of the model. Testing for causality is not presuppositionless, and some of the presuppositions will be included in the models in which causal generalizations are embedded.

When one considers the various statistical means of testing for causality, the same points stand out. Suppose that x and y are correlated and that one wants to determine whether X's cause Y's or Y's cause X's or whether the correlation is due to some common cause of x and y. Suppose that, in the circumstances considered, X's always precede Y's, so that one can (on the assumption that causation never runs backward in time) rule out the possibility that y causes x. To determine whether x causes y or whether x and y are effects of a common cause, one can examine the partial correlation between x and y when one controls for other factors. If the partial correlation does not disappear, no matter what factors one controls for, one concludes that x causes y. If the partial correlation becomes zero when one controls for some factor z, one can conclude that z is a common cause of x and y or that z lies on the causal chain connecting x and y (Simon 1954; Blalock 1964).

While this sketch hardly exhausts the available statistical expedients (see, for example, Granger 1969), it is sufficient to show how much such causal testing depends on prior assumptions. One needs to know what the other relevant factors might be, and one will often need further information to tell whether these are common causes or intervening links. Much of this information will be supplied by the model in which the causal generalization is embedded. Claims about causal orderings can be tested only within a context that specifies possible causal factors and some of the relations among them.

There is thus something right about the assimilation of the testing of causal generalizations to the indirect testing of theoretical claims. But the similarities should not be exaggerated. The context within which one tests claims of causal ordering depends to a very great extent on causal assumptions that are *not* part of the model being tested. Causal generalizations that are part of no explicit model at all can be tested without requiring a general assessment of any theoretical model. Causal testing requires a great many causal presuppositions, but this fact does not imply that one can only tell whether x causes y by means of an overall assessment of some model in which "y" is causally dependent on "x."

4. CAUSAL INSTRUMENTALISM

There is one other way in which one might defend Patinkin's assertions that one can infer that the rate of interest cannot be either cause or effect of the real quantity of money from the fact that "r" and "M/p" are dependent variables (and not causally ordered). What Patinkin may be arguing is that *within the model he is presenting* ("as long as the dependent and independent variables are defined as they are above," 1956, p. 278), it is "meaningless" to regard r as a cause or an effect of M/p, since both "r" and "M/p" are dependent variables. The suggestion that r is a cause of M/p in *Patinkin's model* is as absurd as the suggestion that in *Macbeth* Lady Macbeth's sleepwalking caused Malcolm's and MacDuff's rebellion. The structure of the model is decisive, since Patinkin is only concerned with relations within the model. "Indeed, it is the purpose of the analysis at this level to conduct conceptual 'market experiments' . . ." (Patinkin 1956, p. 15).

This defense comes with a heavy cost, however. Shakespeare could afford to foreclose the possibility that Lady Macbeth's sleepwalking was a cause of the rebellion for artistic reasons, since he did not intend *Macbeth* to be a history of England. Patinkin does not intend his work to be merely an amalgam of fiction and mathematics. It is supposed to apply indirectly or with qualifications or with a healthy margin of error to real economic circumstances. And once Patinkin maintains that his model applies, he cannot infer merely from the fact that neither "r" nor "M/p" is an independent variable in the model that r is neither a cause nor an effect of M/p.

One reason why Patinkin may not recognize the hopelessness of arguing to causal conclusions on the basis of the classification of variables (or of the causal structure of a model) is that he may believe that causal claims are model dependent. There is a variety of *causal instrumentalism*, which is common among economists, at least, and which supports this belief.[4] Many economists believe that one should relativize or confine causal claims to particular models. I call such restriction of causal claims to particular models "causal instrumentalism" since it is analogous to the noncognitive instrumentalist interpretation of theoretical claims proposed by some logical positivist philosophers of science (for discussion see Nagel 1961, pp. 129–40, and Morgenbesser 1969).

Opposed to causal instrumentalism is "causal realism," which maintains that there are true causal generalizations. Causal realists and instrumentalists will also disagree about the interpretation of singular causal claims, but I shall concentrate on causal generalizations. The phrase "causal realism" may suggest a heavily metaphysical view which countenances causal necessity, causal powers, and so forth. Although causal metaphysical realists will be causal realists, causal realism is a modest position. It maintains only that statements like "Striking matches

---

4   Causal instrumentalism has also been advocated with respect to the natural sciences: "Causality is a relation within the realm of conceptual objects. The relation of cause and effect refer to conceptual events regardless of the relation of the latter to reality" (Lenzen, *Causality in Natural Science*, p. 6, quoted in Bunge 1959, p. 5). I discovered the existence of causal instrumentalism among economists when talking with some of them about my paper, "Does the Wage Depend on the Marginal Productivity of Labor?" [later published as Hausman 1990d]. Some of those economists I spoke with were puzzled that I should consider this a question about economic reality. Causal questions, they assumed, were questions about models.

causes them to light" are sometimes literally true. Perhaps there is a cogent argument showing that such statements can only be true if various metaphysical claims about causal necessity are true. In that case, causal realists would have to be causal metaphysical realists. But I am only considering and defending a model causal realism that (a) takes "x" and "y" in the generalization "x causes y" as intended to denote actual events or states of affairs or as intended to refer to kinds of events or states of affairs and that (b) takes full acceptance of such generalizations as a commitment to their truth.

According to the causal instrumentalist, one should not regard Patinkin's simple supply–demand model as showing that the commodity's price and the quantity demanded and supplied causally depend in real economies on the size of the population. Instead one should assert only that there is such a dependence in the particular model (or "conceptual experiment"). One is making no claims about the causal relations among actual economic phenomena; causal claims concern relations among variables within models. The ambiguities in the term "variable" mentioned above make this paradoxical view easier to accept. The so-called experiments which one might perform to investigate the influence of price on quantity violate both the equations of the "reduced form" of the model (1.10) and at least the third equation of (1.7) (or Case 1), since there will generally be an excess supply or demand when price is arbitrarily fixed. To say that "q^D" is not causally dependent on "p" in (1.7) or in Case 1 does not imply that "q^D" might be causally dependent on "p" in another model. Similarly, the fact that the inefficiency of a factory cannot be a cause of its closing is only a feature of some general equilibrium models. The causal instrumentalist is free to work with a diversity of models with different causal structures. On the instrumentalist view, acceptance of a model demands no commitment to the objective truth of any causal claims concerning the world. Causal orderings are features of models only.

I do not know for sure whether Patinkin is a causal instrumentalist, although the quotations strongly suggest that he is; and causal instrumentalists will find his conclusions more defensible. In any event, such relativizing of causal claims to particular systems or models is common. In his influential book, *Causal Inferences in Non-experimental Research*, Hubert Blalock, for example, adopts what he takes to be Herbert Simon's view:[5] "Following Simon, we shall conceptualize causality in

---

5 Simon explicitly repudiates an instrumentalist reading of his views: "We have then two notions of 'direction': the relation of points on a map, and the relation of cities on the globe. Similarly, in the case of causality, we have a relation between variables in a mathematical model (the relation denoted by my term 'cause'); and a relation in the real world between the phenomena denoted by these variables (the relation denoted by the common-sense term 'cause')" (1955, p. 194). Causality is discussed by Simon as a metalanguage concept because the equations of a model do not themselves assert which relations are causal. Causal relations are *shown* by the structure of the equation system; they are not explicitly stated by the equations. This fact does not imply that models do not enable social scientists to offer true non-model-relative, object-language causal generalizations.

terms of simplified models. . . . In other words, there is nothing absolute about any particular model, nor is it true that if two models make use of different variables, either one or the other must in some sense be 'wrong' " (p. 15). ". . . [A] *relationship that is direct in one theoretical system may be indirect in another,* or it may even be taken as spurious" (p. 18). On Blalock's view (as on Theodorson's 1967, p. 143), one might say that "x" is a cause of "y" in some models, "y" is a cause of "x" in others, and that in still others neither is a cause of the other.

5. ASSESSING CAUSAL INSTRUMENTALISM

Most people are causal realists. Indeed, Blalock himself concedes, "However, it will probably be extremely difficult for most persons, including the present writer, to get along without the aid of a metaphysical assumption to the effect that something akin to causal laws operates in the real world and not just in the hypothetical models of the scientist. But such an assumption amounts only to a "pious opinion" and cannot be demonstrated by any methods presently known" (1964, pp. 14–15). In arguing against causal instrumentalism I shall be arguing for a thesis that is so trite and "obvious" that it may appear to need no defense. Surely no one seriously believes that models of unemployment or inflation or racial discrimination can never say anything true or false about real world causes and effects.

Causal instrumentalism is a particularly implausible kind of instrumentalism. Claims about the structure of an atom, for example, explain or predict observable results (perhaps concerning the spectrum of an element) only through a long chain of inferences. There is thus some initial plausibility in regarding statements about atomic structure, as instrumentalists do, as a means for making such inferences. The implications of "x causes y" (unless "x" and "y" denote unobservable events or states of affairs) are, on the other hand, quite direct. Although the testing of causal generalizations, like all testing, will require various auxiliary assumptions, causal generalizations are even less like "inference tickets" or principles for organizing experience than are theoretical claims. There are, of course, also familiar general difficulties with both theoretical and causal instrumentalism that do not need to be repeated here.[6]

6 At least two major difficulties make noncognitive instrumentalism concerning theoretical statements implausible. First, regarding theoretical claims merely as rules for making inferences and thus as neither true nor false seems merely to shift the question. Claims about atoms are not merely inference tickets, they are believed to be reliable inference tickets. Why? Presumably because they are something very like true. Second, the general construal of theoretical claims as metalanguage rules rather than object-language assertions has little basis in the behavior of scientists, except insofar as they are influenced by instrumentalist philosophers. In particular circumstances with respect to particular theories, a "local" instrumentalism can be sensible (see Gardner 1979). In the twentieth century, the peculiarities of quantum mechanics have led many scientists to interpret particular theories instrumentally. Few scientists have, however, been instrumentalists about scientific theories in general.

Many economists and other social scientists espouse causal instrumentalism, despite its gross implausibility, because they mistakenly believe that there are compelling philosophical objections to interpreting causal generalizations realistically. The most effective defense of causal realism is to make explicit and refute the arguments that lead economists and social scientists to maintain that causal claims concern the structure of models only. The arguments for causal realism (why else should policies be based on causal generalizations?) are obvious.

In the works of writers like Blalock and of philosophical critics of causal realism like van Fraassen (1980, pp. 115–18) and Beauchamp and Rosenberg (1981, pp. 240–46), one can find five main arguments supporting causal instrumentalism:

1. The first is a strict empiricist worry that causal generalizations are not conclusively verifiable. They thus appear unwarranted to a strict empiricist or to a logical positivist (as do claims about atoms or electrons). But if the instrumentalist is right and causal generalizations are not true or false, one need not be concerned. If causal generalizations concern features of models and merely provide ways of conceptualizing the world, perhaps they need no verification. But the strict empiricism that thus motivates causal instrumentalism is untenable. The point is by now too well known to require elaboration: no scientific claims are conclusively verifiable (see, for example, Quine 1969; Suppe 1977, pp. 3–118).

2. But even more moderate empiricists have had qualms about the testability of causal generalizations. Why? Suppose one accepts an empiricist analysis of causality like Hume's. On one interpretation of Hume, the only properties of the causal relation are spatial contiguity and constant conjunction of cause and effect and temporal priority of the cause. The only difficulty in veryifying Humean causal generalizations is induction, which is an unavoidable difficulty with all generalizations and which worries only extreme empiricists. Moderate empiricist social scientists could thus dissolve their qualms merely by employing a properly empiricist notion of causality. The causal instrumentalism of moderate empiricists thus arises from an apparent philosophical inconsistency. Neither consistent moderate empiricists nor consistent anti-empiricists need give up talking about objective causal relations.

Moderate empiricist social scientists have sometimes been inconsistent in just this way. This inconsistency is not, however, the result of confusion or lack of philosophical training. Simultaneous equation systems provide information about the likely effects of various possible happenings or interventions only if causal relations, relations of mutual dependence, and the "spurious" relations between effects of a common cause can be distinguished, and one can judge the direction of the causal relations. But Hume's notion of causality often does not permit such distinctions to be drawn, since there is rarely any explicit temporal ordering among the variables. Hicks, for example, maintains that "contemporaneous causation" is "the characteristic form of the causal relation in modern economics" (1979, p. 62). But if simultaneous equation systems support no causal conclusions, they will be by themselves of very little use in policy making.

There are two ways around the difficulty which do not require a non-Humean notion of causality (Asher 1976, p. 11). Time can be explicitly introduced. Alternatively, one can have an implicit theory or set of beliefs concerning time orderings upon which causal judgments may be based. There are practical difficulties with the first option (Asher 1976, p. 27), while the second option is not rigorous or precise.

Not only are the possible ways of reintroducing temporal orderings unsatisfactory, but economists often regard relations as causal without possessing any solid view of the underlying dynamic processes. Causal claims seem to rest more on an asymmetrical notion of determination or effectiveness than they do on time ordering (Strotz and Wold 1960, p. 418; Blalock 1964, p. 10; Goldstein 1967, p. 154). But notions of simultaneous causation, determination, and effectiveness may not seem empirically respectable. Hence the retreat to causal instrumentalism.

A more familiar difficulty with Hume's concept of causality also plagues social scientists. On Hume's view, the only difference between an absolutely constant conjunction (with temporal priority and spatial contiguity) and a causal relation is psychological.[7] Later empiricists have attempted to find a more secure and objective distinction by developing the notion of a scientific law and stressing the hierarchical systematization of laws into theories. These efforts are of little use to social scientists, who possess rough and ready causal generalizations, but who are noticeably short on universal laws. Distinguishing between a mere correlation and a causal connection is often a pressing practical problem. With few laws to provide guidance, there seems to be in Hume's notion of causality little that licenses drawing any distinction at all. Beauchamp and Rosenberg, for example, argue that without "universal and uniform laws, there is no Humean causation, anywhere" (1981, p. 102).

These moderate empiricist qualms reveal, I believe, the inadequacy of traditional empiricist analyses of causality, not the illegitimacy of the causal generalizations social scientists offer. Experimental interventions and statistical manipulations both bring empirical evidence to bear on the assessment of causal generalizations.

7 One plausible interpretation of Hume denies that he attempts to replace the traditional conception of causality as involving a necessary connection between cause and effect (Mackie 1974, p. 20; Beauchamp and Rosenberg 1981, pp. 10ff, 139–45). On this interpretation, Hume is instead showing that we only have evidence of constant conjunctions (with temporal priority and spatial contiguity). Some of our beliefs concerning causal connections thus go beyond the evidence. On this interpretation, causal instrumentalism is a modern restatement of Hume's position. Instead of regarding the necessary connection which is involved in our concept of causality as a psychological propensity to pass from the idea of the cause to the idea of the effect (Hume 1748, pp. 64–84, 86), social scientists regard causal connections as features of the organization of conceptual models. In either case, a crucial difference between causal and noncausal regularities lies with us.

Such assessment is, as I have stressed, very far from presuppositionless, but there are no grounds for the complaint that such assessment does not rest on empirical evidence at all. An adequate empiricist account of causal priority and of causal generalizations must do justice to the reality of such empirical testing. Recent empiricist work on causal asymmetry (see Mackie 1974, ch. 7; and my 1984a) and on imperfect generalizations (see Mackie 1974, ch. 3) offers new possibilities. In any event, the difficulties here lie with traditional and overly narrow empiricist accounts of causation. There is no reason here to deny that social scientists can offer true causal generalizations.

3. Perhaps in presenting the above two arguments, I have misconstrued the qualms of causal instrumentalists. They may be more concerned about the objectivity of causal claims than with their verification. In fact, it seems to me that the most serious arguments for causal instrumentalism challenge the objectivity of causal generalizations (see also argument 5 below). Blalock comments, "In brief, many of the objections to causal thinking reduce to the two points that the notion of cause and effect is far too simple to describe reality, with causal laws being much more a property of the observer than of the real world itself" (1968, p. 161). On Hume's account of causality, there is no objective distinction between cause and effect when they are simultaneous, and, in any case, the only objective difference is temporal. The effectiveness or the determination of causes reflects only our subjective propensities. On the manipulability theory of causal priority espoused by Collingwood (1940), Gasking (1955), and von Wright (1975) (and sometimes defended by social scientists who are impressed with the immense practical importance of manipulability), the difference between cause and effect is ineluctably anthropomorphic. Causes are like levers that enable us to move effects. "z is a cause of y if, by hypothesis, it is or 'would be' possible by *controlling* z indirectly to control y, at least stochastically" (Strotz and Wold 1960, p. 418). Abstracting from our ability to act and from the pragmatic orientation of potential actors, all there are in the world are regularities among kinds of events or states (Wold 1969, p. 459; Orcutt 1952, p. 307; Kaplan 1965, p. 145).

If Humeans or manipulability theorists are right, it seems that no causal generalizations, at least concerning contemporaneous causes and effects, are objectively true.[8] Since causal generalizations are nevertheless undeniably important for our actions, perhaps one should regard them as important features of the way we conceptualize the world — that is, as features of models. Qualms about the objectivity of causal ordering can thus provide a third argument for causal instrumentalism.

But Humeans and manipulability theorists are not right. Whether x causes y (even where x and y are simultaneous) is an objective fact. The procedures em-

8 Beauchamp and Rosenberg (1981) do not regard themselves as causal instrumentalists, but they conjecture that there is no objective asymmetry between cause and effect (pp. 236–46) and they accept a causal instrumentalist reading of Hume (see note 7).

ployed to test for causal ordering are sufficient argument for the objectivity of that ordering (Bunzl 1984). Whether it is indeed the case that whatever influences x influences y, but not *vice versa*, does not depend on anything peculiar to human action or on the pragmatic orientation of a human actor. Observed correlations or the outcomes of controlled experiments are facts about the world, not about our pragmatic stance; and they do not depend on any metaphysical peculiarities of human action. In experimenting we do, of course, act, intervene and manipulate; and our ability to act and to experiment is of the greatest practical importance. In no other way can we so easily convince ourselves that the events which are affecting x and y are not caused by x or y or by causes of x or y. Even if indispensable in learning about causal ordering (which is dubious – see Miller 1971, pp. 274–81), our ability to act is in no way constitutive of causal ordering.

4. Neither empiricist qualms about the verifiability of causal generalizations nor worries about the objectivity of causal priority provide good arguments for causal instrumentalism. But these are not the only concerns that have driven social scientists to causal instrumentalism. Consider the following comments of Blalock's:

Quite obviously, the notions of antecedent causes and intervening variables are always relative to the particular variables selected in the theoretical system. If we do not admit this fact, we immediately become involved in endless debates over ultimate or original causes, or over the numerous possible causes that have been inevitably left out of our causal system. It is for this reason that we must again emphasize, at the risk of being repetitious, that we prefer to think in terms of causal models that represent highly oversimplified versions of the real world. (Blalock 1964, p. 20)

Blalock's argument begins with two significant facts. First, causal claims are in fact often made by sociologists and economists within the context of particular models. This fact is explained by a second one: claims like "Bad harvests cause high food prices" are not themselves and do not imply true *universal* generalizations of the form, "Whenever harvests are bad, food prices (after some time interval) will be high." On the other hand, the generalization, "Given the axioms of model M or in model M, whenever harvests are bad, food prices will be high," is true (usually logically true). The second fact explains the first as follows: by introducing various restrictions by means of the axioms or assumptions of a model (and committing oneself to the model), one can infer universal causal generalizations. Making causal claims within models avoids the slop, qualification, and imprecision of causal claims concerning real phenomena.

One way of interpreting Blalock's argument is thus that causal generalizations are only true given the hypothetical circumstances laid out in one model or another (see also Theodorson 1967, pp. 146–47). Unless one construes causal generalizations instrumentally, one must judge them false and deny their value.

For example, an increase in the price of a commodity (like coffee) causes (in a model) relatively more of substitute commodities (like tea) to be consumed. This is a significant generalization, but because of various interferences or disturbances, it will sometimes be disconformed. The fourth argument for causal instrumentalism maintains that one can only appreciate the force and significance of such inexact causal generalizations if one construes them as assertions confined to particular models only.

This argument (which may not be Blalock's) is a poor one. Social scientists who argue as above (as some implicitly do) want to have their cake and eat it too. There is no way to maintain *both* that causal generalizations enable one to predict and explain phenomena and to maintain that they are only concerned with the structure of models. Without qualifications the generalization that a price increase results in a relative increase in consumption of substitutes is not true. It is convenient to lay the qualifications aside and develop with logical precision theories or models in which this generalization figures. But the generalization is a descriptive claim about the world. It is of value in explaining only if with qualifications and excuses it is true. Nor will it do to say that the model is an "ideal type" that is significant for the contrasts between its claims and the real world (Weber 1904, pp. 90–91) – why accept it as a point of contrast? The fact that few generalizations are true without qualifications (or *ceteris paribus* clauses) is no argument for instrumentalism (for further discussion see Hausmann 1981b, ch. 7).

5. It may be unfair to attribute the last argument to Blalock. In the last quotation he may be making a different point. It sometimes seems that whether x or y depends on which variables one includes in a model.[9] But if whether x causes y depends on which variables one happens to include in a model, it cannot be correct to interpret "x causes y" as the causal realist does (see van Fraassen 1980, pp. 115–18).

Let us consider more carefully the poor Jones family who eat so many potatoes precisely because they are poor. Employing consumer choice theory, the quantity of potatoes the Jones family demands, q, is a function of the Jones family income, y, the Jones family utility function, u_J, and the price vector, p. q is taken as causally dependent on p, y, and u_J. The Jones family's poverty (y) is one cause of

9 What one counts as *the* cause is highly context dependent (see Gorovitz 1969). Collingwood gives a nice example, "For example, a car skids while cornering at a certain point, strikes the kerb, and turns turtle. From the car-driver's point of view the cause of the accident was cornering too fast, and the lesson is that one must drive more carefully. From the county surveyor's point of view the cause was a defect in the surface or camber of the road, and the lesson is that greater care must be taken to make roads skid-proof. From the motor-manufacturer's point of view the cause was defective design in the car, and the lesson is that one must place the centre of gravity lower" (1940, p. 188). The context-dependence of claims concerning *the* cause is, however, of little importance. Even though the county-surveyor, for example, may regard *the* cause of the accident as a defect in the road surface, he or she may concede that the driver's carelessness and the defective design of the car were causes or causal conditions, too.

their large potato consumption. Indeed it might be regarded as *the* cause, if their utility function is unexceptional.

But when one shifts to a general equilibrium perspective, p and y become dependent variables. If it were the case that p and y, although not independent variables in the general equilibrium model, were nevertheless exogenous relative to the subsystem in which the Jones's potato consumption were determined, there would be no difficulties.[10] p and y would still be causes of the Jones's consumption of potatoes in the general equilibrium account.

Matters are not, however, so simple. In ordinary general equilibrium models, q, p, and y are all functions of (e_t, u_t, P) $(t = 1, \ldots T)$, where e_t and u_t are respectively the endowment vector and the utility function of the tth economic agent, T is the number of agents, and P is the production set. There is no subsystem in which q is endogenous and p and y are exogenous. The variables are instead mutually dependent. So it seems that the Jones's poverty causes their high potato consumption in the model of consumer choice, while their poverty does not cause their potato consumption in the general equilibrium model. Thus it seems that causal claims are relative to the model one works with.

The conclusion would not follow if either the model of consumer choice or the general equilibrium model were disconfirmed and judged invalid. It would be silly to deny that flipping a light switch causes a light to go on merely because somebody can make up an utterly implausible model in which there is no relationship between switches and lights. But although economists have reservations about both the model of consumer choice and about general equilibrium models, both models enjoy a considerable measure of acceptance. Does the fact that economists make use of both models show that causal realism must be rejected?

No. If one were to deny that x is a cause of y whenever x is, to any extent, however slight, dependent on y, then one must take the general equilibrium model as showing that the Jones's poverty is not a cause of their potato consumption. But if one took such a purist line, one would also deny that the model of consumer choice was valid. Suppose that if the Joneses consumed no potatoes, their income would be .01% higher and their tastes themselves slightly different. Surely it would be silly to deny for this reason that their tastes and income are causes or causal conditions of their consumption. The existence of *some* mutual dependence − which is all general equilibrium model (if it is valid) reveals − does not falsify all causal generalizations. The general equilibrium model is thus

10 In a market with a nonatomic continuum of traders (Aumann 1964), one can add the Jones family with their endowment density without having any effect on prices. p and y are thus exogenous relative to q and can be exhibited as causes of q. In general equilibrium accounts with a nonatomic continuum of traders, the causal conclusions of the theory of consumer choice still explicitly hold. This feature of Aumann's work gives one reason to contest Georgescu-Roegen's characterization of it as "one of the incriminating *corpora delicti* of empty mathematization" (1979, p. 318).

"approximately compatible" with the model of consumer choice. If the causal relations in the two models could not be made compatible, then one could not regard both as explanatory. Both might be useful (as Ptolemy's model of the earth-centered solar system is useful for navigation) but the conflicting causal claims cannot both be acceptable.

Either the Jones's poverty causes their potato consumption or it does not – regardless of which variables the theorist chooses to include in a particular model. Leaving out relevant variables, one may make mistaken causal claims. Considering variables and relations that are not really significant may lead one to find unimportant mutual dependencies; but whether a causal generalization is in fact true does not depend on the range of variables considered. There is no good reason to be a causal instrumentalist.

CONCLUSION

The general assertion, "x is a cause of y if and only if 'x' is exogenous relative to 'y'," states two truths. First, in constructing models, their causal ordering should mirror the causal ordering of the world. If x is a cause of y, the model should reflect this fact by displaying "x" as exogenous relative to "y" (although this demand may conflict with other desiderata in model construction). Second, one can infer what causal claims a model makes about the world by studying the causal ordering of the model.[11] That "x" and "y" possess a certain causal ordering in a particular model is, however, not *evidence* that x causes y. The causal ordering of the model *reflects* (if the model is a valid one) rather than establishes the world's causal order.

That "x" is exogenous relative to "y" is a feature of a particular model. But the model or applications of the model are incorrect unless x is in fact a cause of y. Causal generalizations are true or false descriptive claims. Such claims are in general testable and objective, even if cause and effect are simultaneous. Neither the qualifications implicit in such claims nor the apparent dependence of such claims on the range of variables considered give any good reason not to interpret causal generalizations realistically. The fact that we successfully rely on such generalizations to guide our conduct is an adequate defense of causal realism.

Causal models are instruments for systematizing and articulating causal knowledge. One employs such models to make objective causal claims and one assesses such models in terms of the correctness of the causal claims they make. If "x" is exogenous relative to "y" and the model is well-confirmed, then one can infer that x causes y – not because the structure of a well-confirmed model establishes the truth of causal claims, but because the model would not be well-confirmed (except by experiment mischance) if it were wrong about the causal facts.

11 With some qualifications. See note 2 above.

10

Classical wage theory and the causal complications of explaining distribution

1. INTRODUCTION

For at least half a century classical political economists were largely in agreement on wage theory. The demand for labor was determined by the so-called wage fund or wages fund, while Malthusian population theory accounted for the supply of labor. Classical wage theory attempted to explain wages in a given period, to identify those factors which would influence the trend of wages over time and to account for the eventual level of subsistence wages in the approaching "stationary state" in which economic growth would cease.

Modern economists have repudiated virtually all of classical wage theory. They no longer regard the supply of labor as determined by the responsiveness of the laboring population to sub- or super-subsistence wages. Nor do they accept the existence of a wage fund. Instead they subscribe for the most part to a marginal productivity theory of demand for labor and to more complicated theories of the supply of labor. Although I do not want to defend classical wage theory, I think that there are some interesting methodological lessons to be learned from it and that the marginal productivity theory which succeeded it, considered as a theory of average wages and of the distribution of income, is no improvement. As we shall see, there are formidable difficulties in the path of any (causal) explanation of the distribution of income. We shall also see that, in constructing and assessing explanations in economics, it is important to pay attention to the causal structure of such explanations.

In section 2, I shall introduce classical wage theory, while in section 3 I shall talk in general terms about supply and demand explanations. In section 4, I shall show how supply and demand explanations of wages run into difficulties which, as we shall see in section 5, classical wage theory, although unacceptable for other reasons, escapes. Finally in section 6 I shall have something to say about John Stuart Mill's famous recantation of classical wage theory in 1869. What is most interesting about classical wage theory is its causal structure – the example it provides of an alternative to modern equilibrium analysis.

I would like to thank Professor H. S. Gordon for his careful and helpful criticisms.

129

2. CLASSICAL WAGE THEORY

Classical wage theory was a theory of "average wages" and of the distribution of income between workers and nonworkers, not a theory of wage differentials. The classical political economists assumed that they could talk about a single input into production called "labor," and I shall follow them in this. Nominal wages are the money earnings of laborers. Real wages are the goods that workers and their families consume.

According to classical wage theory, in each production period the number of laborers (which was equated with the supply of labor) is fixed, and so are the stocks of wage goods, which are largely foodstuffs harvested annually (but see section 6 and footnote 7). Wages are just a quotient. As Nassau Senior put it in 1830, ". . . the rate of wages depends on the extent of the fund for the maintenance of labourers, compared with the number of labourers to be maintained" (1830, pp. ii–iv). Half a century later, Henry Fawcett writes, ". . . wages in the aggregate depend upon a ratio between capital and population" (1883, p. 131). Note that Senior and Fawcett are not just insisting on the arithmetical truth that average wages equal aggregate wages divided by the number of laborers. This arithmetical truth might enable one to *calculate* average wages, but it certainly would not enable one to *explain* wages. Although the stock of wage goods available at the beginning of the production period (which is what the classical economists called "the wages fund") comes to equal the aggregate wages paid in the period, the wage fund is also one of the factors which *determines* aggregate wages.

Aggregate real wages clearly cannot be larger than the wages fund, but they also cannot (in "equilibrium") be smaller. To see why aggregate wages cannot be less than the wages fund, let us follow the classical economists and simplify by supposing that capitalists advance to workers stocks of wage goods and that employers of servants and unproductive laborers also pay them in kind. Since there are profits to be made by putting laborers to work or pleasures to be gained from hiring servants, excess stocks of workers' consumption goods will give rise to a competition among employers and an increase in wages (Mill 1871, Bk. II, ch. XII, sec. 1, p. 362; Longe 1866, p. 21). But until the composition of output and thus the stocks of worker's consumption goods can be changed, aggregate wages are fixed. Individual wages are the quotient of the wages fund (demand) divided by the number of workers (supply).

In the longer run, neither the number of workers nor the wages fund is fixed. Both are growing. Wages will increase or decrease, depending on whether the supply of labor or the wages fund increases more rapidly. Classical wage theory should, I believe, be regarded as fundamentally a dynamic theory of temporary equilibrium, which is devoted to identifying those factors which influence the changes in wages over time. The wages fund increases when investment increases and when inventions increase the productivity of labor, particularly in the wage-good sectors. An increased demand for servants would have an ambiguous effect on the wages fund. If it went along with a decrease in savings and investment, the output of wage goods and thus the wages fund would decrease. But a demand for servants, instead of luxury goods, would increase the demand for worker's consumption goods and would lead to an increase in the wage fund. In any event the classical economists were in fact in the habit of first mentioning direct demand for labor services and then (as in the quotation above from Fawcett) ignoring it. I shall follow them and simplify by assuming that all workers are employed by capitalists. With some possible, but unlikely exceptions, the wage fund increases with investment and improvements in productivity.

Classical political economists were convinced that limited supplies of land must eventually choke off this economic growth (Ricardo 1817, ch. 6, pp. 139–40). And even while such growth could be sustained, economists feared or expected that the labor force (the supply of labor) would at least keep pace with the wages fund. In Mill's words, "We must, therefore, in considering the effects of the progress of industry, admit as a supposition, however greatly we deprecate as a fact, an increase of population as long-continued, as indefinite, and possibly even as rapid, as the increase of production and accumulation" (1871, Bk. III, ch. XXIV, sec. 4, p. 699). Unless the rate of increase of the labor force could be held down, increases in the wages fund would not improve the condition of the average worker.

Classical wage theory thus has apparent immediate practical implications. It says that there are only two ways to increase wages: increase the wages fund (by increasing saving and investment or by technological innovations) or slow the growth of the labor force. To quote Mill once more, "The condition of the [laboring] class can be bettered in no other way than by altering that proportion [between capital and population] to their advantage: and every scheme for their benefit, which does not proceed on this as its foundation, is, for all permanent purposes a delusion" (1871, Bk. II, ch. XI, sec. 3, p. 350). The nineteenth-century political economists believed that the most practical way to increase the rate of growth of the wages fund was to eliminate as many of the obstacles in the way of untrammeled competition as was possible. Schemes to raise wages by legislation or trade union agitation, which in effect increase these obstacles, must inevitably fail. In Francis Walker's words, "The amount of it [the wage fund] cannot be increased by force of law or of public opinion, or through sympathy and compassion on the part of employers, or as the result of appeals or efforts on the part of the working classes" (1876, p. 138, but see footnote 7 below).

Interferences with the workings of the market which attempted to benefit workers by regulating or supplementing wages were held to be particularly injurious. Not only would the consequent decrease in profits slacken the pace of accumulation, but the higher wages would spur the growth of population. Although thus powerful anti-union ammunition, it is worth noting that classical wage theory was in fact seldom used to attack unions (perhaps because economists doubted whether unions were powerful enough to make a serious attempt to raise average wages).[1]

Instead, in Mill's writings and to a great extent in the writings of both his contemporaries and his immediate predecessors, concerns about population growth were predominant. To ease the pressure of population, economists urged "restraint" and emigration. John Stuart Mill also argued that the increase in population might be slowed if women were emancipated, since they would have other occupations and would not consent to bear and to care for so many children (1871, Bk. IV, ch. VII, sec. 4, p. 760). In his more optimistic moods, Mill hoped that a fairly lengthy improvement in the circumstances of laborers (which might be brought about by emigration) might accustom workers to living better and provide them with the education and the prudence needed to limit their numbers and thus to preserve and perhaps even to increase their gains (1871, Bk. II, ch. XIII, secs. 3, 4, pp. 380–82).

With some exaggeration, Francis Walker summarizes the practical implications of classical wage theory as follows:

> If the workman would not give up when told to enlarge his dividend [to increase output and thus the wage fund], he was struck dumb on being informed that his only alternative was to lessen his divisor [the number or workers]. The divisor aforesaid being flesh and blood, with certain attachments to home and life, and with a variety of inconvenient affections, was not to be lessened so easily. If the workman turned from words to blows, and went out "on strike" with a view to better his condition, it was regarded as the act of an irrational animal whose instincts, unfortunately, were not politico-economical. (1876. p. 143)

Among the classical economists, there was little investigation of the details concerning the demand or supply of labor (Taussig 1896, p. 163; Blaug 1978, p. 195). What really mattered about classical wage theory was that aggregate wages would grow as the economy grew, but that permanent improvements in the circumstances of workers depended on a limitation of their numbers. The bogeyman of overpopulation so fascinated or terrified most economists that they paid scant attention to the more immediate factors which might affect wages.

The above, in a nutshell, is classical wage theory and its policy implications. By the end of the nineteenth century, this theory was in complete disfavor. Mill had recanted his previous espousal in 1869. Others (for example Cairnes 1874,

---

1 This claim is argued especially by Blaug (1978, p. 195); Schwartz (1972, p. 71), and Taussig (1896, pp. 104, 194–95) and is borne out by my own reading. The claim is disputed by Breit (1967b, pp. 512–13) and Gordon (1973, pp. 21–23). Applications to trade unionism seem to become more frequent in the second half of the nineteenth century.

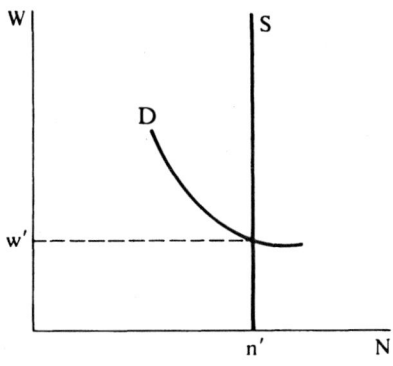

Figure 1

Part II, chs. 1–3, and even Taussig 1896) continued to defend a wage-fund doctrine, but with so many qualifications that little content remained. By the end of the first decade of the twentieth century, James Bonar could remark that "The wages fund theory is the crowning instance of an untrue abstraction . . . and it has probably done more injury to the reputation of economic theory than any other generalization ever received into economics textbooks and then expunged from them" (1911, p. 75; quoted in Breit 1967b, p. 509).

Merely to make explicit the heroic assumptions upon which classical wage theory relies is enough to explain this repudiation. But before saying anything more about classical wage theory, I want to consider in some detail the difficulties which confront any attempt to explain wages and the distribution of income in terms of the supply and demand for labor. After these difficulties are recognized, we will be in a much better position to appreciate the merits and deficiencies of classical wage theory.

3. SUPPLY AND DEMAND EXPLANATIONS OF WAGES

The amount of labor that workers will be willing to supply is, of course, a function of many variables besides the wage; and so is the amount of labor that employers demand. One can assume, however, that these various influences are roughly independent or separable, so that one can treat supply of and demand for labor as functions of a single variable – the wage rate – although, of course, these functions will shift with changes in the other determinants of demand and supply. According to classical wage theory, the situation can be represented by the graph in Figure 1. D is a demand curve for labor, a graph of the demand function. It is a downward sloping hyperbola with unitary elasticity, since the total amount of wages paid is a constant equal to the wages fund. S is the fixed ("perfectly inelastic") supply of labor. In general, of course, demand curves need not have unitary elasticity, nor need supply curves be perfectly inelastic, although economists do assert that in ordinary circumstances demand curves will be downward sloping, while supply curves will be upward sloping. In the general case one will, of course, have the familiar Marshallian "cross."

It is conventional to measure the quantity demanded or supplied along the horizontal axis, although quantity (which in this case is number of units of labor) is in fact the dependent variable. Wages are measured along the vertical axis. At the intersection of the demand and supply curves the amount of labor sought by employers equals the amount offered by workers. The "equilibrium" amount of employment will be n' and the equilibrium wage w'. In supply and demand theories, of which classical wage theory is a special case, one explains wages and employment, in principle at least, in terms of the supply and demand of labor and in terms of the market processes that adjust wages to equalize the amount of labor supplied and the amount demanded. Such causal explanation requires that the demand and supply functions show how much labor would be demanded and supplied at various prices, that demand and supply be determinable prior (in at least a causal sense) to the determination of the wage, and thus that there is a general, but not necessarily perfect, separation between the forces that affect demand and the forces that affect supply (Friedman 1953b, p. 57).

Of course, as everybody knows, in the real world there is often involuntary unemployment (excess supply) as well as occasional excess demand. The supply and demand apparatus does not attempt to explain what wages will actually prevail at any moment. Instead one has a sketch of an explanation of the *equilibrium* level of wages around which actual wages will fluctuate and toward which actual wages will tend. In classical wage theory one only has such equilibrium accounts of wages in a particular period (or of wages in the eventual stationary state). The course of wages over time requires a dynamic theory of the trends in such successive temporary or one-period equilibria.

In modern economics this concern with developments over time has been muted. When contemporary economists consider what will happen with a shift in supply, for example, they do not usually ask the dynamic question: "What will be the chain of consequences?" Instead they are concerned with the (comparative statics) question, "If equilibrium were reached, what would be the new levels of wages and employment?" The fact that supply and demand theories are theories of economic equilibrium and not of actual (disequilibrium) states of the economy is, as we shall see below, of central importance.

As mentioned above, the supply of and the demand for any commodity or service depend on many other things besides the price of that commodity or service. Demand for hairpins, for example, will depend on the price of hairpins, but it will also depend on fashions, on incomes, and on the prices and properties of other commodities like hair sprays or permanents. In writing a simplified function that portrays demand for hair pins as a function of just one variable, the price of hair pins, one is assuming that these other causal factors are not significantly influenced by changes in the particular price.[2] There will always be *some* influence of the price and quantity of hairpins on the other variables that affect demand for hairpins, but it is reasonable to treat the influence of these other variables as separable. These remarks apply, of course, equally to supply functions. The amount of any commodity or service that producers or owners will supply is obviously affected by changes in techniques of production or by changes in the prices of other inputs.

What one holds constant or treats as a separable causal factor affects the nature of the equilibrium explained. Marshall introduced the useful, but potentially confusing distinction between short- and long-run equilibrium prices (1930, Bk. V., ch. III, sec. v). The difference is mainly on the supply side. In the short run, the number of hairpin factories, for example, is fixed. Supply can only be increased by measures like working overtime or double-shifts. Economists thus argue that short-run supply curves will be upward sloping – only at a higher price will more be produced. In the "long run," on the other hand, much less is taken as fixed; even factory capacity can adjust. Long-run supply curves should thus slope upward (if at all) much more gently.

The intersection of a demand curve and short-run supply curve thus indicates what the prices and the quantity exchanged will be, holding constant or treating as separable, factors like plant capacity, while long-run equilibrium price and quantity are determined holding constant or regarding as independent only the basic givens (like tastes and technology) and factors which are assumed to be largely independent, like prices of unrelated commodities. "Long-run" thus has very little to do with real time. Over any real long-run of time, tastes and technology and other prices will change considerably. Long-run equilibrium explanations are not devoted to saying what will *happen* over any long time period, but to saying what prices and quantities would be, assuming full adjustment of the production process (within the limits of the given knowledge of technological possibilities). Carrying Marshall's distinctions with them, contemporary economists have in fact sometimes misunderstood classical wage theory. Equilibria are important in classical wage theory: there are both temporary (one-period) equilibria and the Marshallian long-run equilibrium of the eventual stationary state. But

2 There is some disagreement about what other causal factors one should hold constant. See particularly Friedman (1953b). Both Friedman (1953b, pp. 48, 59–63, 90) and Buchanan (1958, esp. p. 159) insist that *ceteris paribus* stipulations must be consistent with general equilibrium analysis. From the Marshallian perspective that seeks "an engine for the discovery of concrete truth" (1885, p. 159; quoted twice in Friedman 1953b, pp. 56, 90), it is not clear (to me at least) why "approximate consistency" would not often be enough.

the main concern of the classical economists was with the "long run" in an entirely different sense. They were interested in trends over time, not fundamentally with long-run equilibria.

Demand and supply explanations are thus causal explanations, in which for any price causally prior supply and demand functions give rise to amounts demanded and amounts supplied. Differences in amounts demanded and amounts supplied are translated through the (prior) mechanism of the competitive market to price changes. The equilibrium price is the price that equalizes demand and supply. Modern demand and supply explanations are not concerned with any actual sequence of events over either a short or a long period of time, but with equilibrium prices and quantities. Both demand and supply for any commodity or service, including labor, will depend on a great many other things than just the price of that commodity or service, but these other factors are assumed not to vary significantly with prices in order that one can separate out the causal influence of an individual price on demand and supply from the causal influence of other prices, incomes, tastes, technology, and so forth.

4. THE CAUSAL COMPLICATIONS OF EXPLAINING DISTRIBUTION

There is nothing wrong in principle with asserting that demand and supply of hairpins are, *ceteris paribus*, functions of the price of hairpins – where the other things assumed unchanging include other prices, incomes, tastes, and technology. But there is something wrong in principle – indeed something self-contradictory – about asserting that demand and supply of labor are, *ceteris paribus*, functions of the wage rate. It is well known that not only the price level, but also relative prices depend significantly on wages. I am in fact concerned here exclusively with the dependence of relative prices on wages. One cannot in general sensibly consider what demand would be, were the wage larger than it is, prices being what they are, because if the wage were larger, relative prices would not be what they are. Of course, prices may not *change* immediately with changes in wages, but remember that what is being attempted is an explanation of equilibrium wages. The *ceteris paribus* condition built into the supposed labor demand and supply functions can never be satisfied. The causal structure is incoherent: the demand and supply functions depend on wages and employment as well as *vice versa*. Those functions do not and cannot state how much labor would be demanded or supplied at various wage rates.

One might argue, however, that with a slightly different construal of demand and supply functions, these difficulties disappear. Why not take the demand for (supply of) labor function to state how much labor would be demanded (supplied) at a given wage, at the relative prices which correspond to that wage? Instead of holding prices constant, let them adjust.

This suggestion has the drawback that it divorces the demand for (supply of) labor function from the projections of individual employers and laborers concerning how much labor they would seek or offer at different wage rates, since these individual projections do not take price changes into account. But a more serious difficulty remains. Relative prices depend not only on wage rate, but also on the *amount* of employment. Both the size and composition and the demand for goods and the relative cost of production depend on the size of the employed labor force and its total expenditures. The amount of labor which would be demanded or supplied at any given wage, w^*, depends, among other things, on what prices are. But the prices depend not only on the wage but on how much labor is actually employed. Demand and supply can only be defined *after* wages and employment are already given and cannot be used to explain wages and employment.

To clarify this point, suppose that the labor market were a particularly simple sort of market somewhat like that depicted in Figure 1 with the supply of labor some fixed quantity, n'. In this case there is no problem defining a supply of labor function or drawing a supply curve. Since supply does not depend on wages or prices, we need not worry about the dependence of prices on wages and on total employment. Consider now what happens when one tries to define a demand function in which, unlike the special case of the wage fund doctrine, aggregate wages are not determined by the output of the previous period. One way to define a demand function would be to take employment as a given, n'. For each wage rate one can then calculate what prices would be, given that employment is n'. Given the particular wage and those prices, one can say what the demand for labor would be.

But the resulting function would not correctly state the demand for labor if the supply of labor shifted. Since this putative demand curve is derived on the assumption that employment is n', it will typically have to shift. One thus cannot derive equilibrium wages and employment from a new given supply of labor and this putative demand curve. Such a curve has no role in an explanation of wages or employment. Only one point on the curve – the actual wages and employment before the shift in supply – is of any significance.

But there is one other possibility. For each given amount of labor supplied, let us suppose that there is one and only one wage rate for which the amount demanded will equal the amount supplied. (There is, incidentally, no reason why this supposition should be true). One can then trace the locus of all of these pairs of equilibrium wages and employment. This graph may slope downward to the right, although it need not. Why not regard this curve, which Don Patinkin calls a "market equilibrium curve" (1956, p. 45), as the demand curve?[3] The intersection of this curve and any given supply does correctly "determine" equilibrium wages and employment.

A market equilibrium curve and a supply curve *may* jointly enable one to *deduce* equilibrium wages and employment, but they do not enable one to *explain* them. Indeed they are often not even sufficient for the deduction of equilibrium wages and employment, since when supply is a variable function of price the "supply" and the "demand" curves will usually be the identical market equilibrium curve. Market equilibrium curves do not show how much labor would be demanded or supplied in a given market at wages other than the equilibrium wage. They show instead what equilibrium employment is at other wages. Market equilibrium curves are given only *after* equilibrium prices and quantities are determined. They are not causally prior to equilibrium prices or quantities, and they thus have no role in an explanation of *how* equilibrium prices and quantities are determined. The mere fact that market equilibrium curves can sometimes be used to *deduce* equilibrium prices or quantities does not establish that they have any explanatory role.

There is in general no way to define supply and demand functions that can be used to explain equilibrium wages and employment. The basic problem is that labor is such a ubiquitous input that just about everything else in the economy depends on how much of it is employed and how much it is paid. There is no way, in Herbert Simon's (1953) terminology, to "causally order" the determination of the values of various economic variables in such a way that labor supplied and demanded can be known while wages and employment remain to be determined (see also this volume, Chapter 9). One cannot isolate some small set of proximate causes of equilibrium wages and employment in the way that one can isolate the main causal factors upon which depend the price of hairpins and the quantity of hairpins exchanged. The only equilibrium account of wages and employment that could be acceptable would be a general equilibrium account in which wages and employment were determined by tastes, technology, the initial endowments of commodities and resources, and the basic institutional constraints of the market. But, as I have argued elsewhere (1981a), current general equilibrium theories are at best sketches of such explanations or promissory notes for such explanations.

Let me mention two criticisms that the argument above faces. First one might object that although prices are sensitive to both wages and employment, this fact

3 In the course of validly criticizing Patinkin's construction of an aggregate demand curve for money (1958, p. 263), Buchanan mistakenly argues that a market equilibrium curve "is the only meaningful demand curve for money which may be derived for the whole economy" (1958, p. 263). If he is right, then there is in fact *no* meaningful economy-wide demand curve for money. His grounds for regarding the market equilibrium curve as a demand curve is that it enables one to predict what will happen if supply changes. But he overlooks the explanatory role of demand curves, which, as I argue in the text, market equilibrium curves cannot play.

138

makes supply and demand explanations of wages impossible only if this sensitivity is appreciable. If demand and supply functions for labor which ignored price changes were not too far off, one could still offer supply and demand explanations of wages and employment.

This objection is in principle perfectly reasonable, but the onus is on the objector to show that the sensitivity of prices to wages and employment is sufficiently low that one can continue to define approximate supply and demand curves. I have seen no such demonstrations, and I have elsewhere used some simple models to show how significant the dependence of prices on wages and employment is likely to be (1990d). It is also worth pointing out that this defense of supply and demand theories of wages turns out to be a defense of the labor theory of value. If prices are not sensitive to wage changes (and thus to changes in the rate of interest), then they are well approximated by labor values.

Second, one might object that the entire criticism rests upon my taking the notion of "labor" as a single input too seriously. Once it is recognized that there are many varieties of labor, one recognizes that explaining the various wages these varieties of labor are paid presents no special problems. But the difficulty with this objection is that once one retreats to offering separate explanations for the compensation paid to different kinds of labor – which may be an entirely sensible move to make – one has also abandoned the attempt to offer any simple unified theory of the distribution of income between workers and nonworkers (which may also be quite sensible). Insofar as one is considering supply and demand theories of wage determination as theories of the distribution of income, one is forced to theorize in terms of a single ubiquitous input called "labor."

5. THE CAUSAL STRUCTURE, VIRTUES, AND VICES OF CLASSICAL WAGE THEORY

There is thus a general problem in explaining distribution. To offer a causal explanation, one must take certain features of the economy as causally prior to the distribution of income between capitalists and workers – as already determined while the wage and the amount of employment remain to be determined – where this precedence is at least causal, if not temporal as well. But supply and demand for labor do not in general possess such causal priority. Note that this is not just the familiar point that economic variables are simultaneously determined. The "givens" in a typical general equilibrium model, although not in any sense earlier in *time,* can nevertheless be regarded as *causally* prior to the variables whose values are determined in the general equilibrium solution.

It is interesting to notice, however, that classical wage theory can be regarded as an answer to this critique. If it were otherwise acceptable, it would show that supply and demand for labor are indeed both temporally and causally prior to the determination of wages. To clarify this point, let me present a fragment of a mathematical restatement of classical wage theory that I have developed elsewhere:

In an extremely simple one-commodity model where capital consists entirely of advances of some consumption commodity, "corn," to workers, one can write the following highly simplified "supply" and "demand" functions for labor (see my unpublished essay, "A Modern Restatement of Classical Wage Theory"):

$$N_{t+1} = N_t[1 + c_t(w_t - w^*_t)] \tag{S}$$

$$w_{t+1}n_{t+1} = w_t n_t(1 + S_t r_t) \tag{D}$$

(S) is a simplified restatement of Malthusian population theory. It says that the current $(t + 1)$ supply of labor depends on the supply of labor in the last period times a growth factor which reflects the difference between actual wages in the last period, w_t, and subsistence wages, w^*_t, and the responsiveness of population to this difference, c_t, which will be some positive number. (D) states that the current wages fund is equal to the wages fund in the last period plus net investment, where net investment equals net output or income (the rate of profit, r_t, times capital, $w_t N_t$), times the capitalists' propensity to save or invest, s_t. Although the classical economists had little to say about the extent to which wage changes would lead to the substitution of other inputs for labor, it is possible to include substitutability (and considerations of marginal productivity) in the model (Hausman 1983a, sec. 3; Hahn 1972, p. 82; Hollander 1968; Samuelson 1951, p. 328).

To discuss how wages will change over a long period of time requires that one say something about how c_t, w^*_t, s_t, and r_t will change over time and about the extent to which they depend on contemporary or earlier wages and employment. But all these questions may be postponed in considering wages in any given period. Aggregate wages and labor supply are entirely determined by features of the previous period. Aggregate wages are simply the wages fund. Average wages are the quotient of this wages fund divided by the given supply of labor.

Classical wage theory thus purports to explain in principle what wage will clear the labor market in the given period. If the labor market does not clear, wages can be higher or lower than the wages fund divided by the number of laborers. So we have an explanation of *one-period equilibrium* wages in terms of supply and demand of labor. No causal difficulties arise, however, because both supply and demand are fixed in the period before. On the view of causation that I have defended elsewhere (1984a), causes need not necessarily precede their effects in time; but causation remains, of course, an asymmetrical relation. The temporal precedence of the determinants of the wage rate in classical wage theory neatly and decisively establishes this causal asymmetry.

Although classical wage theory is a theory of the market-clearing wage, there is no implication of stationary or general or long-run equilibrium. Other markets need not clear. Both supply and demand in succeeding periods may (and typically will) differ. Since population and the wages fund are fixed when the period begins, they may be regarded (in combination with the competitive processes of the labor market) as determining wages and employment in the particular period. The causal structure of classical wage theory in its one-period application is thus simple and sound.

This conclusion may appear completely uninteresting, since the assumptions of classical wage theory, thus far left implicit, are so hard to swallow. The goods that workers consume are not harvested only once a year; they flow on to the market in streams of varying steadiness throughout the year. The portion of output that workers may consume is not fixed. Aggregate wages can be immediately increased by lessening the consumption of nonworkers. The amount of labor supplied (as opposed to the population of laborers and their dependents) is not independent of wages. In times of business crises, as even classical wage theorists like J. S. Mill pointed out (1871, Bk. II, ch. XI, sec. 2, p. 345), capitalists may hoard rather than invest, and total wages paid may be less than the wages fund. Finally, workers do save and may thus be paid partly in claims to future output.

Although I sympathize with the above objection, I should point out that there are ways in which one can continue to defend a highly qualified (and rather uninteresting) short-run wages-fund theory. Since workers in fact save comparatively little, it is perhaps reasonable to ignore their savings. It may be reasonable to separate theories of business crises from theories of what would happen in their absence and thus to assume full employment and complete distribution of the wages fund (Pigou 1949, p. 174, points out, however, that, contrary to classical wage theory, inventories of consumer goods, after an initial increase, *fall* during recessions). When concerned with the distribution of income, we may be interested in wages per member of the labor force, the population of which one can regard as more or less fixed at any given time. Given the number of workers compared to the number of nonworkers and the differences in much of their consumption, the flow of goods that workers consume, while not fixed, cannot vary both rapidly and appreciably. Finally, even though there is a flow of wages, rather than a stock, production is a roundabout and time-consuming process. To increase the flow of wage goods will require a considerable time period. And, in any case, as will be discussed further in section 6, in its long-run applications, classical wage theory does not rely on the wage fund being rigidly fixed anyway. What remains after all the needed qualifications are made are the less than exciting truths that to increase real wages will affect investment, and to do so appreciably without reducing employment takes time (Taussig 1896, Part I, esp. pp. 82–96).

But the classical political economists were not particularly interested in what might be possible within any given period. Their attention was instead often focused on the long run – not on any Marshallian long-run equilibrium, but on what was likely to happen over the succeeding fifty or one hundred years. Book IV of Mill's *Principles of Political Economy* is appropriately titled "Influence of the Progress of Society on Production and Distribution." How would the wages fund, the size of the labor force, and the amount of wages change? Apart from theories of the stationary state, the classical economists offered no theory of a long-run equilibrium wage or of a long-run equilibrium amount of employment (see Hahn 1972, pp. 88–89). Wages and employment would change from year to year – there is, in their quite sensible view, no single wage or level of employment to be explained. Their inquiry was directed instead toward the factors responsible for changes (particularly general trends) in wages, profits, rents, employment, output and so forth.[4]

One might also propose a proportional growth model that bears a superficial resemblance to classical wage theory. Dropping all time references from (S) and (D), except those on N, and setting supply and demand equal to one another, one can solve for an equilibrium wage and for an equilibrium rate of employment growth (which is equal to the rate of growth of the wage fund).

But such a theory has little to recommend it. To take (S) and (D) as stating supply and demand for labor, *ceteris paribus*, where the other things taken to be unchanging include subsistence wages, the rate of profits or interest, and capitalists' propensity to save, commits even more blatantly exactly the same causal error that oversimplified purported explanations of stationary equilibrium wages in terms of supply and demand commit. Moreover, such a proportional growth model is completely out of step with the aims, interests and convictions of the classical economists. They believed that the rate of profit or interest is not only a decreasing function of the wage rate, but that it must decrease (ignoring technological improvements) with increases in the labor force (which demand more extensive or more intensive agriculture which lowers profits). The propensity of capitalists to save was taken to be a decreasing function of the rate of interest, reaching zero at some small positive interest rate.

At the end of the development lay the stationary state – an economic state in which the rate of profits was so low (because of diminishing returns in agriculture) that there was no net investment and no economic growth. As J. S. Mill especially appreciated, the economy does not, however, march off relentlessly toward some inevitable stationary state whose character we are powerless to influence. The stationary state that society arrives at depends on the subsistence demands of

4 This construal of wages-fund theory was suggested by comments of Joseph Schumpeter's (1954, esp. pp. 666–67, 669). Yet in his long footnote 50 on p. 667, he suggests an equilibrium interpretation that has been explicitly developed by William Breit (1967b, pp. 523–28). I think that economists have generally failed to take sufficient notice of the dynamic nature of classical wage theory. I argue the point in section 2 of my unpublished "A Modern Restatement of Classical Wage Theory."

workers. These may be large or small depending on the extent to which economic growth is soaked up by an increasing labor force. Classical wage theory was a schema for identifying the crucial factors influencing the growth of capital and population and the trend of wages. It is a dynamic causal theory of long-period developments, not a theory of long-run equilibrium.

6. MILL'S "RECANTATION" OF CLASSICAL WAGE THEORY

One of the most remarkable events in the history of classical political economy occurred in 1869 when, in a review of a book by William Thornton, Mill restated some of Thornton's criticisms of classical wage theory and retracted his life-long espousal of it (1869, pp. 642–46). Francis Longe also published a confused attack on classical wage theory in 1866, but he seems not to have influenced Thornton or Mill. Mill's recantation is a fascinating episode for both the historian and the philosopher of science. The fact that it is generally labelled a "recantation" itself raises questions: Does one *recant* one's commitment to a scientific theory?

What makes the episode particularly fascinating is that the doctrine is one that is central to Mill's economics, and the criticisms Thornton offered seem to virtually all commentators weak and confused. To add to the puzzlement one should feel at Mill's retraction is the fact that in the last revision of the *Principles of Political Economy,* which Mill made about a year after his recantation, he made few changes in his exposition and defense of classical wage theory![5]

There are lots of theories about Mill's actions. Some have felt that Mill simply blundered in his retraction, and that his blunder can be explained in part by his desire to help Thornton (whom he liked) or his distress at becoming fully aware of anti-union and inhumane applications of classical wage theory – at becoming aware that, in Francis Longe's words ". . . it excludes altogether the influence of liberal principles from that field of social action, where it is for the interest of society that they should be ever most influential" (1866, p. 8). Others have tried to find reasons for Mill's change of heart, although not necessarily very good ones:

5   In the "Preface to the Seventh Edition," Mill remarks, "Since the publication of these [earlier editions], there has been some instructive discussion on theory of Demand and Supply, and on the influence of Strikes and Trades Unions on wages, by which additional light has been thrown on these subjects; but the results, in the author's opinion, are not yet ripe for incorporation in a general treatise on Political Economy (p. xxxi)." The most substantial change I notice in the body of the *Principles* occurs in Book V, ch. X, sec. 5. In discussing unions, Mill had originally written "But if they aimed at obtaining actually higher wages than the rate fixed by demand and supply – the rate which distributes the whole circulating capital of the country among the entire working population – this could only be accomplished by keeping a part of their number permanently out of employment." In the seventh edition, the sentence is replaced by "They would also have a limited power of obtaining, by combination, an increase of general wages at the expense of profits. But the limits of this power are narrow; and were they to attempt to strain it beyond those limits, this could only be accomplished by keeping a part of their number permanently out of employment."

that he confused monetary and real analysis (Ekelund 1976, esp. p. 67), that he came to have doubts about the existence of a fixed period of production (Schwartz 1972, p. 95), or that he realized dimly that the wages fund doctrine was inconsistent with the assumption of fixed input coefficients (Hollander 1968).

Since a large part of Thornton's critique (and Longe's too) was devoted to questioning supply and demand analysis, one might suspect that confusions or worries about the causal structure of such theories might have a role in this famous episode. In fact, with great generosity one can extract from Thornton's bewildering and mediocre discussion one interesting and germane point. Thornton may argue that, since actual trading takes place typically at nonequilibrium prices, there is no point to theories of equilibrium (1870, pp. 47n, 66–67n, 81–82).[6] In other words, Thornton seems to criticize classical wage theory not because it is too little like the neoclassical theories which succeeded it, but because it is too much like them. It relies on the notion of an equilibrium, albeit a partial and temporary one. Thornton seems to argue against all such theorizing – there is no way to abstract from the detailed day-to-day influences on wages (1870, esp. pp. 81–82).

Although Mill did not explicitly glean this particular point from Thornton's book (which is, given the confusions in Thornton's exposition, hardly surprising), he seems to some extent to have accepted it with respect to the labor market (*not* with respect to markets in general) (1869, pp. 645–46, 657–58). The main point in Mill's recantation, which is independent of his confusion of real and monetary analysis, seems to me to be the following:

The less he [the capitalist] expends on the one [his labourers], the more may be expended on the other [himself], and *vice versa. The price of labour, instead of being determined by the division of the proceeds between the employers and the labourers, determines it.* . . .

. . . and the law of wages, on the side of demand, amounts only to the obvious proposition, that the employers cannot pay away in wages what they have not got. On the side of supply, the law as laid down by economists remains intact. (1869, p. 645, my emphasis)

The portion of the output of consumption goods in period t that constitutes the wages fund of the next period is not fixed in period t and not independent of wages in period $t+1$. One cannot regard the wages fund as causally prior to

6 Longe does not attack supply and demand theories in general, but argues that the supply and demand apparatus is misapplied in the case of labor. There is, perhaps, some echo of Thornton's argument (1866, pp. 24–27); but Longe's discussion is at least as confusing as Thornton's. He argues that demand and supply are misapplied because in wages-fund theory they are not variable functions of wage rates and because "demand" is a fund (of money on Longe's interpretation) (1866, pp. 30–35). Taussig (1896, p. 252) seems to think that Longe has a valid point here. I disagree. My discussion of Mill's recantation might be regarded as an elaboration and a clarification of Schumpeter's claim that Longe's and Thornton's argument boils down to the claim "that there is little point in inserting aggregate wages as a 'proximate cause' that, as such, plays a role of its own" (1954, p. 670).

wages. They are mutually determining in the one-period labor-market equilibrium, and thus no real explanation of wages in terms of the supply of and the demand for labor can be given.

It is important to realize that Mill is not only arguing that wages can be increased in a given period at the expense of capitalists' consumption (the details of which claim Marshall 1930, p. 825, ably criticizes). To argue only that it is not absolutely impossible for unions to raise wages is not to concede much (Gordon 1973, p. 18); it still might be universally inadvisable for them to do so.[7] One can still argue that action to increase wages will slow accumulation, increase population and thus harm the workers. As one of the lesser lights of nineteenth-century political economy put it:

There is only a certain produce to be divided between capitalist and labourer. If more be given to the labourers than nature awards, a smaller amount will remain for the capitalist; the spirit of accumulation will be checked; less will be devoted to productive purposes; the wage fund will dwindle, and the wages of labourers inevitably fall. For a time, indeed, a natural influence may be dammed back; but only to act, ultimately, with accumulated force. In the long run, God's Laws will overwhelm all human obstructions. (Stirling 1869, pp. 26–27; quoted in Breit 1967b, p. 512)

But Mill is not only conceding that wages can be increased above their "natural" aggregate market-clearing or "equilibrium" level. He is claiming instead that classical economics has no good explanation for wages at all. He is questioning whether there is any single equilibrium wage and whether, if there were, real-world competitive labor markets insure that such a wage is paid. Moreover, even if workers were paid "equilibrium" wages, Mill appears to doubt that there is any causally prior demand for labor which can figure in an explanation of wages. The policy conclusions drawn on the basis of classical wage theory condemning collective action to raise wages are thus completely unjustified. Mill would certainly concede that there is a trade-off between wages and economic growth (although he does not stress the point in his review of Thornton); but there is no reason to believe, given the imperfections of the labor market and the dependence of workers' subsistence demands on their actual wages, that efforts to raise wages are always or even usually harmful to the interests of workers in general.

7   In fact, a number of historians of economics have argued that the classical economists did not really insist on a wages fund which was *fixed* even in a single period (Taussig 1896, pp. 214–15; Schumpeter 1954, p. 666; and Breit 1967b, p. 510). Gordon has disagreed (1973, p. 15n). Mill vacillates. In the original sentence quoted in footnote 5, he is committed to a fixed wages fund (and see also 1871, Bk. II, ch. xiv, sec. 7, p. 404). Yet in at least one passage (1871, Bk. II, ch. xii, sec. 1, 2, pp. 362–63), Mill seems to regard an increase in aggregate wages within a single period as entirely possible. Thornton may have regarded his own critique as mainly directed against the fixity of the wage fund, since he makes the following large concession to classical theory, "If the increase of wages obtained trenched very far upon profits, the growth of capital would infallibly be checked, and more or less of the capital already invested might very probably be withdrawn from business" (1870, p. 301).

Homilies to the working class concerning the harmfulness of attempting to increase wages are as unjustified as are homilies concerning the absolute impossibility of doing so. But (and here I am speculating), Mill is not sure what one should replace the wages-fund doctrine with. He did not change his exposition in the *Principles of Political Economy*, I suggest, simply because he did not see how to reformulate his whole theory of distribution. Mill's sympathies for the laboring classes led him to see that some of the abstractions of classical wage theory were unreasonable; but the very same sympathies (along with his unshakeable Malthusianism) made him cling to its general analysis of the long-run course of the economy.

Classical wage theory did not collapse because of the argument I have attributed to Mill, which no one at the time formulated very explicitly or attempted to answer. It collapsed because the abstractions it involves are extreme and perhaps unhelpful, because it failed to say anything about the contribution of additional labor to additional output (although this deficiency could have been remedied), and because economists both lost interest in the dynamic questions that it attempted to answer and became engrossed in the new puzzles thrown up by the emerging marginal productivity analysis.

It is ironic that, if my interpretation is correct, Mill recanted his espousal of classical wage theory on the basis of criticisms that apply much more forcefully to its successor. Classical wage theory did, to be sure, rely on supply and demand to explain a temporary equilibrium in the labor market; and one may reasonably doubt whether one can define causally prior demand and supply functions even within a single period. But twentieth-century theory attempts an explanation in terms of supply and demand of wages in a stationary or proportional growth equilibrium. These demand and supply theories are incapable of explaining wages and employment because supply and demand for labor functions cannot be fixed prior to the determination of wages and employment. I am proposing no resurrection of classical wage theory – its difficulties are many and apparent. But its dynamic and straightforward causal structure is interesting in its own right and as a contrast to twentieth-century equilibrium theory.

11

Supply and demand explanations and their *ceteris paribus* clauses

This paper argues that supply and demand explanations are causal explanations and that it is helpful to recognize this fact explicitly, for then one can appreciate that the variables impounded in the *ceteris paribus* clauses attached to supply and demand curves are other *causes*. One can then specify clearly the conditions of membership of a *ceteris paribus* clause: 1) include all those factors that within the given time period significantly affect the amount supplied or demanded but; 2) do not include any factors that themselves within the given time period significantly depend on the price of the particular commodity or service. Note the vague word "significantly." If one insists on the general interdependencies established in general equilibrium analyses, one must reject partial equilibrium analyses altogether, but to do so would rule out work that may be enlightening and useful. Such theoretical purism is also indefensible, since general equilibrium analyses rely on similar causal approximations. This analysis of *ceteris paribus* clauses is helpful in understanding where supply and demand analysis or comparative statics goes wrong, as in traditional functional distribution theory.

A severe frost cut Brazilian coffee output in 1976 to less than one-third of its previous level. During 1976 coffee prices were much higher. The simple and relatively uncontroversial explanation is that buyers competing with one another for the decreased supply of coffee bid up its price. According to Adam Smith, when the quantity of a commodity

. . .which is brought to market falls short of the effectual demand, all those who are willing to pay. . .[its natural price] cannot be supplied with the quantity which they want. Rather than want it altogether, some of them will be willing to give more. A competition will immediately begin among them, and the market place will rise more or less above the natural price, according as either the greatness of the deficiency, or the wealth and wanton luxury of the competitors, happen to animate more or less the eagerness of the competition. (1776, p. 56)

This is a sketch of a causal explanation. The decreased supply and the actions of buyers and sellers on a market are causally responsible for the increase in price.

The research for this paper was supported by the National Science Foundation (No. SES 8007385), the General Research Board of the University of Maryland, and the Institute for Advanced Study. Gregory Clark, Ronald Findlay, D. W. Hands, Axel Leijonhufvud, Isaac Levi, Donald McCloskey, Martin Osborne, audiences at Carnegie Mellon University, the Institute for Advanced Study, Columbia University, and Southern Methodist University as well as various anonymous referees have offered many helpful criticisms and suggestions. Susan Byers assisted me with the research on the history of marginal productivity theories.

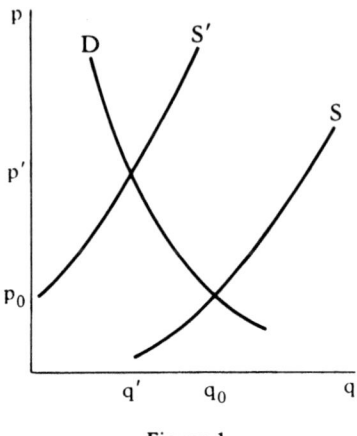

Figure 1

The actual story is of course much more complicated. Any moderately detailed history of the 1976 coffee price increase would have to consider questions of international trade, transportation, and exchange rates, the role of wholesalers and retailers, and their expectations concerning the consequences of the frost, the effect on different grades of coffees, the possibilities of employing different methods of roasting coffee beans and brewing coffee, the extent of substitutability between coffee and tea, and so forth. But the simple supply and demand explanation surely captures the heart of the story.

This paper will examine in detail such simple supply and demand explanations as they are incorporated into neoclassical economics. Toward the end of the paper I shall offer a few words of cautious appraisal of neo-Walrasian high theory; but most of this essay is internal to neoclassical theory, whether it be Marshallian or Walrasian – an examination of its logic and structure.

A modern economist would dress up the above explanation for the increase in the price of coffee in the familiar graph above.

In figure 1, D is a curve showing the market demand function – a mapping from coffee prices to quantities per unit time of coffee demanded. Following Marshall, quantity is plotted on the horizontal axis and price on the vertical axis, even though in contemporary neo-Walrasian thought, price is the independent variable and quantity demanded or supplied the dependent variable.[1] A market demand function is supposed to be in some way the sum of individual demand functions; and both are designed as improvements on Adam Smith's colorful talk

---

1 For interesting discussions of why Marshall transposed the axes, see Gordon (1982) and Leijon-hufvud (1974).

148

of the factors animating the eagerness of the competition among the buyers. D slopes downward to the right, which is an instance of the law of demand: *ceteris paribus*, people demand more of a good at a lower price. S is the initial (prefrost) market supply function for coffee. Since we are considering a short run, in which there is no possibility of planting more coffee trees in Uganda and then harvesting the beans, S slopes sharply upward. Supply is quite inelastic in the short run. q_0 is the initial amount exchanged per period and p_0 the market-clearing price. S' is the supply function following the frost. It is considerably to the left of S. The new equilibrium price is p', which must be higher than p_0, since the demand curve slopes downward. The new total value of the coffee sold, $p'q'$, may be larger or smaller than old total value, p_0q_0, depending on the elasticity of demand.

Although more abstractly told, one has here the same story as at the beginning of the paper. The modern economist is offering a causal explanation of the price increase in which the shift in the supply function coupled with the fixed demand function and the given market mechanism are the causal or explanatory factors. Not all explanations are causal, but supply and demand explanations are supposed to state what *influences* or *determines* prices and quantities exchanged. Furthermore, like causes, the explanatory factors here can be used to manipulate the market outcome. Someone who wanted to have his or her coffee at a lower price could learn from this explanation to try tampering with the market mechanism or to try spreading the news that coffee is a carcinogen. Supply and demand explanation such as this one are causal explanations.

I have belabored this rather obvious point, because economists are suspicious of causal language. There are two main reasons for these suspicions. First, many economists regard talk of causes as a commitment to *single-factor explanation*. Although few economists would deny that the frost led to the price increase, most would stress that there are other crucial influences and that in other circumstances the frost need not have had the same effect. Economists thus prefer to speak in terms of "influence," "determination" or "dependence" rather than in terms of cause and effect. But economists' talk is consequently ambiguous between causal and mere mathematical influence, determination and dependence. One is better off relying upon old-fashioned talk of causal explanation, causes, causal factors, and so forth. In using such language, I am not concerned with which among the various causal or explanatory factors should be called a "cause" as opposed to a "causal condition," nor am I concerned with the context-sensitive question of which among the various causes should be regarded as *the* salient cause. In using causal language I am in no way denying that many factors are causally relevant to economic outcomes. In Hicks's terminology (1979, p. 13) I am concerned with "weak causality." Although I shall often talk of causes, because any alternative would be ambiguous or cumbersome, my concern is with causal generalizations and causal explanations, not with singular causal claims. No analysis of causation or causal explanation will be offered, because the assumptions made here about them are consistent with all the prominent analyses.

The second reason why economists may be inclined to deny that supply and demand explanations are causal is that equilibrium or comparative statics analyses, of which supply and demand explanations are instances, are often *distinguished* from dynamic and explicitly causal accounts. Instead of tracing the chain of consequences of the Brazilian frost though various markets, neoclassical economists attempt to say what price and quantity would be in "equilibrium" – that is in that state where there is no excess demand for coffee. Such partial equilibrium explanations differ from paradigm cases of causal explanation since they abstract from the actual sequence of events and the causal relations in that sequence. There is no explicit mention of time ordering, which according to Hume and others is essential to a causal relation. In the resultant static equilibrium, the supply and demand functions, the market institutions and the equilibrium price and quantity are all regarded as simultaneous, even though the former three are supposed to explain the latter two.

Although the distinction between dynamic and comparative statics accounts is an important one, both may be causal. The causal structure of comparative statics analyses is straightforward. In the background in such analyses is an implicit temporal story in which the parameter shift whose effects one is exploring precedes the establishment of a new equilibrium. In abstracting from the actual course of adjustment to the initial shock, one is assuming that the adjustment process has little effect on the final outcome. When this assumption is mistaken, one's explanation will be incorrect. But making such an assumption and then leaving the intermediate steps out does not make the explanation noncausal. Even those who insist that causes must always precede their effects can regard supply and demand explanations as causal.[2]

Having now, I hope, established that supply and demand explanations are causal explanations and allayed economists' fears of such metaphysical talk, I want to examine the structure of neoclassical supply and demand explanations in more detail, clarify the nature of the *ceteris paribus* clauses these explanations carry, and make precise the relations among fundamental theory, such supply and demand explanations and specific general equilibrium accounts. I shall also show how unclarity concerning the causal structure of supply and demand explanations can lead to mistakes in economic theorizing. This paper is *not* a general treatment of

2 Many philosophers (and indeed some economists too – see Hicks 1979, p. 62) find analyses of causation inadequate that require causes by definition to precede their effects. On accounts of causation such as those offered by Ehring (1982), Lewis (1973a), Sanford (1976) or me (1984a) temporal priority is not built into the analysis of causal priority. On each of these analyses (as well as on many others in contemporary philosophical literature) supply and demand explanations are unproblematically causal. But see Sober (1983).

causation in economics, for it is not concerned with questions of identifiability nor with the problems of inferring specifically causal conclusions from statistical data.[3]

According to fundamental neoclassical theory, economic phenomena are to be explained in terms of the maximizing efforts of individuals, given tastes, endowments with resources and abilities, and the set of production or technological possibilities. In the background is a set of institutional constraints. One great mathematical accomplishment of twentieth-century economics has been to demonstrate that when tastes, endowments, and technology satisfy certain conditions, then individual maximizing efforts can be consistent – that there exists a general equilibrium (where there are no excess demands on any market). Most theorists concede that some of the givens upon which the properties of the resultant general equilibrium depend, such as technology, are themselves influenced by dependent variables such as factor prices (Hicks 1979, p. 58); but as a first approximation (which is seldom or never relaxed) tastes, initial endowments, and production possibilities are treated as primitives that have no economic explanation and are not dependent upon any economic variables. These primitives may, of course, change. But such changes are just exogenous shocks, whose consequences, but not causes, are open to economic investigation. General equilibrium primitives are the ultimate or underlying causes of economic phenomena.

In principle, fundamental neoclassical theory leads to the view that there is just one big explanatory claim to be made (and then adjusted for each exogenous shift in tastes, technological possibilities, endowments, or institutional environment). Indeed some general equilibrium theorists have rejected, at least by implication, all supply and demand explanations because of their inconsistency with a strict general equilibrium perspective. Christopher Bliss articulates what turns out to be the basis for such a rejection as follows: nothing can be an economic cause unless it is a "primitive" – that is, unless its analysis or explanation is "largely outside the domain of theoretical economics as such" (1975, pp. 29, 34, 120). Not every primitive is a cause of each economic phenomenon, but if x is a primitive and an "alteration in its specification might necessitate an alteration of" y, then x is a cause of y (1975, p. 34). In the book on capital theory from which I am quoting, Bliss is not concerned to present or defend a general account of causal explanation in economics. I quote him only as one example of a brief and unsatisfactory treatment of the subject.

In the passages cited Bliss is concerned to show that specific marginal *products*

---

3 On causality mainly as relevant to questions of identifiability, see Koopmans (1949), Simon (1953), Strotz (1960), Strotz and Wold (1960) and Wold (1954; 1960). On questions concerning the inference of causal relations from statistical data and, to a lesser extent, on questions of identifiability, see Engle et al. (1983), Geweke (1982; 1984), Granger (1969; 1980; 1985), Leamer (1984), and Sims (1972; 1980).

(not marginal *productivities* or supply and demand functions) cannot be regarded as causing or explaining prices – which is entirely correct. But the argument proves too much. Marginal concepts are in Bliss's view nothing but "optional extras" (1975, p. 37) merely because they are not primitives. For only primitives can supposedly be causes. Bliss is in effect dismissing the possibility of intermediate causes between the economic primitives and the particular variables to be explained. The same reasoning would demonstrate that supply and demand functions, which are certainly not primitives, cannot be used to explain either.

This implication of Bliss's discussion follows from *both* his criterion for judging the causal ordering or models[4] and from his commitment to general equilibrium models. But such theoretical purism will not do. Surely claims such as, "Jones eats lots of potatoes because she is poor" may be true even though Jones's poverty is not an economic primitive. And indeed it is possible, at least approximately, to causally order (in Simon's sense [1953]) the basic general equilibrium model. For example, suppose that one adds Jones with Jones's tastes and her tiny endowment to an ongoing economy. The economy's price vector may be almost completely unaffected. In this case Jones's endowments and the more or less given prices jointly determine her income. Her tastes, her income, and the prices then in turn determine her consumption. Her income can thus be causally between the general equilibrium primitives and her consumption. In this way the standard theory of consumption is "approximately consistent"[5] with a full general equilibrium account and represents a partial causal ordering of a general equilibrium model. Supply and demand explanations are an extension of such partial and approximate causal ordering.

To get some useful grip on questions such as why the price of coffee increased and thus to use economic theory as an "engine for the discovery of concrete truth" (Marshall 1885, p. 159), economists often need to be able to treat single markets or small groups of markets in isolation. But markets are, of course, not isolated. Supply and demand depend on many other variables besides the price of coffee. To treat them, for the purposes of an approximate, but hopefully useful analysis, as functions of the price of coffee only, is reasonable only if the other factors that influence supply and demand remain constant or if one takes into account the shift in supply or demand caused by a change in these other variables. Economists conceptualize this issue, *which essentially involves separating different causal factors*, in

4 Although Bliss is not explicit on the point, he has proposed a criterion for judging the causal structure of a particular model, not a criterion for judging the causal ordering of the world. Any other interpretation of his views would make the answers to causal questions depend on where one draws the boundaries of economics or on whether one takes a variable in a particular model to be exogenous – which gets things exactly backward. In constructing a model, one decides whether to consider some feature as primitive or exogenous by judging whether it is causally dependent on the other factors considered (see Chapter 9).

5 A continuum of traders (Aumann 1964) permits exact consistency.

terms of defining the *ceteris paribus* conditions for supply and demand functions.[6] Coffee supply and demand functions state how much coffee would be demanded and supplied at various prices, other things being equal. These other things are other *causes*, which are, in Hicks's terminology (1979, pp. 13–14), assumed to be "separable" and indeed "additive."

In discussing *ceteris paribus* clauses in the context of supply and demand explanations, I shall follow the literature and focus on demand curves. The conditions on membership in the *ceteris paribus* clause of the demand function for some commodity or service are simple: One would like the *ceteris paribus* clause for a demand curve to include: 1) all those factors besides the price that within the given time period significantly affect the amount of the commodity or service demanded; and 2) none which are themselves within the given time period significantly affected by the price. "Significantly" is, of course, a vague word, but if one is to have any hope of defining demand as a function separately of price and of other factors impounded in a *ceteris paribus* clause, one must seize opportunity to simplify the causal structure.[7]

The justification of these two general conditions on membership in the *ceteris paribus* clause of a demand curve is straightforward. If one leaves a significant causal factor out, then one will sometimes be mistaken about the quantity demanded, even though, supposedly, all other things are equal. If, on the other hand, one includes a factor that is significantly affected by the price of the commodity or service, then one's *ceteris paribus* clause can never be satisfied. As price varies, one should move along a single unshifting demand curve. Demand

6 *Ceteris paribus* clauses may also be regarded as vague excuses that may enable one to reconcile the commitments of economists to certain statements, which one might regard as fundamental "laws" of economics, with the same economists' recognition that these statements are not true. See my 1981b, Chapter 7. But there is the alternative of taking the specification of disturbances or interferences that economic theory *itself* provides more seriously. On such a view, the other things which must be equal consist of tastes, technology, endowments, and institutional structure. The *ceteris paribus* clauses in specific applications of neoclassical economics would then reflect its commitment to a particular structure of causal explanation. As better defined and delimited, such *ceteris paribus* clauses are more scientifically respectable. Although they may still function as excuses, they are not excuses for all occasions. They do not, for example, explain away apparent instances of non profit-maximizing activity on the part of firms or entrepreneurs. Note also that these constrained *ceteris paribus* clauses have no place in specific *general* equilibrium explanations or predictions. In maintaining that tastes, technology, endowments and basic institutional structure are the *only* relevant causal factors, one is eschewing the vague all-purpose excuse of some totally unspecified disturbance or interference.

7 The extent to which one variable depends upon another is an empirical question, although, like other empirical questions, it cannot be answered in a completely presuppositionless way. An econometrician who is undecided whether a particular coefficient is small enough that it may be treated as zero may estimate the value of that coefficient. But in carrying out that estimation, the econometrician will need a model in which other coefficients are regarded as small enough that they can be regarded as zero. But the inability to read causal structure out of the unvarnished facts does not mean that questions of causal structure are not empirically answerable. Theoretical and causal presuppositions are essential, but they are also correctible in further inquiries.

and supply curves may shift because of a change in one of the variables in their *ceteris paribus* clauses, but they should not *shift* merely because the price of coffee changes. In short-run supply and demand explanations, one may also include in the *ceteris paribus* clause of a demand function factors (such as coffee acreage) which are very sensitive to the price of coffee, but which take a long time to adjust.[8]

Milton Friedman suggests that one also include in one's *ceteris paribus* clause those variables which do not affect demand (1953b, p. 58) at all. But one specifies the content of a *ceteris paribus* clause precisely to make explicit possible disturbances or interferences, not to list irrelevant variables. Although it may not be worth the trouble to remove irrelevant variables from a *ceteris paribus* clause, it is desirable to do so, since one need not worry about the effects of changes in their values.

There is one further complication. Demand for coffee also depends on variables such as the price of tea, which cannot be regarded as unchanging in the short run as the price of coffee varies, and which thus do not qualify for membership in the *ceteris paribus* clause. There are two options here: either one *provisionally* includes such factors in the *ceteris paribus* clause anyway and then later corrects one's solution for "indirect effects," or one may be able to deal with a small number of markets simultaneously.

Finally, since one wants to be able to use a demand curve to explain the change in prices which results from a shift in supply (and *vice versa*) the factors included in the *ceteris paribus* clauses for the supply and demand curve should differ to some extent. Otherwise every shift in supply would be equally a shift in demand, and there would be little point to categorizing factors into influences on supply and influences on demand (Friedman 1953c, p. 8).[9]

8 It should be stressed that although Marshall's short-run thus has a lot to with a short period of time, his notion of long-run equilibrium has little to do with any long period of real history. Over any long time period tastes and technology will change enormously – as Marshall not only recognized, but looked forward to. Unexplained shifts will then carry more of the explanatory burden than economic theory itself. Neoclassical theory has, I suggest, little fruitful application to long periods of time.

9 This analysis of *ceteris paribus* clauses is compatible with the two main positions in the literature concerning demand curves (see Yeager 1960; Friedman 1953b). In the case of the standard Hicksian demand curve the consistency is obvious, apart from the problems with substitutes or complements. The alternative, "Chicago" demand curve, defended by Milton Friedman, is not so obviously consistent, since the real income of coffee drinkers depends on the price of coffee. But provided that one makes the proper compensation for the income effect of the change in the price of coffee, Friedman's variables can satisfy the general conditions on membership in the *ceteris paribus* clause of a demand curve.

It is worth pointing out that Friedman's defense of his demand curve as analytically superior to the standard demand curve is unsuccessful. Friedman argues that the Hicksian demand curve is inconsistent with general equilibrium. For example, if a government subsidy shifts the supply curve for some commodity to the right, more of the commodity will be consumed. But given the *ceteris paribus* clause, where will the resources come from to produce the additional amount of the commodity (1953b, pp. 60–61)? Other endowments must appear from nowhere without affecting

We can at last articulate the structure of the supply and demand explanation for the coffee price increase. The economist assumes that there is an initial equilibrium in which at the market price the amount demanded equals the amount supplied. There is then a change in some factor other than the price of coffee upon which the amount of coffee supplied depends – in other words in one or more of the variables included in the supply function's *ceteris paribus* clause. In 1975, for example, there was an abrupt drop in the endowment of ripe and healthy coffee beans. Presumably such a drop has some effect on the demand for coffee as well. This small effect may be ignored, although it need not be.

The drop in the endowment of coffee beans causes a leftward shift in the supply function. At the old equilibrium price less coffee will be supplied than will be demanded. The market mechanism somehow increases the price of coffee until the amount demanded equals the amount supplied. One must also consider indirect effects of the new coffee price on tea or cream prices and the feedback consequences of these effects on coffee prices. The process of price adjustment may be lengthy and rocky. There is no guarantee that adjustment mechanisms will ever find the equilibrium price, let alone find it rapidly and costlessly, nor that the actual equilibrium will be unaffected by the details of the adjustment process.

In the real world the nonequilibrium prices that prevail in the market at any given moment obviously have a role via the market mechanism in the process of determining equilibrium prices. From an explicitly dynamic perspective, price and quantity bear causal and explanatory relations to one another. One might have expected that these explanatory relations would carry over into the equilibrium analysis, but this expectation is mistaken. In the comparative statics account the explanatory factors reduce to the old demand curve, the shifted supply curve, and the unspecified market mechanism. The relations between equilibrium price and quantity are as epiphenomenal as those between barometer readings and storms. Barring a causal ordering of the model, the values of the variables are simply effects of common causes or explanatory factors. They are mutually or simultaneously determin*ed* rather than mutually determin*ing*.

Unlike specific equilibrium or disequilibrium prices or quantities, or specific marginal products, marginal rates of substitution, scarcities, etc., supply and demand *functions* may thus have a role in explaining prices. Supply and demand explanations should be acceptable to any neoclassical theorist provided that the particular supply and demand functions are causally prior to the equilibrium prices and quantities they are supposed to explain. They will be causally prior if

prices or incomes. But Friedman's demand curve is at best only more explicit about its inconsistency with general equilibrium theory. As one moves along one of his demand curves some of the general equilibrium primitives must change in order to keep the real income of the demanders constant. Those who insist on strict consistency with general equilibrium analysis (unreasonably, as I shall argue) had better not soil their hands with supply and demand curves at all.

and only if the causal factors which affect the supply and demand for a given commodity or service (apart from its price) are to some degree of approximation independent of its price, so that the *ceteris paribus* condition can be met. I cannot resist here a plug for my construal of causal priority (1984a), which makes independence among the various causes of a given effect central to the difference between causes and effects.

The apparatus of supply and demand leads to problems when the *ceteris paribus* conditions cannot be met − that is, when other causal factors which influence supply and demand themselves depend on the price. In such cases economists sometimes make mistakes, which the explication of this paper can help them to avoid.[10] I shall comment briefly on a venerable example.

Functional distribution theory is the attempt to explain the distribution of income to the owners of the principal factors of production: capital, labor, and land. Neoclassical functional distribution theory, like the classical theory which preceded it, has traditionally explained distribution in terms of supply and demand. For brevity let me focus on the theory of wages. Demand for labor depends on the marginal productivity of labor,[11] and it is a decreasing function of the wage because of diminishing returns. Theories of the supply of labor are more varied and controversial and will not be discussed here. A textbook example of a supply and demand account of wages might be a simplified explanation for the higher wages of workers and the lower rents of peasants after the black death in terms of a dramatic shift in the labor supply curve.

Like supply and demand explanations generally, such accounts are supposed to be causal explanations. Yet economists are uncomfortable in regarding the marginal productivity of labor as in any sense one of the causal factors responsible for the wage.[12] In many cases this discomfort stems from the recognition that the

10   Applications of IS-LM analysis provide interesting instances of such causal mistakes. For a relevant, although I believe somewhat flawed, discussion of IS-LM analysis see Leijonhufvud (1983).

11   Since demand curves are typically defined on the *ceteris paribus* assumption that other prices (rather than input quantities) are held constant, marginal productivity curves will not, strictly speaking, be demand curves. (See Bronfenbrenner 1971, p. 137.) There are several different marginal product concepts: marginal physical products, marginal value products, marginal revenue products (Chamberlin 1936), and marginal *net* value of physical products (Bliss 1975, pp. 95−100). When no single marginal product can be defined, input price will lie between the value of the decrease in product when one fewer unit of input is used and the value of the increase in product when one additional unit is used.

12   Most modern theorists would dissociate themselves completely from the claims made by some nineteenth-century theorists that the marginal productivity of labor is *the* cause of the wage. (See Böhm-Bawerk 1888, pp. 223−24; Carver 1894, p. 400; J. B. Clark 1902, pp. 106, 160, 162, 167, 180, 187; Taussig 1939: Volume II, p. 56; Wicksteed 1894, p. 10). But the most common reason for this rejection is that marginal productivity provides only an account of the demand for labor and that to explain wages, one must also consider the supply of labor (see, for example, Machlup 1963, p. 208). But to say that marginal productivity cannot *by itself* determine wages is not of course to say that it is not *one* of the causal determinants of the wage. And many reputable theorists have

marginal productivity of labor is not an economic primitive.[13] But as already stressed, this fact is not sufficient grounds to reject supply and demand explanations of the distribution of income, for marginal productivities may be explanatory intermediaries in causally ordered general equilibrium models. Hicks, for example, asserts, "as these things [the ultimate determinants of marginal productivity] change, so the marginal product of labor changes with them; and these changes in marginal productivity exert pressure, in one direction or the other, upon the level of wages" (1932, pp. 18–19).

Yet modern supply and demand explanations of the distribution of income remain problematic. Since, as Ricardo already recognized, relative prices depend significantly on the wage rate, one cannot impound relative prices in the *ceteris paribus* clauses of labor demand and supply functions.[14] In general one cannot sensibly consider what demand for labor would be, were the wage larger than it is, prices being what they are, because if the wage were larger, relative prices would not be what they are. Prices may not *change* immediately with changes in wages, but remember that what is being attempted is an explanation of equilibrium wages. The *ceteris paribus* condition built into supposed labor demand and supply functions can never be satisfied. The causal structure is awry; the supposed demand and supply *functions* depend on equilibrium wages and employment as well as *vice versa*.

maintained that marginal productivity is one of the determinants of the wage. (Examples are Blaug 1978, pp. 460–61; Carver 1904, pp. 153, 165; Douglas 1927, p. 73; Dunlop 1957, p. 9; Fellner and Haley 1946, p. vii; Hicks 1932, pp. 18–19; McCormick 1969, pp. 64–65; Machlup 1963, p. 208; Marshall 1930 p. 532; Pierson 1965, p. 278; Samuelson 1973, p. 541; Wood 1889, p. 14). Walras makes the surprising claim (1926, p. 145) that "*rareté* is the cause of value in exchange" (see also 1926, p. 307). Many economists have argued that the notion of marginal productivity applies mainly or even exclusively at the level of the firm (Alam 1970, p. 240; Bronfenbrenner 1971, p. 186; Durand 1937, p. 746). But at the level of the firm, marginal productivity figures in an explanation of employment, not of wages, which the firm finds more or less "given." Mark Blaug makes the puzzling claim that marginal productivity thoery "is a theory of wages on the industry level, the supply of labour to the industry being given" (1978, p. 460).

13 Those who have denied that the marginal productivity of labour influences the wage (at least if causal influence is taken to be an asymmetric relation) include Alam 1970, p. 248; Bronfenbrenner 1971, pp. 136–37, 172–73, 188; J. M. Clark 1931, p. 69; Commons 1893, p. 179; Friedman 1962b, pp. 173–76; Hutchison 1953, p. 319; Jaffé 1954, pp. 512–13; Robertson 1931, p. 222; Rothschild 1954, p. 30; Schultz 1929, p. 514; Schumpeter 1954, p. 943; Walras 1926, pp. 417, 495; Weintraub 1958, pp. 14–17. Given terminological and conceptual difficulties and the fact that few economists address the causal questions explicitly, most of the attributions in this and the preceding footnote required considerable interpretation on my part. In his lengthy book on the historical development of marginal productivity theory, George Stigler (1941) never directly faces the causal question. Neither does Hicks in his *Theory of Wages* (1932). I would argue, however, that both Hicks and Stigler believe that the marginal productivity of labor does influence the wage (see Hicks 1932, pp. 18–19 quoted below in the text).

14 Classical theorists avoided this problem, since they took the supply of labor to be given by the population of laborers, while the demand for laborers was taken to be *determined by* the "wages fund," which consists of the preceding harvest (see Chapter 10). Supply and demand for labor were thus regarded as fixed before the wages of a given period were determined.

The point is a simple one, although it is presented here in an unfamiliar way. Questions of functional income distribution are general equilibrium questions. Partial equilibrium accounts such as a supply and demand explanation of the distributional consequences of the black death will not do. Not only can one hardly suppose that the demand function for labor will remain unchanged with the loss of one-third of the population (which suggests the futility, but not necessarily the incoherence of the analysis in terms of supply and demand), but, more importantly, one cannot suppose that relative prices will remain unchanged as wages and employment change. And since one cannot define a demand for labor function, the dramatic decrease in the population of laborers does not automatically imply higher wages. [15]

Defenders of a traditional partial equilibrium treatment of functional income distribution have two possible responses. First, they might reasonably object that supply and demand explanations of wages are impossible only if the sensitivity of prices to both wages and employment is appreciable. If demand and supply functions for labor which ignored price changes were not too far off, one could still use them to explain wages and employment. But the onus is on the defender of traditional income distribution theory to demonstrate that prices are sufficiently insensitive to changes in wages and employment that one can continue to define approximate supply and demand curves. Arguments like those of Durand (1937, pp. 750ff), Archibald (1960), Fisher (1971), Simon (1979) and Thurow (1975, chapter 3) suggest that the influence of wages and employment on prices is significant. One should also note that this defense of supply and demand theories of wages turns out to be a backhanded defense of the labor theory of value. If prices are not sensitive to wage changes and thus to changes in the rate of interest, then they may be approximated by labor values.

Secondly, defenders of traditional functional distribution theory might reasonably object that the entire argument rests upon taking the notion of "labor" as a single input too seriously. There are many varieties of labor services, and explaining the prices of these presents no special theoretical problems. [16] Yet in the retreat to offering separate explanations for the wages of different kinds of labor (which may be a sensible move to make), one has also abandoned traditional functional distribution theory.

One might search for another construal of supply and demand explanations that is consistent with interdependencies among the labor market and other markets.

---

15 In Cambridge models of capital reversing, a shift to a technique that is *less* labor-intensive may lead to *lower* wages.

16 This objection downplays constancies in the relative wages of different occupations, and there is, apparently some evidence of such constancies. According to Reddaway (1959, especially 40), the structure of relative wages among different kinds of labor is not very flexible. Phelps Brown reports that the relative wages of English masons, carpenters, and laborers, for example, remained constant for more than five centuries (1962, p. 132).

For example, one might treat the demand for labor as a function of both wages and relative prices, or one might try treating the price change as an indirect effect whose reciprocal action on wages has to be taken into account. But these *particular* proposals will not do since supply and demand for labor depend not only on the wage rate, but also on the amount of employment. The size and composition of the demand for goods and the relative cost of production depend on the size of the employed labor force and its total expenditures.

Some theorists have, however, proposed a more radical way of redefining demand and supply curves. Suppose that one regards some or all of the general equilibrium primitives as functions of a parameter, k. Suppose further that for each value of k there is a unique equilibrium. One can then derive a reduced form relation that shows the equilibrium values of wages, employment and prices to be explicit functions of k and of any primitives which are independent of k (which are *ceteris paribus* variables here). Such a reduced form relation, although rather differently described, is called by Don Patinkin, a "market equilibrium curve" (1956, p. 45). Suppose, to simplify matters further, that one takes k to be the total endowment of labor services, which one also takes to be the completely inelastic supply of labor. Since the market equilibrium curve now correctly states *ceteris paribus* for each value of the supply of labor what equilibrium wages will be, why not take the market equilibrium curve itself to be the demand curve? James Buchanan argues that demand curves should always be understood as such market equilibrium curves (1958, pp. 263–64). According to Buchanan (1958, p. 264) and Milton Friedman, the purpose of a demand curve is to enable one to predict correctly the new equilibrium that will result with a change in supply. Since market equilibrium curves enable one to do just this, Buchanan argues that demand curves should be interpreted as market equilibrium curves.

A market equilibrium curve and a given supply of labor may jointly enable one to *deduce* equilibrium wages and employment, but one should not jump to the conclusion that market equilibrium curves have any role in *explaining* wages and employment nor to the conclusion that market equilibrium curves are demand curves. One can deduce the height of a flagpole from the length of its shadow and the angle of elevation of the sun, but one has not thereby explained why the flagpole has that height. One can deduce the wage share of national income from the nonwage share, but such a deduction explains nothing.[17] A mathematical dependency is not automatically a causal or explanatory dependency.

Unlike an ordinary demand curve, a market equilibrium curve is not a partial equilibrium tool. It does not summarize the preferences and choices of those on one side of a particular market and it bears no direct relation to the demand for labor functions of individual firms. Instead it is a function showing what wages

17 The first example has been much discussed in the philosophical literature. See Bromberger (1966) and Hausman (1982a). The second example is Bliss's (1975, p. 34).

would be, given adjustments in all markets. The best way to appreciate this point is to consider the general case where equilibrium wage and employment are both variable functions (*ceteris paribus*) of the parameter, *k*. Here the supposed supply and demand curves coincide. The determination of *which general equilibrium one is in* is not a determination of a price or quantity through the forces of supply and demand in any single market.

The market equilibrium curve is an artifact of a particular factoring of a general equilibrium account of wages and employment: first one derives the market equilibrium curve as a function of *k*, then, given *k*, one derives the equilibrium values of the variables. One might reasonably question the usefulness and the explanatory power of such a factoring, but let us turn to the more basic question: is any general equilibrium explanation of the distribution of income possible, whether it is so factored or not? For the only viable way of theorizing about the distribution of income appears to be from a general equilibrium perspective. Since the mathematical and data demands of completely disaggregative general equilibrium theories render them infeasible (Hahn 1973; Hausman 1981a), the only real options for treating problems like income distribution theory are simplified aggregated general equilibrium theories where one includes only a fairly small number of commodities, inputs, and representative agents.

But such models rediscover the problems of defining *ceteris paribus* clauses in questions about the proper kind and degree of aggregation. For aggregation presupposes that the relations among the diverse units that are treated as one are not themselves significantly affected in the short run by the variables one is attempting to explain.[18] For example, if one attempted to use a one-commodity model to explain the change in distribution following the black death, one would be implicitly assuming that the mix of commodities produced and their relative prices do not depend on wages. So a one-commodity general equilibrium model of income distribution is as unacceptable as a simple supply and demand account, and for the same reason. The problems of choosing a suitable aggregative general equilibrium model and of defining demand and supply curves with satisfiable *ceteris paribus* clauses are variants of the same problem of causal analysis. The aggregative general equilibrium approach provides more flexibility than the standard partial equilibrium approach, although at the cost of somewhat greater complexity.

Thinking of supply and demand explanations as causal explanations and of the conditions that define supply and demand functions and their *ceteris paribus* clauses as causal conditions will hardly revolutionize neoclassical economics. Indeed,

18 One can devise an index in order to insure that some of the relations between the commodities one is aggregating will be independent of the variables one is attempting to explain. But one will then need special justification to apply conventional generalizations such as decreasing returns or constant returns to scale this commodity index.

implicitly and none too clearly this is how economists already think of them. But clear thinking about the tools of supply and demand curves and of comparative statics in general requires an explicit appreciation of their causal structure. This paper breaks no new philosophical ground and says little that is philosophically controversial. But this lack of philosophical originality is a *virtue:* the meagre and truistic philosophical basis of this analysis of the causal structure of supply and demand explanations makes the analysis much more readily available to current economic practice than would a more original and controversial philosophical account. In fact, I have some philosophically controversial things that I could say about causation and causal explanation (1982a, 1983a, 1985a, 1986a), but the theses defended in this paper do not presuppose any particular philosophical theory.

In closing let me step back from contemporary neoclassical economics and offer one general reflection on the basic neo-Walrasian theoretical enterprise. As I have suggested throughout this paper, to reject partial equilibrium analyses because they are not strictly logically consistent with a many-commodity general equilibrium approach reflects a misplaced theoretical purism. Good sense demands that one be willing to regard weak causal connections as nonexistent in order to permit supply and demand analyses.

But the purism of general equilibrium theorists is not only misplaced; it is not theoretically defensible. In regarding tastes, technology, and endowments as economic primitives, the general equilibrium theorist is already making exactly the same kind of causal approximation that partial equilibrium analyses require. Both kinds of theories disregard the dependence of tastes, technology and endowments on specifically economic variables such as prices, and both abstract from the complications of adjustment processes and of nonequilibrium trading. Supply and demand explanations merely add to the list of causal approximations by disregarding the small influences on the values of other economic variables exerted by the price and quantity one is attempting to explain. Only if these influences were, as a matter of empirical observation, never small, would partial equilibrium analyses be unacceptable.

Although supply and demand explanations thus do make more causal approximations than do general equilibrium analyses, it seems to me that the causal approximations in supply and demand explanations may actually be less problematic. For there is an interesting tension or conflict in the causal approximations that are common to general and partial equilibrium theories. In both cases one abstracts from: 1) the causal dependence of general equilibrium primitives on economic variables; and 2) the complications of adjustment processes. But the former leads one *toward* a short-run application, where this reciprocal dependence of "primitives" on economic variables is most likely to be negligible, while the latter leads one *away from* the short run, where the complications of adjustment processes are likely to be significant. In some partial equilibrium analyses this tension may not be serious, since the process of adjustment in a single market may be fairly straightforward, and a short-run application unproblematic. But are there many applications of general equilibrium theory in which one can reasonably abstract simultaneously from adjustment processes and from the reciprocal dependence of economic variables on general equilibrium primitives?

In conclusion, I would urge economists to think explicitly about the causal claims they are making and to use the apparent guidance offered by general equilibrium theories cautiously.

PART III

Cases and puzzles

Although there is no way to avoid the "big questions" of theory assessment, much of the most interesting and valuable work in economic methodology focuses on detailed issues. The four essays in this part are all examples of narrowly focused work, although in many cases they also support more general conclusions. Chapters 12, 13, and 15 all help to fill out the general picture of economic methodology sketched and defended in Part I, and Chapter 14 develops themes concerning explanation discussed in Part II. Each of the essays attempts to understand how economists address a particular problem. Philosophical categories and tools are used as a guide for generalizing and abstracting, but not as a rigid set of pigeonholes into which economic theory and argument must be made to fit.

12

What are general equilibrium theories?

A little philosophy of science can be a troubling thing. Simplified treatments of philosophy of science maintain that scientists formulate generalizations or theories, derive implications from them, and retain these generalizations or theories (albeit with some caution) as long as they pass the experimental tests. This story is heavily oversimplified, and its general inadequacies are familiar and shall not be repeated here. But this story is both well-known and a simplification of a truth, not mere error.

If one accepts this oversimplified vision of science, much work in theoretical economics is hard to understand, for it clearly does not consist in the presentation and examination of testable theories. Much of it is, instead, better interpreted as conceptual development, and not a less significant part of empirical science for this interpretation.

In this paper I shall focus on a particular stream of theoretical work in economics concerning which controversy and dispute have raged. The elegant theories of general equilibrium which have been developed during the past three decades have left many economists puzzled, since they appear to have little to do with real economies. Gerard Debreu in his classic *Theory of Value* states that his theory is concerned with the explanation of prices (1959, p. ix). Others as distinguished as Kenneth Arrow and Frank Hahn deny that general equilibrium theories are explanatory (1971, pp. vi–viii). Moreover, some prominent economists (Blaug 1980, pp. 187–92) and prominent philosophers (Rosenberg 1983) have argued that work in general equilibrium theory is not empirical science at all. I shall here offer a philosophical interpretation of what those mathematical structures called general equilibrium theories are. I shall defend their cognitive worth and their place within economics, although I shall concede that they are without explanatory power.

To understand what general equilibrium theories are, one must first understand what *equilibrium theory* is. General equilibrium theories are applications of (and thus *not* identical to) equilibrium theory. They are, as will be discussed later, the result of combining equilibrium theory with auxiliary hypotheses of the right sort. "Equilibrium theory" is my name for the fundamental theory of microeconomics. Although economists do not use my terminology, most regard what I

This paper derives from my 1981a and my unpublished 1982 [Chapter 2 above]. Ed Green provided useful criticisms during the lunchtime seminar where a version of this paper was delivered.

call "equilibrium theory" or "the basic equilibrium model" as fundamental to virtually all economic theory. They hope to be able to reduce, or at least relate macroeconomic theories to equilibrium theory. They hope to be able to augment the basic equilibrium model to deal with questions of economic growth and change. This is the model they rely on in specific empirical research and in many welfare recommendations. When one has succeeded in saying what equilibrium models are, one has largely succeeded in saying what neoclassical economics is.

Among the various assumptions common to different neoclassical models, one can distinguish two different kinds. Some, like "Agents' preferences are transitive" or "Entrepreneurs attempt to maximize profits," should be regarded as the fundamental "laws" of neoclassical economics – although they are, to be sure, very messy and problematic. Other assumptions like "Commodities are infinitely divisible" or "Agents have perfect information" have (when taken to be claims about the world) narrower scope and are not regarded as assertions or discoveries of economics. Economists are pleased when these simplifications can be relaxed. Although such simplifications are essential in most economic theorizing and are common constituents of neoclassical models, they are not really assertions of economics nor are they, I suggest, part of fundamental economic theory or of the fundamental assumptions of equilibrium models. I think one can best understand what neoclassical economics is by focusing on its fundamental laws or principles.

"Equilibrium theory" is my name for these fundamental laws or principles. It is helpful to divide them into four groups:

(1) *Utility theory:* Individuals have complete and transitive preferences and choose that option that they most prefer.

(2) *Economic preference:* Individuals prefer "larger" commodity bundles to smaller. Commodities possess diminishing marginal utility or diminishing marginal rates of substitution for all individuals.

(3) *Production:* Increasing any input (other inputs held constant) increases output at (eventually) a diminishing rate. Increasing all inputs in a certain proportion increases output in the same proportion. Entrepreneurs or firms attempting to maximize profits.

(4) *Equilibrium:* An equilibrium that reconciles the activities of individuals (in which there is no excess demand on any market) exists.

Although utility functions are often immediately defined as ranging over commodity bundles, it is helpful to recognize that utility theory is much more general. It might be regarded as a way of making specific the idea that people are instrumentally rational. Many economists regard it as defining rationality. Utility theory is silent concerning the content of preferences and does not imply that individuals are egoistic or that there is some sensation or entity called "utility" which is the sole or ultimate goal of individual action. To say that

166

agents are utility maximizers is to say no more than that they do what they most prefer.

"Nonsatiation," the generalization that individuals prefer more commodities to fewer, identifies the options that individuals face with commodity bundles. It implicitly declares individuals to be self-interested or mutually disinterested. All they care about is the absolute size of the commodity bundles they wind up with. "Economic rationality" might be (and often implicitly is) defined as utility theory plus nonsatiation. Diminishing marginal utility is sometimes thought (quite implausibly) to be part of economic rationality. But it is simply an empirical generalization about people's preferences for mixes of commodities.

Diminishing returns to a variable input is, like diminishing marginal utility, a fairly well-founded empirical generalization. Constant returns to scale, on the other hand, is one of the principles or laws with which economists are least happy. More than any other in the list, it is included largely because it is needed for mathematical proofs of the existence of equilibrium. Profit maximization is a mare's nest of its own (see, for example, Friedman 1953c). Obviously there is something to it, but there is plenty of evidence of its incorrectness.

The claim that an equilibrium exists might seem an odd candidate for a fundamental "law" of neoclassical ecnomics, since it is never, or virtually never, stated as an assumption in neoclassical models. Instead, the existence of equilibrium is something to be proven. But it is not something that incidentally happens to be provable in a great many neoclassical models. The models are constructed so as to permit one to prove that some sort of equilibrium can obtain. Even though the proposition makes its explicit appearance typically as a theorem, it remains a fundamental "law" of neoclassical economics.

The various constituent claims of equilibrium theory might be regarded as the basic principles or laws that neoclassical economists have discovered. Or, if one wants to postpone questions of assessment, one might regard them merely as the fundamental assumptions in neoclassical models and leave aside questions about the applicability of such models. They are not all equally central and significant. Various simplifications such as perfect information or infinite commodity divisibility will also be common constituents of neoclassical models, but, as mentioned above, such simplifications are not as essential to neoclassical economics as are the propositions of equilibrium theory.

Taken as geniune assertions about the world, the four groups of propositions discussed above make up equilibrium theory, the fundamental theory of neoclassical economics. They are an articulation of a basic vision of economic life that was around long before neoclassical economics was. In that vision, which can already be found in Adam Smith, individuals are thought of as rational and self-interested and as interacting only through voluntary exchanges. Smith and his intellectual descendants then sought to show how the result of such exchanges is a systematic and beneficial organization of the economy. To point out that equilibrium theory is an articulation of this vision is not automatically to criticize it.

Fundamental models do not by themselves enable one to say much about the world. What makes the basic equilibrium model significant is that it forms the core of partial and general equilibrium analyses. In partial equilibrium models, markets are assumed to be isolated from one another and there is often (largely implicit) aggregation, as in the common assumption that there are only two commodities. General equilibrium models often avoid such isolating and aggregating assumptions and attempt to deal with the general interdependence of markets – although, of course, truly heroic assumptions are needed for the exercise. In any case, both partial and general equilibrium models are augmentations of the basic equilibrium model, which are designed to enable one to come to terms with specific practical or theoretical questions (see Green 1981).

There are two quite different varieties of general equilibrium theories. One of these is of practical use, while the other is quite abstract. The first kind is exemplified by input–output models. By assuming, for example, that there are constant production coefficients and that demand will show special constancies, one can set up a model of an economy with perhaps a hundred different commodities and industries and, with the help of a computer, investigate how it operates. Practical general equilibrium theories raise no questions that do not arise equally with respect to partial equilibrium analyses.

Theories of the second kind, which I shall call "abstract general equilibrium theories," place no limitations on the interdependence of markets or on the nature of production and demand beyond those implicit in the "laws." When economists speak of general equilibrium theory, it is usually this abstract variety that they have in mind. It is abstract general equilibrium theory with which I am concerned in this paper. Given the abstractness and lack of specification in abstract general equilibrium theory, many economists regard it as the fundamental theory of contemporary economics. As the previous discussion suggests, this seems a mistake. Equilibrium theory is the fundamental theory. General equilibrium theory is a particular application of the fundamental theory.

What confuses matters is that applying equilibrium theory as the general equilibrium theorists do serves no clear explanatory or predictive purposes. Nor are these theorists attempting to develop a theory of a more specific subject matter within economics. The stipulations they make concerning information, markets, and the like are ill-suited for any such purposes. Theories of intertemporal general equilibrium assert or assume that agents have complete and accurate knowledge concerning the availability and prices of commodities and concerning the production possibilities both in the present and the future! They also stipulate that there is a complete set of commodity futures markets on which present commodities (or titles to future commodities) can be freely exchanged for titles to future commodities of every kind and date (see Koopmans 1957, pp. 105–26; Malinvaud 1972, ch. 10 and Bliss 1975, ch. 3). Since such claims render the theory so obviously either false or inapplicable to real economies, little testing can be done. Furthermore, the fact that reality does not satisfy, even approximately, such assumptions of the theories leaves abstract general equilibrium theories with little if any predictive worth. Given the falsity of stipulations such as perfect information, one wants to know what the point is of abstract general equilibrium theories.

One further peculiarity of abstract general equilibrium theories is that they take the form of existence proofs. One demonstrates that the axioms (which include reformulations of the claims in the first three groups above and stipulations or auxiliary hypotheses of the kinds discussed) are sufficient conditions for the existence of an economic equilibrium. Abstract general equilibrium theories thus seem to have the form of explanatory arguments where the explanandum is the existence of an economic equilibrium. Yet construing general equilibrium theories as explanations of economic equilibria with various properties is implausible, since there is no fact of equilibrium to be explained.[1] Such peculiar theories thus appear to be without explanatory power. What then are they doing as such a prominent part of a supposedly empirical science?

This is a difficult question upon which leading theorists disagree. Some believe, mistakenly (as argued at greater length in ch. 7 of my 1981b) that general equilibrium theories serve at least in part to explain prices (Debreu 1959, p. ix; Malinvaud 1972, p. 242). C. J. Bliss denies that abstract general equilibrium theories "represent reality," but claims that nevertheless they are a good point of departure and a good guide to which concepts are central and fundamental (1975, p. 301). Although Bliss's view suggests important truths, it is misleading. Many economists, particularly when they are concerned about how to justify their theories, are tempted to say that they only provide some sort of logic of economic phenomena or that they are merely bags of tools into which theorists dip when convenient. These claims have a certain truth to them, which I have tried to capture by distinguishing equilibrium theory from its applications and hinting at a distinction between models and theories (see my 1981b, ch. 3). These claims do not, however, resolve problems of justification. If an economic theory is only a logic or bag of tools or a guide to which concepts are central, we still need to ask whether it is a good logic or a good bag of tools or a good guide. If, as in the case of general equilibrium theories, there are no empirical applications, we have no way of answering these questions.

There is, however, more to the attitude toward general equilibrium theory that Bliss and others hold than the above argument recognizes. General equilibrium

1 This is an overstatement. Portions of economies may in exceptional circumstances approximate equilibria. On rare and special occasions general equilibrium theories may thus be applicable and explanatory. If these theories have real importance, it is not for this exceptional applicability.

theory may be of great heuristic value (see Green 1981). Although heuristics is itself a complicated subject, one can show that general equilibrium theories have been of heuristic value merely by showing that they have, in fact, helped in developing valuable empirical economic theories. Notice that the heuristic value of general equilibrium theories is independent of the existence proofs (the arguments) that such theories provide. Where general equilibrium theories have been most valuable has been in the invention of conceptual and mathematical devices (dated commodities, for example) which are useful in other theories.

Yet it seems to me that the existence proofs that general equilibrium theories provide are themselves also of value. Roy Weintraub argues that the existence proofs show that the "hard core" of neoclassical economics, which includes the claim that there are equilibrium states, is consistent, and that without such proofs the general research strategy of neoclassical economics would be futile (1985a, 1985b, esp. ch. 7). But the mere consistency of the "hard core" propositions of neoclassical economics or of the "laws" listed above (which embody these propositions) can be established in very simple models and does not require the sophisticated mathematical work of the past four decades.

My views are closest to those expressed by Kenneth Arrow and Frank Hahn. They largely deny that general equilibrium theories say anything about real economies, but they insist, rather unclearly, that they remain a serious and valuable part of economics (1971, pp. vi–viii).

Since the eighteenth century many economists have believed that, given reasonably favorable conditions, self-interested voluntary exchanges lead to coherent and efficient economic organization. Yet the theories which economists have possessed have not enabled them to explain how this order comes about nor even to show how it is possible that such order could come about. Economic theorists might thus reasonably be in doubt concerning both whether their theoretical framework captures the crucial features of the economy and whether it is likely to lead them to an adequate theory. In pursuing and developing equilibrium theory, will one ever be able to explain how self-interested individual action within certain institutional constraints can lead to coherent economic order? Do theorists really have a grip on the most important and central economic regularities? Will economists ever be able to understand whether the results of individual actions are truly efficient and whether they lead to the achievement of other goals we might have?

In proving the existence of equilibria under various conditions, I take the abstract general equilibrium theorists to be providing explanations in principle of the characteristics of possible (although imaginary) economic states. In doing so they demonstrate that equilibrium theory is capable of explaining at least some sorts of complicated economic equilibria, and thus they give one reason to believe that economists are on the track of an adequate general economic theory. This sort of an explanation of a possibility needs to be distinguished carefully both from explaining "How possibly?" in the sense of Hempel and Dray and from any discussions of the feasibility of economic equilibria. Hempel's and Dray's view is that sometimes things happen contrary to our expectations which need explaining (away) (see Hempel 1965, pp. 428–30). But economists are not trying to show that the existence of equilibrium is consistent with prior beliefs. Nor, despite Hahn's claims (1973, p. 324), are abstract general equilibrium theorists concerned with how or whether a competitive equilibrium is practically possible or feasible. We do not need all this theory to know that real semicompetitive capitalism does not regularly achieve full employment. If one did need general equilibrium theories for the purpose, they would not help anyway, since the existence proofs that the theories provide show only what conditions are sufficient for competitive equilibria, not what conditions are necessary.

The abstract general equilibrium theorists have shown that were the world very much simpler than it will ever be, economists could use their laws to explain in principle how economies work. If one regards the resemblances between the imaginary worlds of the theories and actual economies as at all significant, these demonstrations give us reason to believe, in Mill's words (1843, Bk. VI, ch. III, sec. 1), that economists know the laws of the "greater causes" of economic phenomena. Theorists thus have reason to believe that they are on the right track. We should regard the existence proofs as providing this sort of theoretical reassurance, not as explanations. Note in addition that these abstract general equilibrium theories may help to improve current economics. By progressively weakening and complicating the stipulations needed in order to demonstrate the existence of more complex equilibria, economists come closer to being able to apply the theory to real economies.

13

Arbitrage arguments

Consider the following famous argument, which motivates accepting the hypothesis of rational expectations.[1]

(RE: Rational expectations argument) I should like to suggest that expectations, since they are informed predictions of future events, are essentially the same as the predictions of the relevant economic theory. . . . If the prediction of the theory were substantially better than the expectations of the firms, then there would be opportunities for the "insider" to profit from the knowledge – by inventory speculation if possible, by operating a firm, or by selling a price forecasting service to the firms. The profit opportunities would no longer exist if the aggregate expectation of the firms is the same as the prediction of the theory: . . . (Muth 1961, pp. 316, 318)

This is a powerful argument, although some reasonable doubts may remain. The phrase "the predictions of economic theory" is elliptical in an important way, for economic theory makes predictions only with the help of information concerning initial conditions, which may not be shared by various economic agents. Furthermore, it might be the case that economists cannot make a killing not because the expectations of firms match the predictions of economic theory, but because the expectations of firms are superior to economic theory. One is also reminded of Keynes's strikingly successful efforts on the stock market on behalf of King's College. But clearly there is something to the argument – enough to convince many talented economists to take seriously the rational expectations hypothesis.

(RE) is a simple instance of a general form of argument that is much used and sometimes abused not only by economists but by others as well. Arguments of this form I shall call arbitrage arguments because they turn crucially on the possibility of exploiting disequilibrium exemplified by arbitrage. What is the form of arbitrage arguments, and when is it reasonable to be persuaded by them?

I would like to thank Michael McPherson and Jonathan Pressler and members of the audience of "Philosophy of Science II," especially Cristina Bicchieri, Bert Hamminga, and Philippe Mongin, for helpful comments.
1 Actually, as Cristina Bicchieri pointed out in discussion, one is forced to a stronger conclusion. For if agents are rational and, on average, their expectations match those of economic theory, then this information, too, will be used and the expectations of individuals will collapse to the average expectations. In more recent work, it is assumed that everyone's expectations are rational. Philippe Mongin pointed out that this argument contains itself in one of its premises – see premise 4 of the reformulation. This self-reference reduces the argument's persuasive power, although it does not, of course, render it invalid.

Let us first reformulate (RE) as a logically valid argument:

(RE')

(1) (existential premise) The expectations of some firms match the predictions of economic theory.

(2) (fitness premise) If the expectations of firms that match the predictions of economic theory are in some domain more accurate than expectations of other firms, then these firms will, *ceteris paribus*, make larger profits than firms whose expectations do not match the predictions of economic theory.

(3) (equilibrium premise) It is not, for the most part, the case that firms run by economists or that employ relatively many economic consultants make larger profits than other firms.

(4) (adaptation premise) The predictions of economic theory are *ceteris paribus* more accurate than expectations generated in any other known way.

(5) (indicator premise) Firms run by economists or that employ relatively many economists as consultants have expectations that match the predictions of economic theory.

Therefore

(6) (conclusion) *Ceteris paribus*, the expectations of firms for the most part match the predictions of economic theory.

As stated this argument would not satisfy a logician's account of validity.[2] The interpretation of *ceteris paribus* clauses is a tricky matter and the vague quantification of "for the most part" needs clarification. But it seems to me that provided that the *ceteris paribus* clause in the conclusion encompasses the *ceteris paribus* clauses in the premises, one is stretching only a little in regarding (RE') as a strictly valid argument — that is, as an argument in which it is logically impossible for all the premises to be true and the conclusion to be false. It is helpful to recast an argument so that it is logically valid. For in that case, all questions about its *soundness* can focus on the truth of the premises.

2 Ignoring the *ceteris paribus* and "for the most part" qualifications, and simplifying, one can rewrite the argument in the first order predicate calculus as follows:

(1)	$(Ex)Hx$	existential premise
(2)	$(x)\{[(Hx{\rightarrow}Ax)\&{\sim}(x)Hx]{\rightarrow}Fx\}$	fitness premise
(3)	$(x){\sim}Fx$	equilibrium premise
(4)	$(x)(Hx{\rightarrow}Ax)$	adaptation premise

thus

(5)	$(x)Hx$	

where the domain of quantification is restricted to firms, "Hx" should be read "x has expectations matching the predictions of economic theory." "Ax" should be read "x has more accurate expectations than firms whose expectations do not match the predictions of economic theory," and "Fx" should be read "x makes larger than average profits." In simplifying the formal structure I have made use of a stronger equilibrium premise (3) and have omitted reference to indicators.

In arbitrage arguments typically authors state merely that some firms *could* possess the property that would give them a competitive advantage, but without the premise that some firm actually *does* possess that property (which in this case is possessing expectations that more or less coincide with the predictions of economic theory), the argument would not be logically valid. One might instead formulate arbitrage arguments as counterfactuals with premises concerning what could happen and conclusions concerning what would; but it is better to avoid the ambiguities and unclarities that counterfactuals introduce. Thus the somewhat strange formulation of premise (1), which I have called the existential premise.

The names for (2) and (4) are borrowed from biology, where they are used in the sense employed here. It may seem a waste of time to saddle (2), the fitness premise, with a long antecedent that is then asserted in the adaptation premise, (4), but, as we shall shortly see, arbitrage arguments can be used to argue against analogues to the antecedent of the fitness premise, (2), just as easily as they can be used to argue that all agents must possess some property or other. Note the *ceteris paribus* clause. If, for example, it turned out that firms whose expectations match the predictions of economic theory were generally led by timid and muddleheaded individuals, then it might not be the case that these firms would earn higher profits. The *ceteris paribus* conditions in (2) and its analogues in other arbitrage arguments are often ill-specified and hard to satisfy.

The equilibrium premise, (3), is in principle a straightforward empirical claim. Note that no one is asserting that *no* firm run by an economist makes extremely high profits, just that on average firms obviously led by the wisdom of economic theory do not do better than firms not so led.

(4), the adaptation premise, simply makes explicit the presumed superiority of economic theory. It is, as we shall see, often the weakest link in an arbitrage argument in economics. There might be some question about whether the *ceteris paribus* clause in (4) is necessary, given the usual stochastic construal of "accuracy" in rational expectations equilibrium. But it might be the case that somebody's predictions are more accurate than those derived from economic theory not because of luck, but because he or she has actually discovered a better theory. It is, in any event, safer to regard the clause as present. In other arbitrage arguments the *ceteris paribus* clause in the adaptation premise will be more significant. (Note that the *ceteris paribus* clause in (6) is needed regardless of whether one regards (4) as carrying such an implicit qualification.) (5) is an indicator premise that operationalizes the idea that those whose expectations match the predictions of economic theory will make larger profits than those whose expectations do not by telling us whose expectations match the predictions of economic theory.

The conclusion to the argument, finally, inherits both the *ceteris paribus* clauses of the fitness and adaptation premises and the "for the most part" clause of the equilibrium premise, (3). All one can validly conclude from these premises is that, other things being equal, the expectations of firms will be distributed around the predictions of economic theory with whatever systematic differences permitted by the degree of approximation in the equilibrium premise.

Is (RE') sound — that is, are premises (1)–(5) true? (1), the existential premise seems acceptable in contemporary applications of the hypothesis of rational expectations. Surely it is the case, for good or ill, that some firms take the relevant economic theories seriously and are guided by them. If in applications of the hypothesis of rational expectations to the past, however, it is supposed that the expectations of firms matched the predictions of economic theories which were not yet known, then the existential premise might be dubious. Appearances to the contrary, the fitness premise is far from obvious. If one's knowledge of the future is extremely weak and defective, improvements will not necessarily lead to competitive advantage. One might, for example, find an analogue here to the theory of the second best. Further questions might be raised concerning the extent of the fitness, given the extent of the superiority of knowledge of the future.

The equilibrium premise, (3), seems to be a straightforward and reasonably well-supported empirical claim. There are, however, empirical complications involved in its confirmation: if the fitness conferred by the wisdom of economic theory is fairly small, then it might be impossible, given the noise in the data, to detect the larger profits firms with such wise expectations make.

There is obviously some dispute about the truth of (4), the adaptation premise — that is about the predictive value of economic theory — although most orthodox economists seem convinced of the predictive value of orthodox theory (and similarly for nonorthodox theorists and their own theories).[3] As we shall see shortly, it is also possible to make a rather precarious arbitrage argument for the truth of this premise. Finally, although one might quibble about the indicator premise (5), it clearly seems reasonable to take firms that are evidently guided by those schooled in economic theory as firms whose expectations match the predictions of economic theory. In considering the argument one must also consider the *ceteris paribus* clause in the conclusion, for Muth and others downplay this important qualification.

So (RE) is neither absurd nor obviously sound. It may reasonably persuade people to take its conclusion seriously and to seek further evidence. To account for the persuasiveness of Muth's argument, it is thus not necessary to follow McCloskey (1985, chap. 6) in stressing the role of rhetorical devices such as analogy. On the other hand, the existence of such a valid and arguably sound

---

3 One must be careful concerning the notion of "accuracy." Predicting that the weather tomorrow will be the same as it is today may be more accurate than are professional weather forecasts in the sense of frequency of correct predictions, but such predictions will, of course, miss all weather changes; and the losses from such errors may be much larger. To speak sensibly about accuracy requires some specification of the loss function for error.

argument does not imply that there are no extra-logical means of persuasion at work here. There is no reason why any argument may not *both* stress an analogy and be logically sound.

Not all arbitrage arguments have just this structure. To show some of the possible complexities, consider the following famous argument in population genetics, originally due to R. A. Fisher (1931, pp. 158ff). Here is Hamilton's formulation:

(1:1 Sex ratio argument [my name])
  (1) Suppose male births are less common than female.
  (2) A newborn male then has better mating prospects than a newborn female, and therefore can expect to have more offspring.
  (3) Therefore parents genetically disposed to produce males tend to have more than average numbers of grandchildren born to them.
  (4) Therefore the genes for male-producing tendencies spread, and male births become commoner.
  (5) As the 1:1 sex ratio is approached, the advantage associated with producing males dies away.
  (6) The same reasoning holds if females are substituted for males throughout. Therefore 1:1 is the equilibrium ratio. (Hamilton 1967, p. 477)

1:1 differs from (RE) in two main ways. First, it is concerned with the equilibrium sex ratio in the population, not necessarily with the equilibrium sex ratio among offspring of particular members of the population. In equilibrium, if there are as many organisms producing offspring in the ratio N:M as there are producing in the ratio M:N, then there will be no selection pressure against either of these ratios. In contrast, the (RE) argument is concerned with the behavior of the individual members of the population of firms. It supports a more refined conclusion. Second, different behavior is adapted to circumstances of disequilibrium than in circumstances of equilibrium, while in (RE) theories optimal behavior often varies little, and, in any case, disequilibrium scarcely obtains.

Let us then reformulate Hamilton's argument so that it roughly parallels (RE') and then use this reformulation to suggest a general schema for arbitrage arguments.

(1:1')
  (1) (existential premise) In any population, some pair of organisms will produce male and female offspring in whatever ratio is best adapted to the particular environment in which the population finds itself.
  (2) (fitness premise) If for some N, M, in some environment, a pair of organisms that is genetically disposed to produce male and female offspring in the ratio N:M has *ceteris paribus* more grandchildren than aver-

age, then *ceteris paribus* the genes for producing offspring in that ratio will spread.

(3) (equilibrium premise) It is not for the most part the case that genes for producing offspring in the ratio N:M are spreading.

(4) (adaptation premise) If the ratio of males to females in the population is larger (smaller) than 1:1 and N < M (N > M), then a pair of organisms that tends to produce male and female offspring in the ratio N:M has in that environment, *ceteris paribus*, more grandchildren than average.

(5) (indicator premise) Pairs of organisms that produce male and female offspring in the ratio N:M are genetically disposed to produce male and female offspring in that ratio.

Therefore,

(6) *Ceteris paribus,* the ratio of males to females is close to 1:1.

Apart from the slack of the *ceteris paribus* clauses and the "for the most part" of (3) and the "close to" of (6), this is a logically valid argument. Given the negation of (6), and (1), (2), (4), and (5), it follows that (3) must be false. Hence one can vividly infer (6) from (1–5). (5) is, of course, badly oversimplified, although (I hope) in a harmless way.

The differences between the 1:1 and (RE) arguments show up in the adaptation premise and in the less specific conclusion. Although there may well be some forms of arbitrage arguments that have a more complicated structure, let me now venture the following first stab at a general form for such arguments.

Arbitrage Argument Schema:

(i) (existential premise) For any feasible environment e and any property H in a set of properties $\{H(e)\}$, some individuals x (in population P) possess property H.

(ii) (fitness premise) For any environment e, property H, and individual x, if the possession of H is adaptive (leads to possession of property A_e) and not all individuals possess H, then, *ceteris paribus*, the possession of H confers a relative fitness on x (x does better than average according to some criterion C).

(iii) (equilibrium premise) It is not in general the case in the actual environment e^* that, *ceteris paribus*, any individual is relatively fit – does better than average according to some criterion C.

(iv–A) (adaptation premise) For all x, in the actual environment e^* the possession of property H^* is adaptive (leads *ceteris paribus* to possession of property A_{e^*}).

or

177

(iv–B)   (diversity premise) Some x in the actual environment e^* do not possess H^*.

Therefore

(v–A)   (conclusion A) *Ceteris paribus*, in the actual environment almost all x possess H^*.

or

(v–B)   (conclusion B) It is not the case that *ceteris paribus* for the most part in the actual environment e^* that possessing H^* is adaptive.[4]

Since (as in the 1:1 argument) different properties may be adapted to different environments, we need to consider a set of properties $\{H(e)\}$ and various environments e including the actual environment e^*. In some cases, as in the (RE) argument, we may be able to draw strong conclusions (*ceteris paribus*) concerning properties of almost all members of the population. In other cases, as in the 1:1 argument, we may only be able to draw a weaker conclusion concerning some property of the population in the actual environment, but we can treat properties of populations as properties of the individuals that make them up. I will discuss and illustrate arguments employing (iv–B) and arriving at (v–B) shortly.

In the case of the argument for rational expectations, the population consists of firms, the properties H consist of the single property (which is also H^*) of having expectations that match the predictions of economic theory. The adaptive property A_t (which, like fitness is not a member of $\{H(e)\}$) is the property of possessing (relatively) accurate knowledge of the future; and criterion C is the rate of return on investment. Given the additional premise that to possess expectations that match the predictions of economic theory is to possess the most accurate expectations, the conclusion that the expectations of all firms match the predictions of economic theory follows. The environment is left implicit, but obviously the

---

4   Here is a formal restatement of the schema. Although it involves second order quantification, particular arbitrage arguments need not:

    (1) $(e)(H)(Ex)He,x$ existential premise

    (2) $(e)(H)(x)\{[(He,x \rightarrow A_fe) \& \sim (x)He,x] \rightarrow_{c.p.} Fe,x\}$ fitness premise

    (3) $(e)_t \sim Fe^*,x$ equilibrium premise

    (4a) $(x)(H^*e^*,x \rightarrow_{c.p.} A_{e^*}x)$ adaptation premise

  or

    (4b) $(Ex) \sim H^*e^*,x$ diversity premise

  thus

    (5a) $(x)_{c.p.,g} H^*e^*,x$

  or

    (5b) $\sim_{c.p.,g}(x)(H^*e^*,x \rightarrow A_{e^*}x)$

I left implicit the restriction of H to $\{H(e)\}$ and of x to some population P. The subscript "*c.p.*" abbreviates "*ceteris paribus*" and the subscript "*g*" abbreviates "generally," or "for the most part." Again I have oversimplified the equilibrium premise (or placed an additional burden on its *ceteris paribus* clause) to make the logical structure as evident as possible.

argument assumes a competitive economy. I left the indicator premise out of the general schema in order to focus on the essential elements.

In the case of the sex ratio argument, the population consists of some population or organisms that reproduce sexually. The properties He,x, consist of the differing genetic tendencies to produce male and female offspring in various ratios. In addition to general features of the environment, e depends on the actual sex ratio in the population. H^* is not the property of producing offspring in a 1:1 sex ratio, but the different property of belonging to a population that produces offspring in a 1:1 sex ratio. A_e is the property of producing more grandchildren than average. The criterion of success, C, is gene propagation.

The general form provides one with a choice. The existential, fitness, and equilibrium premises (which are the core of the argument) jointly imply *either* that the population possesses some property (or that all members of the population do) or that possessing H^* does not make an agent adapted to the actual environment – that is, possessing H^* does not lead it to possess A_e. To conclude that one of the disjuncts is true, the other must be denied, which is accomplished either by the adaptation or the diversity premises. Thus a cynic might prefer to insist on the diversity premise (which is the denial of the conclusion of the argument for the rational expectations hypothesis) and arrive instead at the conclusion that the predictions of economic theory are not more accurate than expectations generated in other ways.

The basic structure of arbitrage arguments should by now be transparent. If there is an equilibrium and a certain trait, which is supposedly advantageous, is found in some members of the population, then either it must be found in all members (or in population features) or it must not in reality be well adapted after all. Such arguments can be made in any domain in which the notions of fitness and of an equilibrium that could be shifted by a comparative advantage apply. Economics and populations genetics are the obvious domains, but there are potential applications to other fields as well, such as anthropology or even chemistry.[5]

Although commentators on economics are often leery of the postulate of equilibrium, it seems to me that the equilibrium premise (within some suitable degree of approximation) is generally fairly robust and unproblematic. So, I suggest, in the case of economics are the existential and diversity premises. The premises to be skeptical of in economic applications are particularly the adaptation and fitness premises, which are either dubious in themselves or problematic on account of their *ceteris paribus* clauses. In evolutionary biology there are also special difficulties concerning the existential premise (Elster 1979, chap. 1), for mutation may never stumble upon adaptations that are obvious to human foresight and intelligence.

---

5 One might, for example, offer an arbitrage argument to the effect that a taboo on eating cows must be advantageous (Harris 1966) or to the effect that a particular low energy molecular state must be universal within a given gas sample.

As Elliott Sober has noted (1983) equilibrium explanations – arbitrage arguments that are employed to explain their conclusions – possess a special power and attraction. Without specifying the causal mechanism or the causal initial conditions that are responsible for the particular state of the population or of its members, an arbitrage argument can show that state to have been more or less inevitable. As a good explanation should, such an argument eliminates mere contingency and shows that what is in fact the case is what one would have expected, if one had known the laws and the relevant initial conditions. Equilibrium explanations are particularly powerful explanations because so little depends on the precise initial conditions.

But the price of this power is a peculiar precariousness. In a more specific causal explanation, one identifies the particular causes or causal conditions upon which the explanandum depends and the law or laws which link cause and effect. Such explanations can easily be incorrect, of course. We may be mistaken in our purported knowledge of the purported laws. We may be mistaken in our claims concerning which causes or causal conditions were present. We may mistakenly believe that the *ceteris paribus* qualifications, which attach to all causal claims, are met. But since the explanation is based on knowledge of the particular causal circumstances, there are limits to such failings. In equilibrium explanations, in contrast, one does not have to identify the causes and the relevant laws; the explanandum is supposed to obtain, *ceteris paribus,* regardless of the particular causal antecedents. But without knowing the particular causal history, one is often in a poor position to check claims of adaptation or to know whether the *ceteris paribus* condition is actually met. In the case of the rational expectations argument, for example, no one checks to see whether particular firms in a particular (disequilibrium) environment that employed neoclassical economic theory actually made better forecasts than did firms that did not employ neoclassical theory. No one checks to see whether in those circumstances the better forecasts actually led those firms to do better. No one does much more than guess whether there were no other "interferences" or "disturbing causes" that led firms employing economic theory to do worse or to make poorer forecasts, despite the predictive virtues of the theory.

Let me illustrate the power and the pitfalls of arbitrage arguments with two rather different examples from philosophy and economics, which are instances of the general schema and show weaknesses at exactly the suggested spots. The first is from a philosophy paper and is an arbitrage argument for the accuracy of the adaptation premise (4) in (RE):

(PS: Predictive success argument) Contrary to Rosenberg's claim, predictive success *is* an important criterion of theory choice in economics. One of the reasons for this is that economic predictions are *consumed* by the business community. . . . The argument is only that the survivability of the traditional approach in such applications indicates that (relative to the available alternatives), its predictive failings are not as great as Rosenberg would have us believe. (Hands 1984, p. 498)

Recasting this argument so that it is (with some differences to be discussed) an instance of the general schema for arbitrage arguments helps one to see clearly where it breaks down and what the general pitfalls of the argumentative strategy are. I suggest the following reformulation:

(PS')

(1)   (existential premise) Some firms do not pay for the predictions of economic theory and instead employ a cheaper alternative means of making predictions.

(2)   (fitness premise) If firms that are not paying for predictions of economic theory are paying less for information that is just as accurate as economic theory, then, *ceteris paribus*, those firms will have higher net revenue.

(3)   (equilibrium premise) In general, firms that do not pay for the predictions of economic theory and employ some alternative do not have higher net revenues.

(4)   (diversity premise) Some firms do pay for the predictions of economic theory.

Therefore

(5)   (conclusion) (1) *Ceteris paribus*, firms that are paying for the predictions of economic theory are purchasing predictive information that is in general more accurate than any cheaper available alternatives.

(6)   (conclusion) (2) *Ceteris paribus*, economic theory makes some predictions that are in general more accurate than any cheaper available alternatives.

The population here consists of firms again. The property some firms have is not paying for the predictions of economic theory. The further advantageous property that may follow is lower costs. The criterion in terms of which agents would do better is net revenue.

So we have an instance of an arbitrage argument. But note that the conclusion here is in effect the adaptation premise (4) in (RE), and it is drawn by denying that all firms avoid paying for the predictions of economic theory rather than by asserting the antecedent of the fitness premise (2). (PS) is problematic because its fitness premise (2) is dubious. Without knowing the causal pathways that make firms that hire economists viable, it is hard to know whether hiring economists might benefit firms in some other way instead.

To illustrate how this might be, consider a parallel argument that one might suppose some medieval proto-economist to have offered. To make this argument, just substitute in the last argument the word "kings" for the word "firms" and "astrological theory" for "economic theory." The evident conclusion is that astrological theory made better predictions than its medieval competitors. How else could kings that employed astrologers have survived?

The argument for astrology strikes almost everyone in much the way that Hands's argument strikes most noneconomists. Those who would defend the predictive success argument for economics, and not for astrology, must distinguish between the two arguments. One might, for example, argue that relations among different kingdoms were out of equilibrium, but surely so are relations among firms. One might argue that possessing an astrologer can be valuable to a king with a superstitious population, even if astrological theory is predictively worthless. But an economist can, of course, be valuable to a firm with a superstitious group of stock holders in just the same way. One might also feel uneasy about detaching the *ceteris paribus* clause from the conclusion. Kings who employed astrologers might also have been more wealthy or enterprising than those who did not. But firms that hire economists are not obviously the same in all other relevant respects as are those that do not. These qualms about the argument for the predictive worth of astrology should also apply to the argument for the predictive worth of economics. Without having to attend to the actual history, it is easy to let one's prejudices hide how unfounded one's premises are.[6]

My second example is Becker's and Friedman's famous argument concerning racial discrimination by firms:

(RD: Racial discrimination argument) A businessman or an entrepreneur who expresses preferences in his business activities that are not related to productive efficiency is at a disadvantage compared to other individuals who do not. Such an individual is in effect imposing higher costs on himself than are other individuals who do not have such preferences. Hence, in a free market they will tend to drive him out. (Friedman 1962, pp. 109–10)

With some additions Becker's and Friedman's argument (RD) fits into the general schema as follows:

(RD')

    (1)   (existential premise) Some firms will hire workers without regard to race.

    (2)   (fitness premise) If a firm that hires workers without regard to race has

---

6 This comment on Hands's argument was prompted by Alex Rosenberg's reaction:
    Hands's argument that economic theory is predictively successful because business and government would not continue to demand, pay for, and consume it if it weren't, has all the merit of an equivalent argument for alchemy. Since alchemists were in demand for over half a millennium, they must have had something worth selling. Survivability arguments have a place in economics. . . . But unguarded ones like this simply give them an undeservedly bad name. (1986, p. 130)

lower labor costs, then, *ceteris paribus,* it will have higher net revenue and will tend to displace those that make smaller profits (or force them to change their ways).

(3) (equilibrium premise) Firms that hire workers without regard to race are not for the most part outperforming those that do not.

(4) (adaptation premise) *Ceteris paribus,* firms that hire workers without regard to race have lower labor costs.

Therefore

(5) (conclusion) *Ceteris paribus,* firms all hire workers with more or less no regard to race (i.e., there is no racial discrimination in hiring).

This argument fits the general schema nicely. The population consists of firms. The property some have is not discriminating against black workers. The further property this one leads to is lower labor costs. The criterion according to which firms with lower labor costs do better is net revenue or general competitive success. Given the existence of equilibrium, it follows (*ceteris paribus* for the most part) that there is no racial discrimination.[7]

I have taken some liberties here with what Friedman says, in order to display clearly the formal similarities with other arbitrage arguments. Friedman may not intend such a strong argument. One might only argue that *eventually* the workings of the competitive market will insure that there will be no discrimination in hiring. Unless the system moves rapidly to equilibrium, this weaker conclusion is consistent with systematic racial discrimination.

Let us focus on the stronger form of the argument, regardless of whether Friedman or Becker intended to make it. Is it sound? The existential premise (1) seems obvious: some firms do not discriminate on the basis of race. (2), the fitness premise, *seems* just as obvious: if not discriminating lowers labor costs, then, *ceteris paribus,* it increases net revenue, and firms with higher profits will, *ceteris paribus,* displace firms with lower profits or force them to change their ways. (4) is plausible as well. And, finally, to the best of my knowledge, the equilibrium claim (3) is true: nondiscriminatory firms are not for the most part displacing those that discriminate or forcing them to change. Yet the conclusion is obviously false.

Where are the unobvious difficulties with the premises? Just where one would expect – in the adaptation and fitness premises and their *ceteris paribus* clauses. As Becker himself points out, there are circumstances in which one should either

---

7 Note that these cost advantages are available even to employers who hire and compensate their workers without regard to race at all and who pay just as well as the firms that do discriminate. For such employers will be able to attract better workers for the given wages. Note that Alchian's (1950) and Friedman's (1953c) early arguments to the effect that firms act as if they were profit maximizers can also be seen as such arbitrage arguments.

reject (4) or note that its *ceteris paribus* condition is not satisfied: Hiring workers without regard to race will not lower one's labor costs if workers of different races do not work well together. Furthermore, the *ceteris paribus* clause in (2) may never be satisfied. As Akerlof (1985) persuasively argues, hiring black workers can considerably increase *non*labor costs, given racial prejudice on the part of only a few suppliers or customers. Such costs would be obvious if one examined the actual causal history that purportedly forced firms to give up their discriminatory ways or that purportedly drove the recalcitrant out of business altogether. Without such study or some good substitute, the *ceteris paribus* clauses in the fitness and adaptation premises will be unjustified guesses.

The strength of sound arbitrage arguments is that they establish that a population or all of its members must have certain traits merely because of the existence of some members with certain traits and a competitive environment. Thus they avoid having to make assumptions about given universal traits of human beings and concerning particular causal paths.[8] If *ceteris* were *paribus* and hiring without regard to race really did lower total costs, then the market would lead toward the elimination of racial discrimination in hiring whether or not a great many employers were racist. Indeed, one apparently needs almost no assumptions at all about the motivation of firms. Those that do not act in order to maximize profits, or hire with regard to race, or make predictions about the future that do not match those of economic theory, and so forth, will simply be eliminated. But the world is a complicated and messy place, and if we do not attend to what is actually going on, our arguments will all too often turn out to be the venting of our prejudices instead of our insights into nature's secrets. If we want knowledge of matters of fact concerning various populations and their members, we're going to have to do empirical research. Even the best attested scientific theory provides few shortcuts here.

Arbitrage arguments only work when their premises are true and the *ceteris paribus* conditions can be met. Thus they will, in my view, have little application to consumer behavior, where the fitness premise will rarely be satisfied,[9] and even

---

8 Sober argues, in fact, that what he calls "equilibrium explanations," which would include arbitrage arguments are not causal at all (1983). Although not specific about the particular causal mechanism, they nevertheless seem to me to be causal explanations.

9 Thus consider an argument such as the following:

    (CM: Consumer mastery argument): Bayer aspirin must be better than its competitors, since people are willing to pay more for it. If it were not better, those people who bought cheaper aspirin would feel just as well and have more money to spend. Others would learn from their example, or, through some experimentation, would learn the lesson themselves. Bayer could not continue charging more for its aspirin unless it really were superior.

The advantages enjoyed by those who do not purchase Bayer aspirin if it were the case that Bayer were no better than other aspirin are weak and uncertain, and only a flimsy mechanism is suggested whereby the competitive outcome is supposed to be a drop in the price of Bayer aspirin or its elimination from the market.

application to firms is dubious. Alchian's and Friedman's argument that firms must behave as if they were profit maximizers has already been forcefully (decisively in my opinion) criticized by Winter (1962). The argument for the rational expectations hypothesis is a relatively strong one, although the presumed predictive superiority of economic theory and the extent of the fitness provided by this superiority can certainly be questioned. The Friedman–Becker argument concerning racial discrimination is mainly of value because the falsity of its conclusion demonstrates the falsity of its premises or the failure of their *ceteris paribus* clauses.

In closing let me add a few meta-methodological remarks. I take it as a truism that good philosophy of science must pay careful attention to what workers in particular scientific disciplines are doing, but that philosophy of science nevertheless remains distinct from history of science. This paper puts some flesh on this truistic skeleton as follows: Although possible, it would be difficult for a philosopher to recognize the sort of theoretical strategy manifested by arbitrage arguments. Only familiarity with the use of such arguments enables one to appreciate their strengths and weaknesses. Yet the training and concerns of philosophers are essential, too – the knowledge and interests that lead to the quasi-formalizations above have a central role; and the ability and willingness to look beyond a particular discipline is also helpful. Finally a normative concern with good argument and the search for knowledge are central to the philosophical project.

Let me end by quoting a particular robust arbitrage argument. I'll leave its criticism to others:

(SS: Self-serving argument) Methodological scrutiny and philosophical reflection on economics must be valuable. Otherwise those who avoid it would be more prominent, earn higher salaries, and teach more students. Over time those who persist in such scrutiny and reflection would see the light, be driven from the profession, or simply die out without replacements. Since such a process is not in evidence, the value of methodological scrutiny and philosophical reflection is established.

14

Explanatory progress in economics

Has there been explanatory progress in the social sciences? Alexander Rosenberg, in his *Sociobiology and the Preemption of the Social Sciences*, regards it as evident that there has been none:

> But we seem no closer to such laws [of human behavior] now, after several score more years of attempting to secure them, than Mill and his contemporaries were. The absence of such laws, or even of successively improved approximations to them, remains a continuing embarrassment to those empiricists who agree with Mill that the methods, and the sorts of knowledge which the application of such methods are to eventuate in, must be broadly the same in social and natural science. . . .
>
> In fact he [Mill] is committed to the same variables in the explanation of human activity that Plato embraced in the *Phaedo* over two millennia before him. . . . Thus Mill's explanation [for lack of progress in terms of complexity of subject matter] is too weak in light of the allegation that no significant progress has been made in the provision of a real *science* of man throughout the whole of recorded history. No progress has been made in spite of the fact that throughout the period we have been acquainted with the explanatory variables presumably required to generate this science. (1980, pp. 2–3)

Rosenberg's explanation for this remarkable failure is that the variables in terms of which common sense explains human action are the wrong variables and that real laws concerning human behavior will come only from neurophysiology or sociobiology.

But Rosenberg's view that there has been no explanatory progress is apparently not shared by historians of economics. At the beginning of his magisterial *History of Economic Analysis*, Joseph Schumpeter writes:

> . . . from the earliest times until today, analytic economists have been interested, more or less, in the analysis of the phenomenon that we call competitive price. When the modern student meets the phenomenon on an advanced level of his study . . . he is introduced to a number of concepts and problems that may seem to him difficult at first, and would certainly have been completely un-understandable to so relatively recent an author as John Stuart Mill. But the student will also discover before long that the new apparatus poses and solves problems for which the older authors could hardly have found answers even if they had been aware of them. This defines in a common-sense and at any rate a perfectly unambiguous manner, in which sense there has been "scientific progress" between Mill and Samuelson. It is the same sense in which we may say that there has been technological

My thanks for badly needed help to Margaret Schabas and an anonymous referee.

186

progress in the extraction of teeth between the times of John Stuart Mill and our own. (1954, p. 39)

More recently and in much the same spirit Mark Blaug writes:

And so, has there been progress in economic theory? Clearly, the answer is yes: analytical tools have been continuously improved and augmented; empirical data have been increasingly marshaled to verify economic hypotheses; meta-economic biases have been repeatedly exposed and separated from the core of testable propositions which they enmesh; and the workings of the economic system are better understood than ever before. (1978, p. 7)

One should, however, also note the words that follow: "And yet the relativists do have a point. The development of economic thought has not taken the form of a linear progression toward present truths" (pp. 7–8).

Rosenberg's views are not necessarily inconsistent with Schumpeter's and Blaug's assertions. For Schumpeter and Blaug do not maintain that economists have discovered more or better *laws,* and Rosenberg does not suppose that there has been no progress in any regard. He is not denying that contemporary economics uses more sophisticated mathematics than economists did a century ago or that some particular projects in economics have made progress toward achieving their particular goals.

Yet some conflict remains, for Schumpeter believes that progress has also been made in solving what he takes to be genuine (empirical) problems concerning price determination, and Blaug believes that "the workings of the economic system" are now "better understood." Moreover, although the quotation from Schumpeter might suggest otherwise, both Blaug and Schumpeter believe that this progress is cumulative.

Are Blaug and Schumpeter right? Has there been *explanatory* progress in economics? Is Rosenberg wrong to suppose that "no significant progress has been made in the provision of a real *science* of man throughout the whole of recorded history"?

The point of the question, for me at least, is not to determine whether the National Science Foundation should have a Division of Social and Behavior Sciences or whether there should be a Nobel Prize in Economic Science. The point rather concerns what attitudes and methods are appropriate to human efforts, such as economics, to understand aspects of human behavior and habits and their implications. Is it coherent, sensible, and helpful to regard explanations in social theories as similar to attempts to explain natural phenomena in terms of testable generalizations? Or should social explanations be conceived of in some radically different way, as, for example, more akin to philosophical reflection?

This essay will tell a historical story that bears on these general questions. Since, as we shall see, Blaug's, Schumpeter's, and Rosenberg's comments can all be regarded as correct with respect to this history, it will show how there can be cumulative explanatory progress in economics *without* progress in the development of laws of human behavior. As this paper will demonstrate, explanatory progress is possible within the conceptual framework of commonsense explanations of behavior, even if Rosenberg is correct in his view that a "real *science*" with "exact" laws that shows the sort of theoretical progress that physics or chemistry have shown requires a different framework.

The issue with which I shall be concerned is an ideological hot potato: How should one explain the existence of profits? As we shall see, this question itself has evolved over time, but the successive answers to it not only differ from one another but show cumulative progress. Since the very meaning of the word "profits" reflects, as I shall explain below, theoretical commitments, I shall use the neutral word "returns."

WHAT QUESTIONS SHOULD ONE ASK?

We are so accustomed to the fact that the returns on money placed in a bank account or invested are generally positive that we are not surprised or amazed. But the fact is a remarkable one. One takes some money and places it in a magic device called a savings account, a bond, or an investment. Then one waits. Some time later some or all of the money may have disappeared – these magical devices are temperamental – but on average the result is that, even correcting for inflation, more money comes out than went in. How does this magic work? How can one understand this process?

If one looks at attempts to explain such returns, the first thing one notices is that the questions theorists have asked about them have themselves changed. One reason why the questions have changed is that the phenomena have. It is, for example, anachronistic (although not necessarily mistaken or uninstructive) to speak of profits, interest, wages, or rents in medieval economies. Consider the first extended discussion of returns in Western culture, which began in the wake of the revival of commerce in Europe in the twelfth century, when such monetary returns grew larger and more common. Scholars of the church were called upon to judge the moral legitimacy of such returns, for interest on money loans had been condemned as morally impermissible usury. Yet rents and physical returns in agriculture had been regarded as harmless. What should one then say of the returns received by merchants? And if these returns should be regarded generally as morally blameless, how could one condemn interest on loans made by such merchants? For in making a loan, a merchant was forgoing the returns that would have been made if the money had been invested rather than loaned (Schumpeter 1954, pp. 103–4; Blaug 1978, p. 31). Cannot these costs of making loans be charged legitimately to the borrower?

The task was not to develop a general theory of such returns. Still less was there any attempt to explain their magnitude. Empirical curiosity about the sources of such returns was driven and bounded by the need to pass moral judgment on practices of particular *individuals* (Schumpeter 1954, p. 162); and it thus did not give rise to any attempts at systematic theorizing. (Indeed, even if the curiosity had been there, the notion that there was such a thing as an economy or an economic system to study was not.) The context was one in which the rich were held to have an obligation to aid the poor and in which the view that market behavior was civilizing and beneficial had not yet been entertained (see Hirschman 1977). The Scholastics' normative concern is thus not at all the same as that which drives people nowadays to pass judgment on capitalism or to ask whether business profits are exploitative. For the concern of the Scholastics was not to judge institutions, let alone whole social systems (had they thought in such terms), but to offer principles for judging the practices of individuals. The modern normative questions, in contrast, demand a comprehensive understanding of an economy and, unlike the Scholastics' concerns, demand systematic economic theory.

The modern normative concerns with the justification of returns hover around most empirical theorizing concerning returns on investments. But even within empirical theorizing many different questions are broached. The question whose history I shall be focusing on goes to the heart of the magic of investment: Why does the provision of mere *capital*, as opposed to various physical things, command a return?

WHAT ARE "RETURNS"?

For more than half a millennium philosophers and then economists have offered explanations for why there are generally positive returns on investment. But one cannot simply list their answers and compare them, for the phenomena studied have changed dramatically, and there has been disagreement concerning what the returns are that one is attempting to explain. Is the problem one that is essentially concerned with *money*, or is the basic problem why there is output that is not only larger in physical units than input but of more *value?* Are the returns on investments *net* returns after all — costs associated with the use of "capital"? What are costs? Physical quantities? Disutilities? Opportunities forgone? There is no clear question "Why are the returns on investments generally positive?" apart from an economic theory to define what is being asked and to provide a framework in which questions about values and costs can be posed and answered.

The Scholastics, for example, did not associate interest on loans with rents (such as there were) and other "returns" in agriculture. They were concerned with monetary returns — interest, and, if Schumpeter and Blaug are to be believed, they explained and justified such interest in terms of a primitive notion of an opportunity cost: If a merchant could expect a certain normal return on investment, then a merchant could charge that amount of interest on a loan (possibly with some adjustment for risk and charitable obligations). Ordinary returns on investments were themselves regarded either as a payment for risk bearing, for some (labor) service, such as transportation, or as a matter of chance. They were typically justifiable and thus permitted by just prices (see Hollander 1987, pp. 16–17).

Although further and more sophisticated theories of monetary interest were developed in the seventeenth and early eighteenth centuries, the main line of explanatory inquiry shifted to the investigation of "physical" returns:

> . . . the phenomenon to be explained was the net surplus of business, which, in turn, was essentially a surplus arising from the use of an assemblage of certain physical goods; for this surplus, cleared of accessories such as compensation for trouble and risk, had to be handed to some other person, . . . hardly required independent explanation. (Schumpeter 1954, p. 331)

Indeed, in this rush to uncover the "real" factors under the veil of financial transactions, economists sometimes overlooked the need, stressed by Böhm-Bawerk (1888), to explain not only the existence of a physical net output but of an increase in *value* as well.[1]

A TERMINOLOGICAL INTERLUDE

Before the eighteenth century, returns were taken to be money interest, while during the eighteenth and nineteenth centuries, returns were generally taken to be the value of output net of rent, wages, and physical inputs. The problem of explaining why returns were normally positive thus became the problem of explaining why there was generally this net output and why the value of output was normally larger than the value of these inputs.

This explanatory task has been conceived of in two quite different ways. The classical economists thought of it as the problem of explaining why there were "normal profits" or why the normal or average rate of profits was usually positive. They recognized that "profits" – in the sense of apparent net business revenues – consisted of various elements. Included were wages of management, risk premiums, windfalls resulting from uncertainty, and rents, as well as "normal" profits.[2]

---

1 Suppose that input and output in a particular industry consist of the same bundle or vector of commodities c. Then the value of the one-period return in period t, r_t, is $o_c p_{t+1} - i_c p_t$, where o_c and i_c are the outputs and inputs and p_t and p_{t+1} are the prices in periods t and $t + 1$. Notice that $o_c > i_c$ is neither necessary nor sufficient for $r_t > 0$.

2 The distinction between risk, which is in principle insurable, and uncertainty, which is not, was not clearly drawn until this century and is due to Frank Knight (1921b). Since risk is insurable, bearing risk involves a definite cost. Facing uncertainty, in contrast, results in "pure" profits or losses.

But the classical economists were concerned to explain why *normal* profits were typically positive.

Neoclassical economists, particularly in the twentieth century, prefer to call "normal profits" "interest" and to conceive of the task as explaining why there is generally a positive rate of interest. At first glance, one might regard this difference as merely terminological, for what earlier economists called "normal profits" can be renamed "interest," and what economists now call "interest" can (at least with respect to business firms) be called "normal profits." But there is an important issue at stake. Both classical and neoclassical economists agree that profits are a residue. Profits are what is left of revenue after all costs are paid. So whether one calls normal or average returns "normal profits" or "interest" turns on whether one regards these returns as a normal excess of revenue over cost or as a cost. Whether one uses the terminology of normal profits or interest depends on how one answers this normatively loaded question. Hence my use of the awkward but (I hope) neutral terminology of "average returns."[3]

THEORIES OF "NORMAL PROFITS"

Ricardo and Marx regarded average returns as a normal excess of revenue over costs (Ricardo 1817; Marx 1867). Other "classical" economists are ambivalent and sometime regard average returns as a cost and hence as interest. Nassau Senior, with his famous "abstinence" theory (1836, pp. 58–59), comes closest to regarding average returns as a cost rather than a surplus, but even he is by no means of one mind on this point. Both views can be found in both Smith and Mill, although Smith was, I think, closer to Ricardo's perspective and Mill closer to Senior's and to later views that average returns are a cost (Smith 1776; Mill 1871).

For both Ricardo and, on my reading, Marx, "normal" or "equilibrium" prices are largely controlled by labor values – the quantity of labor socially necessary to produce something, where labor is measured in time involved in production. Neither faced squarely the difficulties posed by the heterogeneity of labor. Instead, both supposed that all labor might be regarded as some multiple of some basic homogeneous kind of labor service or "power." Their account of prices also applies only to reproducible commodities or services, not to "rare" goods such as works of Greek sculpture. Ignoring the possibilities of waste or accident, the value of reproducible goods equals the value of inputs plus the amount of labor time.

3   Average returns, like interest and profits, are per unit time. At different dates returns per year will typically differ even on investments of the same length, and when they do, then investments of different lengths even at the same date will have different returns per year. The rate of interest per year on U.S. Treasury bonds with a two-year maturity is rarely if ever the same as the rate of interest per year on U.S. Treasury bonds with a one-year maturity.

Since the value of the wage goods – the amount of labor socially necessary to produce them – may be less than the total amount of labor time, there can be surplus value and, hence, profits. In both Marx's and Ricardo's view, wages tend toward or are normally at a socially determined subsistence level, and there is a considerable surplus value that constitutes the profits of the capitalists (and the rent of landlords, too, but I shall avoid discussing the classical view of rent here). Wages can rise above the subsistence level, and profits can be squeezed. But both Marx and Ricardo postulate mechanisms to drive wages down. In the long run, however, both held, although again for different reasons, that the rate of profits would decline.

Actual capitalists may perform a variety of tasks of supervision, organization, market research, etc.; and some of the returns they earn from their enterprises are properly regarded as wages paid for such services. What earns the capitalist her normal *profits* is her capital, which enables her to purchase various inputs and to provide the workers with wage goods or with the money wages to purchase them. What makes these profits possible are the fact that the capitalist, and not the worker, owns this capital – this command over currently available goods – and the fact that there is physical output net of inputs and wages (within a competitive market). So, apart from the general market background (again ignoring rent), the existence of normal profits depends on three necessary conditions: (1) the capitalist's monopoly over the means of production, (2) the existence of a net physical product, and (3) the wage.

But if capitalists hire workers, what keeps the wage from increasing to the point at which there will be no normal profits? Or, alternatively, if workers were to borrow capital from capitalists (by, for example, selling bonds to capitalists), why doesn't competition among capitalists for these bonds drive their price up to the point where they pay no interest? Without a theory of how wages are determined, we have no explanation of why there are normal profits.

Both Ricardo and Marx (on my reading) supposed that the labor market was generally competitive and that, with increased demand for labor, wages increase, while with increased supply, wages decrease. So it is not inevitable that there be a surplus after purchasing inputs and paying wages. Indeed, both believe profits will decline in the long run to a negligible minimum. But if it is possible to pay the workers the socially determined subsistence wage and still have some surplus, either population growth (in Ricardo's view) or labor-saving technological changes (in Marx's view) will increase the supply of labor or decrease the demand for labor to lower the wage.

Such accounts of labor supply or of *shifts* in labor demand do not suffice. Ricardo and Marx must still explain how the demand for labor (or supply of capital) is limited. Otherwise Ricado's larger population could be put to work with no drop in wage, and Marx's labor-saving technological improvements would result only in more output. This final aspect of the theory was developed by the classical economists (although not by Marx) as the so-called wages-fund doctrine, which held that aggregate wages were determined by the fund of wage goods – mainly foodstuffs – available, or, in other words, by the past year's harvest. Marx has no such clear-cut theory, but mentions a number of factors that may impede investment with its consequent demand for labor. Although Senior combined his abstinence theory with an endorsement of the wages-fund doctrine, the central thesis of the abstinence theory, that investment involves a sacrifice of current consumption, could have provided an alternative explanation of how investment and demand for labor are limited.

So normal profits arise because the supply of capital and hence the demand for labor is limited and because using capital to employ inputs and workers in production yields a net output. But this theory has its difficulties. For the account of what limits investment is either the implausible wages-fund doctrine or the diverse factors mentioned by Marx. Furthermore, asking about what determines the supply and demand for capital tempts one to regard average returns as interest, that is, as the cost of capital, rather than as a surplus that those who own capital are able to appropriate to themselves.

NEOCLASSICAL THEORIES OF THE RATE OF INTEREST

As I have interpreted the dominant classical explanations for normal profits, one sees more continuity than change in the shift from classical to early neoclassical theory. The crucial difference lies in the recognition and application of marginal notions and in the consistent and thorough application of the categories of supply and demand. The capitalist *qua capitalist* provides funds to those who manage the firm. *Capital* (as opposed to capital goods) consists of such funds, and thus generalized control over capital goods and the production process (see Clark 1902; Fisher 1906) (although there is a great deal of controversy concerning what capital is).

Demand for capital depends, as implicitly in Ricardo and Marx, on productivity, but now the emphasis shifts to *marginal* productivity. Using more capital (which, among other things, permits one to use more roundabout methods of production that take more time) results in more output, although at a decreasing rate. Supply of capital, as in Senior and J. S. Mill, depends on the costs of deferring current consumption. But once again one needs to focus on the *marginal* preference for current over future consumption. Those who would still buy bonds if their prices were higher or who would invest at lower interest rates receive rents. Moreover, the fact of economic development itself induces a preference for present over future consumption (Böhm-Bawerk 1889). For with no change in tastes, additional consumption makes a smaller addition to total well-being when one is better off, as people should rationally expect to be in the future. Even weighting future and present satisfactions equally, one can expect to get "less bang for the (marginal) buck" in the future (see Kuenne 1971, pp. 25–34).

The general story has been refined and elaborated in dozens of ways.[4] Although controversy abounds, it is fair to summarize the neoclassical view of the rate of interest as, in Irving Fisher's words, "determined by impatience to spend income and opportunity to invest it" (1930).

DISAGGREGATIVE GENERAL EQUILIBRIUM THEORIES OF INTEREST

Indeed, the same general vision carries over into general equilibrium accounts of intertemporal pricing. In typical disaggregative intertemporal general equilibrium theories, there is (at least explicitly) no such thing as *the* rate of interest (Malinvaud 1972, ch. 10; Koopmans 1957, pp. 1–126). Commodities are all "dated," so strawberries today are different commodities than strawberries next week. Since each commodity has a price, one can define a rate of return for every pair of commodities with different dates. Particularly noteworthy are "own rates" of return or interest involving the same *good* at different dates. For example, the one-week own rate of interest for strawberries next week relative to strawberries today is $p_{today}/p_{next\ week} - 1$, where $p_{next\ week}$ is the "discounted" price *today* of strawberries next week. In May, just before the strawberry harvest, the one-week own rate of interest on strawberries might be as much as 75 or 100 percent. In June, at the end of the harvest, the one-week own rate of interest might well be negative, for the strawberry futures price then of strawberries the week following would likely be higher than the price of current strawberries. Each good and pair of periods will have its own own rates of interest. In this account, there is no such thing as *the* rate of interest. Introducing various financial instruments will introduce various rates of monetary interest, but there will still be no such thing as *the* rate of interest.

At first glance it seems as if one has left behind the traditional problems and their

4   For example, Paul Samuelson (1958) vividly pointed out not only that the need to save for retirement can induce a preference for future over present income and thus a negative interest rate, but also that in a growing monetary economy this desire can induce a preference for future over present income and thus a negative interest rate, but also that in a growing monetary economy this desire can induce a positive interest rate. Böhm-Bawerk and the Austrians have argued at length that capital is not an independent input into production and that interest ought not to be regarded as the cost or price of capital. What, according to the Austrians, contributes to production and incurs a sacrifice to provide is "waiting." Others, such as Frank Knight (1936), have questioned the distinction between produced and unproduced means of production and the consequent distinctions sometimes drawn between rents and interest. Knut Wicksell in *Lectures on Political Economy* pointed out the extent to which the value and apparent quantity of capital itself depends on the rate of interest.

purported solutions, but this impression is misleading. For the explanation for each of the own rates of interest, although more complicated because of the interdependence of the various markets, in a sense preserves the traditional neoclassical explanation for why there is a positive rate of interest. In the case of each good and each pair of periods, one can define own (marginal) "technical" and subjective rates of return or interest. It would be misleading to say that the own rate of interest is *determined* by the own subjective and technical rates of interest, for all of these depend on the basic givens to general equilibrium systems – tastes, technological possibilities, and the distribution of initial endowments (Bliss 1975, pp. 32–37). Yet, just as in the traditional neoclassical accounts, one can see how both productivity and impatience are linked to interest rates. The simpler causal story told by the earlier neoclassicals has been *aufgehoben*, transcended, but in a sense preserved as well. [5]

PROFITS OR INTEREST

Are normal returns then best seen as normal profits – a normal excess of revenues over cost – or as interest, the cost of some factor needed in production, be it "capital" or "waiting"? I shall touch briefly on some of the central arguments for and against, without attempting to settle the issue. Doing so vindicates Schumpeter's distinction between the ideological "vision" guiding economics with respect to which progress is problematic or impossible and the analytical accomplishments of the theorizing guided by such visions, which can progress, even with changes in the guiding "visions" (1954, pp. 41ff.).

Three powerful arguments support the conclusion that returns are interest, the cost of some factor needed in production. First, capital – command over present commodities that are not consumed now – (or waiting), like any factor of production, is necessary to the production process, and both its supply and demand depend on the rate of interest. Second, in intertemporal general equilibrium theory, rates of interest are simply intertemporal price ratios. Third, regardless of ownership relations, allocative efficiency requires that there be a rate of interest. Otherwise there will be no limit to the portion of a society's wealth devoted to investment and no general criterion for which investments to undertake in which order.

---

5 Moreover, although in general equilibrium theory one need never mention such a thing as *the* rate of interest, implicitly there is one; see Hausman 1981b, pp. 88–93. Suppose one picks in each period some numeraire (some unit of a commodity whose price is set at one) such that the general price level from period to period remains constant. If one then values input and output in these "contemporary" (as opposed to "discounted") prices, the ratio of the increase or decrease in value to the total value of inputs will, in equilibrium, for each pair of time periods be the same in every productive enterprise; and that ratio will (depending on how one looks at things) be *the* rate of interest or the normal rate of profits.

But there are serious oddities involved in regarding capital as a factor of production whose cost is interest. For, unlike land, or labor, or capital *goods* such as typewriters, the quantity of capital itself must be recalculated with every change in the rate of interest. Moreover, it can be shown that it is *possible* for an increase in the "quantity of capital" relative to the quantities of other inputs into production to be accompanied by an *increase* in the rate of interest (Harcourt 1975; Hausman 1981b). Furthermore, the effects of setting a rate of interest by government fiat differ significantly from the effects of setting other prices.

The issues here are very knotty. But even if this ideologically charged question has not been answered, there has still been considerable explanatory progress in accounting for why there are typically positive returns on investment. Thus explanatory progress in economics, even *cumulative* explanatory progress that bridges different ideologies, does not presuppose ideological progress.

EXPLANATORY CHANGE AND PROGRESS

The history sketched above supports the conclusion that economists currently understand the phenomena of positive returns better than did their predecessors. There is no question that economists are now able to offer better explanations of positive returns than were medieval, classical, or even early neoclassical economists (although one might question whether there were "positive returns" in the modern sense for medievals to explain). There has been explanatory progress, despite the differences in the questions asked and in the description of the explanandum. Notice that even though the "translation" between talk of interest and of normal profits involves substantive theoretical commitments, those who differ with respect to these commitments can still understand one another. Neoclassical economists can find in Marx's *Capital* insights into factors affecting the demand and supply of capital, and Marxists can find in intertemporal general equilibrium theory insights into how the distribution of resources can affect the normal rate of profit.

It seems to me that there are at least seven regards in which there has been cumulative explanatory progress here:

When, with just a little background in philosophy of science, one thinks of explanatory progress, one thinks of the first two dimensions, the discovery of new laws and of new "facts." Although these are not, I think, the main dimensions of explanatory progress with respect to the phenomenon of positive returns, there has been some progress along both of them. Economists have, first of all, come to recognize new regularities. Whether, given their imprecision, one should regard them as "laws" is an issue for another occasion (see Hausman 1981b, ch. 7). In any case, it has not, for example, always been recognized that people generally prefer present consumption to future consumption. How widespread this tendency is, to what extent it itself depends on the existence of positive returns, and so forth, are all subjects of lively controversy. But that there is such a tendency is widely recognized, as is its relevance to the phenomena of positive returns.

This example does not refute Rosenberg's skepticism concerning nomic progress in the social sciences. For it is debatable whether this generalization is a law, and it is even more debatable whether this generalization has significant explanatory force. For, as contemporary economists recognize, an individual's rate of time preference depends on her economic environment, and time preference and the rate of return cannot be regarded simply as cause and effect. Nevertheless, the *impression* Rosenberg gives that the social sciences have been standing in place or, at best, running in circles, is indefensible.

There are many instances of progress along the second dimension, the recognition of relevant new facts. Given changes in the facts of economic life, this could hardly fail to be the case. Even so trivial a fact as that the price of a bond bears an inverse relation to the rate of interest had to be learned. But one also finds new and *improved* perspectives on persistent phenomena.[6] People have not always known that, quite apart from the risk involved, it is costly to make loans or that competitive markets require an equalization of the rate of return. There is no doubt about the increase in this factual knowledge and about the explanatory progress consequent to it.

A third dimension of explanatory progress, the correction of errors, is closely related to the first two. Over the past half millennium philosophers and economists have made many mistaken claims about positive returns, and the correction of those mistakes is progress. Of course, if a new mistake were made whenever an old one was corrected, this progress would not be cumulative or much to brag about. But coupled with progress along other dimensions, the correction of mistakes is real progress. For example, in failing to recognize that the rate of interest equates only with the *marginal* unwillingness of individuals to "abstain" from consumption and to save and invest, Senior made a mistake with important ideological consequences. In correcting that mistake, economists made progress in explaining positive returns.

A fourth dimension of explanatory progress involves recognizing the *relevance* of already known facts and generalizations, rather than discovering new facts or generalizations or correcting old errors. The Scholastics not only had to recognize that merchants could generally expect positive returns on their investments, but they had to recognize the relevance of this fact to the question of whether interest on money loans was justified. Anybody who bothered to ask whether a pint of strawberries today necessarily has exactly the same value as the guaranteed deliv-

---

6 Given how important human perceptions and interpretations of a social phenomenon are to the phenomenon itself, there can be no sharp distinction between perceiving a new phenomenon and interpreting an old phenomenon differently.

ery of a pint of strawberries in one week could give an answer, but it is not obvious that facts such as these are relevant to the phenomena of positive returns. The development of links between disparate phenomena is an important element of explanatory progress.

Closely related to the fourth dimension of explanatory progress is the growth of *systematization*. In integrating accounts of positive returns into the rest of economic theory — that is, (a) employing the same conceptual apparatus, (b) seeing positive returns as instances of broader pricing phenomena, and (c) offering unified explanations of disparate phenomena — there has been explanatory progress. The theory that effects the greatest such systematization — intertemporal general equilibrium theory — is an object of considerable controversy, and this systematization might turn out to be a mistake. But, other things being equal, such systematization is an aspect of explanatory progress.

Sixth (and closely related to this systematization), there has been increasing conceptual articulation and clarification. In their failure to understand marginal concepts, the early classical economists were unable to make some points clearly and correctly. Unless one is committed to a rigid analytic–synthetic distinction, this aspect of conceptual development cannot be sharply differentiated from empirical developments in discovering generalizations, recognizing their relevance, and systematization (Quine 1960), but even if only as a distinctive perspective on basically the same sort of progress, it deserves separate mention.

A final aspect that is present in the history of discussions of positive returns might be called "deepening" or "superseding." Theorists have cumulatively recognized less obvious factors that are relevant to known regularities and upon which known regularities are conditional. The history of accounts of the supply of "capital" is particularly instructive in this regard. The wages-fund doctrine, for example, retains an element of truth once one recognizes the further factors upon which both wages and the wages fund depend. Although most economists recognize the element of "abstinence" or "time preference," most have also come to recognize the extent to which this factor, upon which the supply of capital supposedly depends, itself depends on factors such as the rate of increase in average incomes or on the basic "givens" of general equilibrium theory. The extent to which bearing "risk" is a cost or an element in profits depends on the possible existence of an insurance market and, in turn, on whether the "risk" involves uncertainty, in Knight's sense of the term. Taking seriously the existence of uncertainty raises questions about the tenability of the whole intertemporal equilibrium theoretic account of interest. What is involved in explanatory progress of this sort is not so much the discovery of new regularities or facts or the correction of old errors, but of qualifying old regularities and facts, recognizing their limitations, and in a sense incorporating them, with heavy revisions, into a more general account.

So even with respect to one of the ideologically most sensitive questions in economics, one finds, regardless of one's ideological commitments, explanatory progress. Blaug and Schumpeter are right: Even if the possibilities for resolving the most fundamental ideological difference are limited, there has still been ample analytical and explanatory progress. Yet Rosenberg's skepticism about whether there has been progress toward a *real science of human behavior* may be justified as well, for most of the explanatory progress has not involved discovering increasingly precise and general laws. But one may reasonably question whether a "real science" requires such laws, and even if one decides that it does, one should not belittle or overlook the genuine, cumulative, and multifaceted progress manifested in economics and other social "sciences."

15

On dogmatism in economics:
the case of preference reversals

Standard economic theory incorporates a simple definition or model of *rationality*. An agent A chooses rationally if A's preferences are complete and transitive and if there is no feasible option that A prefers to the one A chooses. A's preferences are complete if for all options x and y either A prefers x to y or A prefers y to x or A is indifferent between x and y. A's preferences are transitive if for all options x, y, and z, if A prefers x to y and y to z, then A prefers x to z and similarly for indifference. Insofar as economic theory attempts to describe, explain, or predict how people actually behave, economists do more than merely define what rationality is. They must in addition maintain that people are to some degree of approximation rational – that is, to some degree of approximation, that the preferences of real people are complete and transitive and that real people choose what they most prefer. These generalizations about preference and choice are called "utility theory," and they play an important role in statistics, decision theory, and even philosophy, as well as in economics.

No one is under any illusion that these generalizations are exceptionless universal laws. Faced with a long series of choices among pairs of options, most of us would probably eventually violate transitivity. Given the reality of ignorance, people may often be unable to rank alternatives at all. But this sort of messy reality does not show that utility theory is not a reasonable first approximation or that it cannot be helpful in predicting and explaining behavior. What should be much more worrisome to economists would be evidence that people's preferences and choices differ systematically from those predicted by utility theory.

What happens when economists are confronted with such apparently disconfirming evidence? If they are students of Milton Friedman's "The Methodology of Positive Economics" (1953c), they will ask whether the disconfirmation concerns phenomena with which they are concerned, and if it doesn't, they will shrug their shoulders and pass on to more relevant issues. If economists are instead committed to the old-fashioned view espoused by Mill (1836) or Robbins (1935), that economics investigates deductively the implications of proven psychological and technological truths, then they will regard the apparent disconfirmation as due to some disturbing cause or other. Economists are often accused of being dogmatists

This essay is drawn from Chapter 13 of my book *The Inexact and Separate Science of Economics* (1992a). I am indebted to Philippe Mongin and Hal Varian and to audiences at the University of Helsinki, the University of Groningen, George Mason University, and George Washington University for criticisms.

of one of these varieties. Let's look at one case to see whether they are. Of course one case *proves* nothing. But it may be suggestive and enlightening nevertheless.

PREFERENCE REVERSALS

One way in which people's choice behavior deviates systematically from that predicted by utility theory involves so-called "preference reversals." Paul Slovic and Sarah Lichtenstein describe the discovery of this phenomenon as follows:

> The impetus for this study was our observation in our earlier 1968 article that choices among pairs of gambles appeared to be influenced primarily by probabilities of winning and losing, whereas buying and selling prices were primarily determined by the dollar amounts that could be won or lost. . . . Subjects setting a price on an attractive gamble appeared to start with the amount to win and adjust it downward to take into account the probability of winning and losing, and the amount that could be lost. The adjustment process was relatively imprecise, leaving the price response greatly influenced by the starting point payoff. Choices, on the other hand, appeared to be governed by different rules.
>
> In our 1971 article, we argued that, if the information in a gamble is processed differently when making choices and setting prices, it should be possible to construct pairs of gambles such that people would choose one member of the pair but set a higher price on the other. We proceeded to construct a small set of pairs that clearly demonstrated this predicted effect. (1983, p. 597)

Lichtenstein and Slovic called the bets with a high probability of winning "P-bets," while bets with large prizes are "$-bets." Given their earlier conjectures, Lichtenstein and Slovic predicted that among pairs of bets with positive expected value individuals who choose the P-bets should often be willing to pay more for $-bets. For example, consider the P-bet (P^*) consisting of a gamble in which one wins $4.00 if a roulette wheel comes up with any number except 1 (that is, with a probability of 35/36) or loses $1.00 if the roulette wheel comes up 1 (that is with a probability of 1/36). Lichtenstein and Slovic paired it with the $-bet ($*) in which one has an 11/36 chance to win $16.00 and a 25/36 chance to lose $1.50. The expected monetary value of the two gambles (that is, the sum of the prices times the probabilities) are respectively $3.86 and $3.85. Lichtenstein and Slovic made the conditional prediction that if individuals preferred the P-bets in pairs such as (P^*,$*), they would be likely to pay *more* for the $-bets. Such reversals are "predicted." A reversal in which an individual prefers a $-bet and prices a P-bet higher is "unpredicted."

The first experiments

In their essay, "Reversals of Preference Between Bids and Choices in Gambling Decisions," Lichtenstein and Slovic report the results of three experiments in which

201

subjects were first asked to choose among bets with approximately the same expected value such as P* and $* above. Then the subjects were distracted with other tasks for about an hour. Finally they were asked to put a price on various bets presented to them one at a time. In the first two experiments, subjects were paid for participating, and there was no actual gambling. In the third experiment, the bets were played, and the subjects were paid their winnings. In the pricing part of Experiment I, subjects were asked to suppose that they owned tickets to play the lotteries and to state the minimum price they would accept to sell their tickets. In Experiment II, subjects were asked to state the highest price they would pay to purchase each lottery. In Experiment III, all choices were repeated three times (with prompting concerning prior choices) and a special device (to be described shortly) was used to give subjects strong incentives to state truthfully and accurately the minimum selling prices for lotteries. In the first experiment nearly three-quarters of the subjects reversed their preference *every time* they chose the P-bet in the pairwise comparison. There were few unpredicted reversals. In Experiment II the results were not as striking, but more than two-thirds of the subjects had a higher rate of conditional predicted reversals than of conditional unpredicted reversals. In Experiment III, which used only 14 subjects, six always made conditional predicted reversals, five sometimes made them, and unpredicted reversals were infrequent. As Lichtenstein's and Slovic's hypotheses concerning choices and valuations of gambles implied, reversals were most frequent 1) when the loss in the $-bet was larger than in the P-bet, which led subjects to prefer the P-bet more often; and 2) when the win in the $-bet was large relative to the win in the P-bet, which led individuals to bid more for the $-bet.

To encourage subjects to reveal their true minimum selling price, Lichtenstein and Slovic arranged in the third experiment to purchase the bet from a subject whenever a chance mechanism generated a purchase price exceeding the subject's selling price. If a subject announced a selling price higher than the probabilistically generated purchase price, then the subject would play the lottery instead. Given this arrangement, there is nothing to be gained by understating one's minimum selling price and there may be real costs, for doing so may result in selling the lottery for less than it is worth to one. To overstate the minimum selling price again brings no additional revenue, and doing so may lead one to play the lottery when one would prefer to sell it at the price offered. (This method is due to Becker, deGroot, and Marschak 1964.)

In the case of bets with negative expected values and improbable, but large, losses, Lichtenstein and Slovic predicted the opposite reversals among those preferring the $-bets to the P-bets. This implication was not tested in the experiments reported in the 1971 paper, but when the above results were replicated in a later experiment (Lichtenstein and Slovic 1973) this additional implication was also confirmed. The later experiment was carried out on the balcony of the Four

Queens Casino in Las Vegas, and the experimental subjects, who included professional gamblers, played with their own money! Once again Lichtenstein and Slovic found frequent conditionally predicted reversals and infrequent unpredicted reversals (see also Lindman 1971).

Apparent significance

Assuming that individuals prefer more money to less, preference reversal apparently involves gross choice inconsistency.[1] As the economists David Grether and Charles Plott point out,

Taken at face value the data are simply inconsistent with preference theory and have broad implications about research priorities within economics. . . . It suggests that no optimization principles of any sort lie behind even the simplest of human choices and that the uniformities in human choice behavior which lie behind market behavior may result from principles which are of a completely different sort from those generally accepted. . . .

Notice this behavior is not simply a violation of some type of expected utility hypothesis. The preference measured one way is the *reverse* of preference measured another and seemingly theoretically compatible way. If indeed preferences exist and if the principle of optimization is applicable, then an individual should place a higher reservation price on the object he prefers. (1979, p. 623)

Suppose I prefer bet a to bet b and place a price of $x on a and a price of $y on b. If we assume that I place a price of $x on a if and only if I am indifferent between a and $x and similarly for b and $y, then I must prefer $x to $y. This equivalence between pricing and indifference is called "procedure invariance" by Tversky et al. (1990, p. 205). If I am indifferent between $x and a, which I prefer to b, and I am indifferent between b and $y, then, by, transitivity, I must prefer $x to $y. If, in addition, I prefer more money to less, $x must be larger than $y. Yet in the case of preference reversals, individuals who prefer P-bets price $-bets higher. So preferring a P-bet and pricing a $-bet higher violates either transitivity or procedure invariance.

GRETHER'S AND PLOTT'S EXPERIMENTS

Not surprisingly, these results were greeted with skepticism by economists. But those who have reacted to them in print have not argued that such results cannot shake their confidence in the fundamental propositions of economic theory. They have shown neither the dogmatism implied by the traditional deductive method nor that which follows from Milton Friedman's argument against considering the

1 But see below, "Further responses by economists."

realism of assumptions. Economists have, of course, considered the possibility that the results are due to disturbing causes or that they arise only because of peculiarities of the experimental setup. But these possibilities suggest experiments rather than providing automatic excuses. Thus Grether and Plott comment,

> There is little doubt that psychologists have uncovered a systematic and interesting aspect of human choice behavior. The key question is, of course, whether this behavior should be of interest to economists. Specifically it seems necessary to answer the following: 1) Does the phenomenon exist in situations where economic theory is generally applied? 2) Can the phenomenon be explained by applying standard economic theory or some immediate variant thereof? (1979, p. 624)

Grether and Plott did not dismiss the results as due to experimental error or economically insignificant disturbing causes. Instead they attempted to see whether in properly designed experiments the preference reversal phenomenon would disappear. Grether and Plott are explicit about how they *want* the experiments to come out, for they say bluntly that the purpose of their experiments was "to discredit the psychologists' works as applied to economics" (1979, p. 623). But whether the fundamental theory can be saved depends on the experimental results, not on methodological fiat.

Accordingly, Grether and Plott constructed a list of possible explanations for the preference reversal phenomenon. On the list are psychological explanations, including two in terms of human information-processing procedures. The first of these is Lichtenstein's and Slovic's, in terms of the different methods devoted to different cognitive tasks, while the second (which is not their view, although it might complement their view), explains the preference reversals in terms of information-processing strategies designed to lessen the costs of decision making. The other possible psychological hypotheses on Grether's and Plott's list cannot explain the data.

In addition, the list includes various explanations in terms of faults in the experiment – misunderstanding among unsophisticated subjects, expectations produced by the knowledge that these were psychological experiments, etc. Grether and Plott do not believe that Lichtenstein and Slovic botched their experiments, but, just to be sure, they try to control for these unlikely sources of the odd results.

How preference reversals might be explained away

Grether and Plott are particularly interested in the following four ways in which economists might attempt to explain or to explain away the preference reversal phenomenon. If supported by the evidence, these explanations would show that the preference reversal phenomenon poses no challenge to economics and reveals no serious flaw in the standard model of economic rationality. The four possible "economic" explanations are:

(1) Poor Incentives: The incentives in the experiment were insufficient to get people to behave as they would in real life when significant decisions have to be made.

(2) Income Effects: As people acquire more wealth they may rationally come to be willing to gamble more. This change in aversion to risk as a result of increases in wealth could contaminate the results in some of Lichtenstein's and Slovic's experiments, in which many gambles were played and wealth changed between separate choices.

(3) Indifference: In Slovic's and Lichtenstein's experiment, subjects were not allowed to say that they were indifferent between the two bets. If subjects were nevertheless indifferent between the P- and $-bets when they said they preferred the P-bet, then there would be less irrationality in pricing the $-bet higher.[2]

(4) Strategic Pricing: Finally, subjects might not be telling the truth when asked to state the minimum price they would accept to sell a lottery. It is often advantageous to ask more than one would truly be willing to accept, and since it is hard to exaggerate the value of the P-bet, this general strategy may account for the reversals.

Grether and Plott endeavored to control for these factors to see whether the conditionally predicted preference reversals would then go away (see also Grether and Plott 1982). Before discussing their experiments, it is worth noting that these alternatives to accepting Lichtenstein's and Slovic's hypothesis are implausible and generally insufficient.

(1) Poor Incentives: Since the same results obtained in Slovic's and Lichtenstein's experiments whether the gambles were played, whether it was the subject's own money, and whether individuals were driven to attend carefully, it is hard to believe that the preference reversals result merely from the weakness of the incentives. And while it would be reassuring to economists if preference reversals went away when the incentives were substantial, it seems to me that economists should still be curious why weak incentives would lead only to the predicted, not the unpredicted, reversals.

(2) Income Effects: It is hard to believe that these could be important, because the results obtained whether the gambles were played or not; and as is noticed in the first excuse, the stakes were low. Furthermore, the

---

2 Levi argues that preference reversals might be due to incompleteness rather than indifference. The "preferences" expressed for the P-bets might reflect their greater security (1986, p. 48).

opposite reversals in the case of bets with large possible losses, which were predicted and observed in the Las Vegas replication, are inconsistent with a purported explanation in terms of income effects.

(3) Indifference: Even if individuals were indifferent between P- and $-bets when they announced a preference for the P-bet, it would still be inconsistent with rational choice theory to price the $-bet higher. Indifference would also not explain the asymmetry between the frequency of conditionally predicted reversals and unpredicted reversals. Furthermore, although Lichtenstein and Slovic did not permit individuals to register indifference, they did ask them to indicate strength of preference on a four-point scale: "slight," "moderate," "strong," and "very strong," and the mean strength of preference indicated was "strong."

(4) Strategic Pricing: Strategic misrepresentation would not explain reversals when individuals were only asked to price gambles rather than to state buying or selling prices, and would predict that when asked to state buying price, individuals would understate the prices of $-bets.

Grether's and Plott's results

So it is not surprising that Grether and Plott failed to make the preference reversal phenomenon go away by controlling for these factors. Here is what happened:

(1) Poor Incentives: To determine the importance of incentives, Grether and Plott varied them. But the phenomenon was unaffected, so the explanation in terms of weak incentives was largely refuted. The fact that incentives had little effect was taken by Grether and Plott as evidence against the explanation in terms of information processing costs, since individuals should devote more care to adjusting for probabilities as the stakes increase.

(2) Income Effects: To control for these, subjects played only one of the gambles (which was chosen randomly) and the order of choosing vs. bidding varied. But the phenomenon persisted.

(3) Indifference: Grether and Plott permitted subjects to register indifference as well as preference, but scarcely any subject ever did, so the phenomenon did not arise from indifference.

(4) Strategic Pricing: Grether and Plott used the same Becker–deGroot–Marshak mechanism as Lichtenstein and Slovic in order to elicit a truthful statement of minimum selling price, and they also compared the result with simply asking people to state what they believed a lottery was worth. The amounts stated when pricing and evaluating were not appreciably different, so the explanation in terms of strategic responses was ruled out.

Thus Grether and Plott state,

> Needless to say, the results we obtained were not those expected when we initiated this study. Our design controlled for all the economic–theoretic explanations of the phenomenon which we could find. The preference reversal phenomenon which is inconsistent with the traditional statement of preference theory remains. (1979, p. 634)

What is surprising to me is not the result of Grether's and Plott's experiment, but why the result should have surprised them. Given how implausible are the alternatives to Lichtenstein's and Slovic's hypothesis, which incidentally managed to predict this phenomenon before it was ever observed, it seems, at least with hindsight, that Grether and Plott should not have expected any different results.

Apparent dogmatism: Grether's and Plott's Conclusions

What then do Grether and Plott conclude? Here is what they say.

> The fact that preference theory and related theories of optimization are subject to exception does not mean that they should be discarded. No alternative theory currently available appears to be capable of covering the same extremely broad range of phenomena. In a sense the exception is an important discovery, as it stands as an answer to those who would charge that preference theory is circular and/or without empirical content. It also stands as a challenge to theorists who may attempt to modify the theory to account for this exception without simultaneously making the theory vacuous. (1979, p. 634)

After the preceding openminded discussion and the striking concession that the preference reversal phenomenon really does appear to be a refutation of a central behavioral postulate of contemporary economics, these words (which constitute the last paragraph in Grether's and Plott's conclusion) are a letdown. It is almost as if they conclude, "Since these awful data cannot be discredited, economists should ignore them, although not without first congratulating themselves for possessing such a splendidly non-vacuous theory." Is this caricature completely unfair? Is their response justifiable?

DOGMATISM, ITS SOURCES AND JUSTIFICATION

Dogmatism is sometimes justifiable. As various philosophers of science such as Imre Lakatos (1970) have pointed out, theories are too valuable and too hard to generate to be easily dismissed even when they face serious problems, unless better alternatives are available.

Moreover, Grether and Plott use their experiments to test the explanations of preference reversal proposed by some psychologists, and they argue that some of these hypotheses are unsuccessful, too (1979, p. 634). So they suggest that they are confronting a mysterious phenomenon rather than rejecting a well-confirmed alternative hypothesis. But, as Grether and Plott concede, Lichtenstein's and Slovic's own hypothesis anticipated the experimental results and is well confirmed by these new experiments. At least at first glance, Grether's and Plott's reaction seems indefensibly dogmatic.

Dogmatism and the deductive method

What explains this dogmatism? A common accusation made against economists is that they are unwilling to take evidence seriously. Up until the 1930s the dominant view of theory assessment in economics was what John Stuart Mill called the "deductive method" or the "method *a priori.*"[3] The idea is that economists can tell by introspection or everyday experience that the causal factors with which economics is concerned are real and significant. Economics is devoted to deducing the implications of these obvious generalizations in particular circumstances. Cases where the theory does not fit the data – that is, where there appear to be disconfirmations – only reveal the influence of interferences or disturbing causes and do not count against the basic theory. This method has been denounced by methodologists as unreasonably dogmatic, although it persists in practice.

Whether or not this method *a priori* is as unjustifiable as it might appear to be, commitment to it does not explain Grether's and Plott's dogmatism. For they do not refuse to take the disconfirming evidence provided by Lichtenstein and Slovic seriously, and they are not content to say merely that the problem must be caused by some interference. On the contrary, here is an instance where respected economists, who are committed to standard economic theory, are prepared to take solid experimental evidence as disconfirming one of the most central claims of economics. But having done so, little is changed.

Dogmatism and the commitment to a separate science

Why? How else might one explain this dogmatism? The reason Grether and Plott give for refusing to move from refutation to theory change or modification is that, "No alternative theory currently available appears to be capable of covering the same extremely broad range of phenomena." This way of defending economic theory is familiar. For example, Tjallings Koopmans writes,

The theories that have become dear to us can very well stand by themselves as an impressive and highly valuable system of deductive thought erected on a few premises that seem to be well-chosen first approximations to a complicated reality. . . . In many cases the knowledge these deductions [from these premises] yield is the best we have, either because better approximations have not been secured at the level of the premises, or because comparable

3   Mill 1836; 1843, Bk. III, ch. 11, Bk. VI, ch. 9; see this volume, Chapters 3 and 4.

reasoning from premises recognized as more realistic has not been completed or has not yet been found possible. Is any stronger defense needed or even desirable? (1957, pp. 141–42)

At first glance this defense seems completely reasonable. The theory is only a first approximation, so disconfirmations are not decisive. And, in any case, theory assessment is comparative. As problematic as economic theory may be, there are no alternatives which provide "better approximations . . . at the level of the premises" and enable one to draw from such alternative premises conclusions comparable to those which can be drawn from accepted theory. Milton Friedman offers a similar defense when he remarks that ". . . criticism of this type is largely beside the point unless supplemented by evidence that a hypothesis . . . yields better predictions for as wide a range of phenomena" (1953c, p. 31).[4] But Friedman's and Koopmans's defenses of economics, like Grether's and Plott's, have a tacit premise: that any good economic theory must, like the accepted theory, have both comprehensive scope and a compact or parsimonious theoretical core. The stipulated standard that an alternative theory must meet is that it "be capable of covering the same extremely broad range of phenomena."

The idea to which Grether and Plott and Koopmans and most economists are committed also goes back to John Stuart Mill. He writes,

Notwithstanding the universal *consensus* of the social phenomena, whereby nothing which takes place in any part of the operations of society is without its share of influence on every other part, . . . it is not the less true that different species of social facts are in the main dependent, immediately and in the first resort, on different kinds of causes; and therefore not only may with advantage, but must, be studied apart. . . .

There is, for example, one large class of social phenomena in which the immediately determining causes are principally those which act through the desire of wealth, and in which the psychological law mainly concerned the familiar one that a greater gain is preferred to a smaller. . . . By reasoning from that one law of human nature, and from the principal outward circumstances (whether universal or confined to particular states of society) which operate upon the human mind through the law, we may be enabled to explain and predict this portion of the phenomena of society, so far as they depend on that class of circumstances only, overlooking the influence of any other of the circumstances of society, . . . (1843, 6.9.3)

Mill is not only proposing that social theorists focus on the most important causes of particular phenomena. He is also maintaining that whole classes of social phenomena (such as economic phenomena) depend "in the first resort" on a small set of causes. Consequently one can aim at what Mill calls a "separate science," a

---

4   Earlier Friedman argued that one can use considerations of scope to choose among "alternative hypotheses equally consistent with the available evidence" (1953c, p. 10). This is perfectly reasonable. But in the later passage quoted in the text, Friedman, like Koopmans and Grether and Plott, is ruling out theories with narrow scope, even if they are *more* consistent with the evidence.

science of economics that explains and predicts all central and significant economic phenomena by means of a single systematic and parsimonious theory (see Hausman 1992a, ch. 6).

Grether and Plott, like Koopmans and Friedman, are committed to this vision of economics as a "separate science." Such a theoretical strategy precludes accepting hypothesis concerning gambling choices and bidding such as Lichtenstein's and Slovic's, for that theory has a narrow scope. Its causal factors are significant for a comparatively small set of phenomena; they are not significant factors in all economic phenomena.

Grether and Plott and Koopmans and Friedman are not just saying that it is reasonable to hang on to accepted theory because there are no alternatives that are better confirmed. Instead, they implicitly demand that any alternative to accepted theory must preserve a peculiarly "economic" realm to be spanned by a single unified theory. They are not merely defending simplicity, unity, and broad scope as methodological desiderata or as criteria to be employed when there are ties or nearties on empirical grounds. Instead, one finds a constraint in operation here against considering a narrow-scope hypothesis, regardless of its empirical vindication.

This requirement seems unjustified. In defense of it in this context, one might argue that since utility theory is a theory of rationality, as well as a set of generalizations about how people in fact behave, it should not have a piecemeal structure. But this is to legislate that the theory of choice must also be a theory of rational choice. There are pragmatic grounds for preferring theories of choice that are also theories of rational choice (Hausman 1992a, ch. 12.), but those grounds must take second place to solid empirical evidence. It would be nice if a better alternative possessed such unity and scope, united positive economics and the theory of rationality, and preserved the peculiar moral authority of economists, but one cannot inflate these methodological desiderata into methodological constraints against considering alternatives, no matter how much better they fit the data.

FURTHER RESPONSES BY ECONOMISTS

It might seem unfair to focus exclusively on Grether and Plott. How have other economists reacted? Among the relatively small number who have discussed preference reversals, none seems to have paid any careful attention to Lichtenstein's and Slovic's hypothesis (that people employ different cognitive processes when pricing than when choosing), and there has been no attempt to incorporate it into economics. There is little theoretical collaboration between economists and psychologists in this area,[5] and the continuing work by psychologists on aspects of preference reversals is not cited by economists.

5 Richard Thaler is a striking exception.

In the decade since Grether and Plott published their results, there *have* been further discussions by economists of the preference reversal phenomenon, and most of them have been published in the *American Economic Review*, certainly one of the most prestigious economic journals. In the immediate aftermath, Pommerehne et al. (1982) and Reilly (1982) tried even harder to make the preference reversal phenomenon go away and were able to reduce the frequency of preference reversals (although in doing so, they also blunted Grether's and Plott's criticism of the information-processing-costs explanation). But the phenomenon cannot be made to go away. Pommerehne et al. found that although experimental subjects can learn from repetition to accept more profitable gambles, they do not learn to avoid preference reversals (1982, p. 573). In a more dramatic demonstration of just how robust the phenomenon is, Berg et al. (1985) ran a series of experiments that exploited the choice inconsistencies by leading subjects through a "money-pump" cycle of exchanges in which they paid money to wind up back where they started. The effect was to decrease the dollar amount of the preference reversals, but not to eliminate them (Roth 1988, p. 1015).[6] All of this confirms Lichtenstein's and Slovic's initial hypothesis.

But economists did not start studying contemporary psychology. Instead, some still tried to explain away the phenomenon. Thus Holt (1986) and Karni and Safra (1987) pointed out that the experimental results may be explained by a failure of the independence axiom, rather than by a failure of transitivity. Since independence is not a part of ordinal utility theory and is not as central to the theory of rationality, this was an encouraging result. With odd preferences for money and a strange function relating degrees of belief to objective probabilities, one can explain the experimental results as (what Karni and Safra call) "announced price reversals" that show no intransitivities. In a similar vein, Segal (1988) pointed out that the preference reversals in some of Grether's and Plott's experiments could be due to a failure of the reduction postulate,[7] which is an even less important part of the theory of rational choice. Since standard economic theory incorporates only ordinal utility theory and does not rely on either the independence principle or the reduction postulate, these alternatives would save economic theory from apparent disconfirmation.

But these ways of "saving" transitivity are implausible and do not account for the details of the data. The purported explanation of preference reversals in terms of a failure of the independence condition requires attributing to people, in an *ad hoc* way, bizarre preferences and subjective probability judgments, for which there

---

6 But, as discussed below, Chu and Chu (1990) report experiments in which repeated and transparent money-pumping did eliminate preference reversals.

7 The Becker–deGroot–Marschak method of getting subjects to state their true selling prices involves in effect a compound lottery. So, if individuals do not relate the values of compound and simple lotteries in the way specified by the reduction postulate, they might show preference reversals without violating transitivity or independence.

is no independent evidence.[8] Furthermore, no single set of such beliefs and preferences can account for the whole series of choices subjects make in the experiments. The purported explanation in terms of a failure of the reduction postulate is just as *ad hoc* and, as noted by Tversky et al. (1990, p. 209), it cannot explain the asymmetry in preference reversals.[9] Tversky et al. also establish that a random mixture of P-bets and $-bets is not preferred to the P-bets and $-bets for sure, as it should be if there is a failure of independence (1990, p. 209). Furthermore, the explanation in terms of a failure of the reduction postulate is refuted by the result that the selling prices elicited by the Becker–deGroot–Marschak mechanism do not differ significantly from the other valuations subjects make.

Although these alternative explanations for the preference reversal phenomenon are of interest mainly as evidence of how unwilling economists are to accept the disconfirmation or to take seriously psychological hypotheses, they have nevertheless been tested. In a recent essay (published in the *American Economic Review*, 1989), Cox and Epstein report the results of tests of the explanations of preference reversals in terms of failures of independence or of the reduction postulates. The paper begins with a misstatement of the preference reversal phenomenon: it is described simply as any inconsistency between the pricing and choice of $- and P-bets rather than pricing $-bets higher than chosen P-bets. The authors do note the point in a footnote (p. 409), in which they mention that a referee pointed it out, but attention to the details of the phenomenon and to the psychological hypothesis that predicts just these reversals seems an afterthought.

To determine whether reversals might be due to failures of independence or of the reduction postulate, Cox and Epstein jettison the Becker–deGroot–Marschak elicitation mechanism. Instead, subjects were asked to price both of the gambles in a pair at the same time, and were told that they would get to play the gamble with the higher price and would be paid a fixed amount for the gamble with the lower price (1989, p. 412). This experimental procedure is faulty, for it makes pricing just a way of stating a choice. Indeed, Cox and Epstein themselves conjecture, "that most of our subjects realized that the particular numbers they stated for prices were irrelevant except for their relative magnitudes. This was evidenced by their comments and by their propensity to state prices such as 1,000 francs for lottery A and 999 francs for lottery B in any given (A,B) pair" (p. 422). The procedure removes the central difference between the *tasks* of pricing and

<hr/>

8   In Karni's and Safra's example, the utility of money function $u(x)$ is $30x + 30$, for $x \leq \$-1$, $10x + 10$ for $\$-1 \leq x \leq \$12$ and $6.75x + 49$ for $x \geq \$12$. The function relating degrees of belief to objective probabilities is $1.1564p$ for $0 \leq p \leq .1833$, $.9p + .047$ for $.1833 \leq p \leq .7$, $.5p + .327$ for $.7 \leq p \leq .98$, and p for $.98 \leq p \leq 1$ (1987, p. 678). Although the general point that concerns Holt and, especially Karni and Safra, is of real interest, it would be an *ad hoc* maneuver to "save" transitivity by attributing such beliefs and utilities.

9   But see the argument of Safra et al. 1990, p. 927.

choosing that led Lichtenstein and Slovic to predict the reversals in the first place, and there is no reason to expect the phenomenon to present itself in these circumstances. Indeed, were Cox's and Epstein's procedure to show the same preference reversals, one would have grounds to doubt Lichtenstein's and Slovic's account of the source of the phenomenon.

Cox and Epstein do not find the standard (asymmetrical) preference reversal phenomena. But they conclude that these results disconfirm Lichtenstein's and Slovic's work. Cox and Epstein write, "However, if the anchoring and adjustment theory is to be immunized to the apparent falsifying evidence of our experiments, it will have to be extended to incorporate more than a message space explanation of choice reversals" (p. 422). What they mean by the "message space explanation of choice reversals" is an explanation in terms of whether bids rather than choices are elicited. But their conclusions are unpersuasive. What matters in Lichtenstein's and Slovic's view is the *task* subjects are asked to carry out, not the way the task is worded. Cox and Epstein find reversals in either direction about one-third of the time, but absent any inquiry concerning how consistently the subjects otherwise choose, it is impossible to diagnose the causes of these reversals.

In the most recent study of which I am aware, there is at last some "good news" for economists. Although (as mentioned above) there is evidence that people do not easily learn to avoid preference reversals, it is hard to believe that people will not learn at all. In the latest experiment results concerning preference reversals, Chu and Chu show how to make people stop showing preference reversals. Slightly oversimplying: Experimental subjects were asked to state their preferences with respect to a *single* pair of a P-bet and a $-bet (such as $[(\$4,35/36),(\$-1,1/36)]$ and $[(\$16,11/36),(\$-1.50,25/36)])$ and to state prices for the two bets. They were then given a certain amount of money. Those who showed preference reversals were then "educated" by the following sequence of exchanges. They had to purchase the $-bet from the experimenter for the price stated, make the exchange of the $-bet for the P-bet, which they claimed to prefer, and then sell the P-bet back to the experimenter for the price they had stated. After the round was complete, they were, of course, poorer by $\$(\$-bet)-\$(P-bet)$. Individuals could then revise their preferences or their pricing and the game was repeated. Few continued to be reversers after two rounds, and after having been educated to stop reversing their preferences with respect to one pair, individuals also avoided reversing their preferences with respect to other pairs. So people do indeed learn. In some environments, irrational behavior is inherently unstable.

Chu and Chu are careful not to leap to conclusions concerning how efficacious is the education provided by actual markets, and the weakness in the general claim that learning makes irrational behavior unimportant is precisely at this point. For markets do not always underline our mistakes so clearly. (If they did, then individuals should have learned not to show preference reversals before the experiments began.) Chu's and Chu's results and the general argument that people will learn provide some hope that phenomena such as preference reversals will not be important factors in economic life. But such hope does not justify dismissing experimental findings of irrationality as obviously insignificant. [10]

Although one sees in this history little evidence of a distinctively dogmatic view of theory appraisal, one does see insularity and dogmatism of a different sort. [11] In particular, economists have shown little interest in or even patience with the hypotheses psychologists have formulated to explain aberrant choice behavior. The reason is, I believe, that the possibilities that valuation might be variegated and that connections between choice and valuation might be complex and indirect threaten the structure of theoretical economics.

The unwillingness to take seriously the theoretical work by psychologists is a little ironic, for although Lichtenstein's and Slovic's hypothesis concerning information processing is not compatible with standard models of economic choice, it can be modeled with similar mathematical tools and combined with much that is standard in economic theory. It owes a great deal to the work of less orthodox economists such as Richard Cyert, James March, or Herbert Simon (Cyert and March 1963; Simon 1959). But to incorporate Lichtenstein's and Slovic's hypothesis within an economic theory would be to move toward a theory of economic behavior with many behavioral postulates rather than few, and with behavioral postulates that apply only to a comparatively narrow range of phenomena. And economists are generally unwilling to surrender their vision of a single unifying economic theory.

Despite attempts such as Holt's, Karni and Safra's, and Segal's to "save" the standard theory, attention among decision theorists and theoretical economists has shifted in the past few years to proposing alternatives to utility theory to account for the perference-reversal phenomenon. Loomes and Sugden (1983) argue that their revision of expected utility theory, "regret theory" (1982) can explain it (see also Loomes et al. 1989). Levi (1986) has suggested that preference reversals may be due to incompleteness in preferences, which ought anyway to be modeled in an adequate theory of rational and actual choice. Machina (1987) suggests that formal choice models involving intransitive preferences can be formulated. Notice that respected economists such as Sugden and Machina are

---

10 For example, Kahneman, Knetsch, and Thaler (1990) argue that the "endowment effect" (valuing something more highly when it becomes part of one's endowment) and the asymmetrical attitude people adopt toward losses as opposed to forgone gains persist even in market environments that provide opportunities to learn. Ausubel (1991) explains the striking failure of competition in credit card markets in terms of the irrational unwillingness of credit-card users to believe that they will borrow on their cards.

11 Notice I am not making any *quantitative* claims about dogmatism. I am not saying that there is too much, or that there is more or less than in some other field. My concern is rather to understand the nature and sources of dogmatism in economics.

willing to consider discarding even such a central postulate of economics as transitivity. What economists refuse to give up is not their theory, but their theoretical strategy. All of these proposals for modifying utility theory cling to the vision of a separate science of economics.

PREFERENCE REVERSALS AND "PROCEDURE INVARIANCE"

The most recent contributions of psychologists concerning preference reversal undermine these alternative theories, for they suggest that preference reversals are not due to a failure of transitivity after all![12] Recall that pricing the $-bet higher than the P-bet violates transitivity only if one assumes that in pricing a bet, an individual is indifferent between the stated price and the bet. Failures of this assumption of procedure invariance rather than failures of transitivity might be responsible for preference reversal. In a recent paper, Tversky, Slovic, and Kahneman point out this fact and report on experiments designed to discriminate intransitivities from procedural variances.

Suppose an individual A is offered a choice between not only P- and $-bets, but also between these bets and some payoff for certain, X. Let $(P) and $($) represent the prices the individual would put on the P- and $-bets, and assume in each case the following preference orderings hold:

$($)

                           P-bet

$X

                           $-bet

$(P)

We know the orderings within the two columns, but we do not necessarily know where items in one column fit in the ordering in the other. Depending on how these are combined, preference reversals in the predicted direction can arise in four different ways (Tversky et al. 1990, p. 206).

(1) Intransitivity: Given procedure invariance, the P-bet goes in the same row as $(P) and the $-bet goes in the same row as $($) and one has the intransitive ranking

$($), $-bet
$X
$(P), P-bet
$-bet

---

12   There is an irony here in the fact that psychologists are defending transitivity against economists. But, as we shall see, the diagnosis of preference reversals offered by Tversky et al. is even less palatable to economists than is surrendering transitivity.

Table 1: *Intransitivity vs. procedure variance*

$-bet	$X	P-bet	P-bet
$X	P-bet	$-bet	$X
P-bet	$-bet	$X	$-bet
intransitivity	overpricing	underpricing	over- and
	$-bet	P-bet	underpricing
10%	65%	6%	18%

(2) Overpricing the $-bet: Subjects are indifferent between $(P) and the P-bet and $X is preferred to both the bets. The consistent preference ordering is:

$($)
$X
$(P), P-bet
$-bet

(3) Underpricing the P-bet: Subjects are indifferent between $($) and the $-bet and consequently both bets are preferred to $X. The consistent preference ordering is

P-bet
$($),$-bet,
$X
$(P)

(4) Overpricing the $-bet and underpricing the P-bet: One consistent preference ordering is[13]

$($), P-bet
$X
$(P),$-bet

Procedure invariance requires one to place the bet and its price in the same row and leads to intransitivity. If it is not assumed, then the bets can be placed in various places in the monetary ranking, and purely transitive preference orderings are possible.

As summarized in Table 1, the four cases above provide testable criteria for intransitivity, overpricing, underpricing, or both over- *and* underpricing as explanations of preference reversals. In a sizeable study, Tversky et al. tested for the frequency of these four patterns. The results (when $X was the expected monetary

13   There are others, for the ranking of $($) and the P-bet and of $(P) and the $-bet has not been specified.

216

value) are written at the bottom of each column. It seems that procedure variance, in particular overpricing of the $-bet, is a much more important factor in preference reversals than is intransitivity.

These data are compatible with Lichtenstein's and Slovic's original explanation for preference reversals. In pricing, agents pay more attention to payoffs than in stating a preference. But this explanation is superficial, and Tversky et al. offer a conjecture with a wider scope. They argue that human thinking is influenced by what they call "scale compatibility." If asked to answer a question about quantities in a particular unit, people give a larger role to data expressed in the same units. Dollar amounts have a greater influence in the pricing task, because dollars are the units in which one prices. So preferences and pricing of bets that involve nonmonetary prices should be much more consistent, as has indeed been shown by a study done by Slovic et al. (1990). And if one examines rankings and pricing of monetary options in which there is no explicit element of risk, similar reversals should be found. This implication is supported by the results of a second experiment by Tversky et al. (1990, pp. 212–14) in which subjects were asked to rank and price options involving different time patterns of incomes. Many who prefer smaller short-run gains place a higher price on larger longer-run gains.

CONCLUSIONS

The implications for economics are disturbing. Tversky and Thaler conclude a recent summary piece as follows:

The discussion of the meaning of preference and the status of value may be illuminated by the well-known exchange among three baseball umpires. "I call them as I see them," said the first. "I call them as they are," claimed the second. The third disagreed, "They ain't nothing till I call them." Analogously, we can describe three different views regarding the nature of values. First, values exist – like body temperature – and people perceive and report them as best they can, possibly with bias (I call them as I see them). Second, people know their values and preferences directly – as they know the multiplication table (I call them as they are). Third, values or preferences are commonly constructed in the process of elicitation (they ain't nothing till I call them). The research reviewed in this article is most compatible with the third view of preference as a constructive, context-dependent process. (Tversky and Thaler 1990, p. 210)

This context-dependence has serious implications, for, as Tversky et al. conclude,

These developments highlight the discrepancy between the normative and the descriptive approaches to decision making, which many choice theorists (see Mark Machina 1987) have tried to reconcile. Because invariance – unlike independence or even transitivity – is normatively unassailable and descriptively incorrect, it does not seem possible to construct a theory of choice that is both normatively acceptable and descriptively adequate. (1990, p. 215)

What seems to be required is the sort of theorizing that has traditionally been most repugnant to economic theorists. The pragmatic preference for a theory of choice that is also a theory of rational choice will have to be abandoned. The hope of a unitary account of all economic choice behavior vanishes. There also seems to be a case here for the sort of subjectivist perspective that contemporary Austrian economists defend. For in eliciting preferences, we must attend to how agents *interpret* our actions and questions (Schick 1987). The independence between belief and preference that is fundamental to standard decision theory is cast into doubt.

Contrast these disturbing implications to Machina's recent (1987) discussion of preference reversal. Although it takes the phenomenon seriously, holds no hope for making it disappear, and indeed seems to urge economists to consider what sort of influence such anomalies may have in real market behavior,[14] Machina's theoretical prescription is to construct a still more general formal theory of utility maximization that permits intransitivities. Piecemeal theorizing that relies on substantive generalizations with limited applicability is apparently not worth considering. But such theorizing seems to be needed.

The general complaisance with which most economists continue to regard the claims of economic theory and their unwillingness to take seriously relevant psychological hypotheses seems hard to defend. The attractions of a separate science run deep, but there is no justification for insisting on such a structure, and doing so creates unreasonable barriers to theoretical and empirical progress.

14 1987, p. 140. Some business-school economists have done so. Mowen and Gentry (1980) have replicated the phenomena among marketing students asked both to choose among investment opportunities and to price them. They also found more frequent reversals among *groups* facing such problems than among individuals (1980, esp. p. 721). In a fascinating recent study confirming the compatibility hypothesis, Schkade and Johnson (1989) actually test for subjects' cognitive processes by studying how they manipulate a computer "mouse" to retrieve information and register reactions.

218

PART IV

Postscripts

Economists have philosophers and economic methodologists looking over their shoulders. Philosophers, in contrast, have to look over their own shoulders. It's a paradoxical but unavoidable task. Chapter 16 explores the paradoxes that arise when philosophy of economics is conceived of as an empirical discipline – that is, as basing its conclusions on evidence provided by psychology, sociology, and the history of science, including especially the history of economics. Chapter 17 then distinguishes philosophy of economics from economic methodology – and thereby explains why economists have *two* spectators looking over their shoulders.

16

How to do philosophy of economics

Although philosophers of science have always been interested in the actual work of scientists, there has been a strong turn in the last generation away from prescribing how science ought ideally to proceed and toward studying more carefully how science has proceeded. In part this turn has been a reaction to previous work in philosophy of science, which to many seemed misguided and largely irrelevant to the sciences. In part this change reflects a general skepticism about the possibility of doing traditional foundationalist epistemology. Such skepticism is itself a reaction to the failure of the foundationalist program of the logical empiricists. The contemporary turn toward careful empirical study of the sciences constitutes a new program for the philosophy of science, which I shall call "empirical philosophy of science" or "the empirical approach to the philosophy of science."

1. EMPIRICAL PHILOSOPHY OF SCIENCE

The credo of the empirical approach may be stated trenchantly and simplistically as follows:

The philosophy of science is itself an empirical science.

All conclusions about the scientific enterprise that the philosopher of science draws are, or should be, scientific conclusions and must be defended in the same way or ways that the results of the sciences are defended. When the philosopher of science makes pronouncements about the goals of science or the basis or bases upon which scientists accept various theories or about any other feature of science, we should regard these pronouncements as scientific claims and assess them as we would assess the various assertions the sciences make.

The empirical approach to the philosophy of science denies that epistemology can be distinct from empirical study of the human cognitive faculties, the history of the human search for knowledge and the general progress of the sciences. In Quine's terminology (1969), epistemology is "naturalized." It aims no longer to justify kinds of knowledge claims in terms of an epistemologically prior (self-evident or indubitable) foundation. In justification we always take for granted

I am indebted to Philip Ehrlich, Michael Gardner, Jonathan Lieberson, Stephen Stich, and Paul Thagard for criticism of earlier versions and to unpublished work of Dudley Shapere.

221

much of our scientific and everyday knowledge. "Justifying" an assertion consists solely of showing that it is supported by evidence in the way or ways that scientific assertions generally are. When our claims to know are challenged, the best we can do is to explain scientifically how we know (or can know) what we do.[1] As empiricists, we accept these explanations ultimately because they help us to organize our experience and are supported by our experience. We have no other ultimate warrant. Our goal is to construct empirical theories of human knowing which are consistent with theories of other subject matters and which explain how we can know all these theories.

The empirical approach to philosophy of science is not purely "descriptive." Although philosophers' claims about sciences should be defended in part by showing their consistency with scientific practice, empirical philosophers of science can still assess the work of scientists and offer advice and instruction. Philosophers of science can sometimes contribute directly to the scientific disciplines they study. What we learn about scientific knowledge acquisition provides the basis for such assessment and advice. Empirical philosophy of science thus does not reduce to history of science. Not all of the history of science is relevant to the questions with which the philosophy of science is concerned. The precise details of how scientific results are reached are only important to philosophers of science when they help them understand how we come to know. On the other hand, there are other sources of evidence (for example, from psychology) about how humans acquire knowledge.

2. THE EPISTEMOLOGICAL CIRCLE

In attempting to study science as an empirical philosopher of science, one falls into a logical circle with at least four forms or manifestations. Such an "epistemological circle" is, in fact, common to every theory of knowledge. Hegel states the predicament well:

We ought, says Kant, to become acquainted with the instrument [of cognition], before we undertake the work for which it is to be employed; for if the instrument be insufficient, all our trouble will be spent in vain. The plausibility of this suggestion has won for it general

1 One might argue that a scientific explanation of knowledge acquisition is inconceivable because empirical scientists cannot explain why some methods of acquiring beliefs justify beliefs while some do not. Determining the *standards* for justified belief is not and cannot be the task of any empirical science. I do not find this claim compelling. A psychologist might, by means of sufficiently cunning experiments, be able to show that certain methods of acquiring beliefs are more likely to lead to true beliefs in certain circumstances than are others. If the psychologist could moreover show us *why* some grounds for believing lead to more reliable beliefs, then he or she would be in a position to explain how in certain circumstances people acquire knowledge. There are obviously many circularities here, but I argue in the body of the paper that they are benign. I thus see no reason to believe it impossible that we can explain how we know what we do.

assent and admiration; . . . In the case of other instruments, we can try and criticize them in other ways than by setting about the special work for which they are destined. But the examination of knowledge can only be carried out by an act of knowledge. To examine this so-called instrument is the same thing as to know it. But to seek to know before we know is as absurd as the wise resolution of Scholasticus, not to venture into the water until he had learned to swim. (1817, p. 14)

Some theories of knowledge find their way through these difficulties easily. If one maintains that there are self-warranting truths, for example, then one can easily meet the demand that we know some of the results of epistemology in order to do epistemology. The empirical philosopher of science, on the other hand, has some serious problems.

The first form of the epistemological circle is perhaps most striking. Empirical philosophy of science is itself a science. In doing philosophy of science empirically, one should thus follow scientific method or scientific methods. But one of the goals of the empirical philosophy of science is to find out what scientific methods are. It thus seems that one must already know at least tacitly what one is supposed to find out.[2] If we do not already know how to do science, how can we find out (scientifically) how to do science?

The circularity is not vicious. Empirical philosophers of science disavow seeking any justification for scientific knowledge other than the broadest possible coherence among our theories, including our theories of knowledge acquisition and our perceptual beliefs. There is thus nothing improper in beginning empirical philosophy of science as it were mid-stream, believing already that we know something tacitly or consciously about how to acquire knowledge. Justification, although philosophically interesting, is not the immediate task. Investigating scientific knowledge in accord with our initial conception of scientific investigation, we improve and articulate this conception (and revise our procedures for carrying out this improving and articulating) as we proceed. We are not guaranteed that we will not be forced to change our minds and our procedures. Although we cannot start learning about the sciences from scratch, we can learn about the sciences. This circle remains disturbing, since many philosophers find it difficult wholeheartedly to eschew searching for justification for our knowledge that goes beyond such broad coherence. Contemporary philosophers show, however, little enthusiasm for any alternative. The talk of "coherence" here should not be misconstrued. Since perceptual claims are for the most part knowledge claims, "coherence" here incorporates a sort of correspondence with "reality."

When one questions the philosophical theses upon which the empirical approach is based, the epistemological circle manifests itself again. Suppose some

2   I doubt that the distinction between "knowing how" and "knowing that" is sharp and significant enough to provide a way out of such circularity, although I cannot argue the case here.

traditional philosopher maintains, as many have, that there is knowledge to be gained in epistemology which is different in kind from the empirical knowledge the sciences provide. Such a philosopher would accuse the empirical philosopher of science of avoiding the real epistemological tasks of assessing and justifying (not merely explaining) our scientific knowledge. In answer to such a challenge, the empirical philosopher of science must either deny that there are any such justificatory tasks or deny that there is any way to tackle them. But on what basis is either of these denials to be made? The grounds must themselves be the results of empirical philosophy of science (or of naturalized epistemology) or an anticipation of those results. But the traditional philosopher of science denies that philosophers ought to rely on (or ought to rely *only* on) such grounds. All empirical philosophers of science can do is to repeat their (scientific) reasons for surrendering the ambitions of traditional foundationalist epistemology. They can, of course, also criticize in detail epistemologies that attempt to do more.

The third way in which the epistemological circle manifests itself is somewhat different. Much of the evidence upon which empirical philosophy of science bases its conclusions comes from the history of science. Unless, however, empirical philosophers of science are content only to describe all cognitive enterprises whatsoever, they must add to the presuppositions of their investigations discriminations between good and bad science, between science and pseudo-science, and between knowledge and conjecture. These initial discriminations are revisable as the inquiry proceeds, but they are indispensable. If an investigation of, for example, an economic theory is to contribute to understanding how humans acquire scientific knowledge, the philosopher must be able to assess that theory. An informed assessment demands that one *do* economics — that one finds out what there is to be learned at present about economies. The philosopher of economics must be a competent economic theorist. Standards to assess scientific work are also needed. Yet the standards of assessment and the methods to be employed in learning about economies can only be anticipated now. In trying to learn more, philosophers need to rely on all the knowledge they think they have, even if some of it is not well founded and turns out not to have been knowledge at all.[3] There are, however, special difficulties when one's subject matter is a disci-

---

3 Since empirical philosophers of science must begin by discriminating knowledge from superstition and science from pseudo-science, is not the way open for astrologers, for example, to begin by regarding astrology as the paradigm of a science? Might they not then come up with an empirical philosophy of science which shows how we can acquire such astrological knowledge? After all, a crucial test, among astrologers, for any philosophical account of science will be whether it successfully shows us how we can know astrology. But if astrologers can invent an empirical philosophy of science that "justifies" the claims of astrology, what does our empirical philosophy of science, which criticizes astrology, accomplish? The argument is deceptive. Alternative philosophies of science are, I suspect, not easily created. Astrologers who attempt to come up with a naturalized epistemology which coheres with both their purported knowledge of astrology and their nonastrological knowledge of the everyday world will face a difficult task. If they find that

pline like economics, whose conclusions are disputed and important to people's material interests. I will return to these last difficulties below.

The fourth form of the epistemological circle concerns the relations between empirical philosophy of science and empirical philosophical investigations of particular sciences. The conclusions of empirical philosophy of science rest largely on investigation of the history of actual sciences. To that extent, empirical philosophy of science in general depends on empirical investigations of particular theories, disciplines, incidents, etc. General conclusions in the philosophy of science must rest on particular inquiries into particular sciences. Yet in order to investigate some limited area in science, one needs a great deal of philosophical apparatus. One has no choice except hesitantly and critically to rely on philosophical models of theories, explanations, laws, confirmations, objectivity, and the like. Once again the philosopher must anticipate the answers to his or her questions. If the conclusions of current philosophy of science were already well supported and already merited the esteem and confidence of philosophers and scientists, these anticipations would not be troubling. But a great deal of "established" philosophy of science is poorly confirmed and has been cast into doubt. In this last form the epistemological circle presents a pressing practical problem. In my own work concerning theories of capital and interest, I have made use of whatever philosophical wisdom I could; but the limitations in that wisdom have been palpable. Yet there is no way to increase our knowledge in the philosophy of economics or the philosophy of science in general except to rely on (while attempting to improve upon) conclusions of the past.

Empirical philosophers of science are caught in at least these four ways in the epistemological circle. Does this fact make dubious an empirical approach to the philosophy of science? Should we worry about whether the conclusions of empirical philosophical investigations of particular sciences are prejudiced by the presuppositions with which they begin? Note that many of these presuppositions come from less self-conscious "investigations" of just the same data (from the history of science and from experience of human learning) that the philosophy of science now examines more systematically. We already know a good deal about the world and about how to get knowledge about the world. Without that knowledge, we could not inquire into the nature of our knowledge and the means of its acquisition – but then we would lack not only the means to carry out such an

epistemology is to be done as a nonastrological science is done, they will discover that their attachment to astrology is irrational. If they develop some other sort of epistemology, they might (in some sense) be able to come up with a coherent body of knowledge. Yet this body of knowledge would have to be so different from ours, that our inability to show the astrologers that they are in error is not so disturbing. Once we deny that there is any certain or self-evident foundation for human knowledge, the possibility of consistent and incommensurable knowledge systems cannot be denied. The fact that the astrologer (or theologian or paranoid) begins with different beliefs does not, however, itself show that such incommensurable knowledge systems can be constructed.

investigation, but also an object to investigate. If we really lacked even tacit knowledge about how to acquire knowledge, we would be unable to find out how to learn by investigating scientifically the knowledge we had. Not only would we not know how to inquire, but we would have little or no knowledge to inquire about. The possibility of doing epistemology arises with the possibility of having serious epistemological questions. One may, of course, have good reasons to suspect bias in particular cases. General doubt about whether we can achieve any knowledge through an empirical approach to the philosophy of science on the other hand merely expresses skepticism about the possibility of human knowledge in general. It may turn out, of course, that in doing philosophy of science we are unable to come up with any interesting general results.

3. PHILOSOPHY OF SCIENCE AS A SOCIAL SCIENCE

The empirical philosophy of science, if itself a science at all, is a social science (where "social science" is understood to include history and psychology). Thus it may be that the structure, methods, etc., of philosophy of science will be unlike those of the natural sciences. Social scientific naturalists argue that, in crucial respects (goals, methods of justification, logical structure, fundamental ontology, or whatever), the social sciences are or should be identical to the natural sciences. Antinaturalists argue for an essential difference in one or more of these respects. The debate over naturalism, as the last two sentences suggest, is exceedingly messy. It seems to me that the empirical approach to the philosophy of science ought not *itself* to prejudge this debate. Both naturalists and antinaturalists ought to be able to adopt empirical approaches to the philosophy of science. Otherwise it is hard to see how the philosophy of science can contribute to clarifying and resolving the many disputes between them. Individual empirical philosophers of science may anticipate the resolution of the debate over naturalism.

The empirical approach to the philosophy of science does not presuppose that the structure, methods, etc. of the social sciences (and thus of the philosophy of science itself) are the same as those of the natural sciences. In fact, philosophers of science rarely study the sciences the way physicists study motion or matter. The actual practice of empirical philosophy of science is diverse. Much of it will remain for the foreseeable future more like intellectual history than like physics. While the object of the philosophy of science is all of science, its structure(s), methodology(ies), and the like should be that of (some of) the social sciences. The worst social scientific naturalists can say of this distinction is that it is empty.

Notice that the question of social scientific naturalism is only a special form of the question of whether the methods, structure, goals, and the like are, at a suitable level of generality, one and the same for all sciences in all historical periods. Although we may sometimes have to beg this general question, we should not forget that it is there. It should not be a condition of doing the philosophy of science empirically that this question have only one answer. Otherwise we could not learn its answer in doing philosophy.

4. HOW TO DO PHILOSOPHY OF ECONOMICS

If the above general view of the philosophy of science is correct, how is one to do the philosophy of economics? How is one to answer a much debated question like: "Is microeconomic theory a good scientific theory despite the fact that its basic lawlike claims appear to be false?"

The general *technique* – to study the works of economists and philosophers which develop, apply, and discuss the theory – is certainly not novel. In the actual course of such study the philosopher of economics will have to rely heavily on the tentative results of contemporary philosophy of science and on initial judgments concerning the nature and worth of economic theory and of economics as a discipline. Merely to classify and to order what one finds when reading economics books, one must have some idea of what a science is, what a theory is, what count as laws, and so forth. The richness of philosophical work on the natural sciences and the extent of its influence makes it tempting to suppose that a moderate naturalism is correct. Economists talk about their own work in many ways. They write, for example, about "principles," "models," "theories," "assumptions," and "definitions" and make use of previous work by epistemologists and philosophers of science. To interpret their comments and to describe accurately what they have done, one needs to know a great deal of philosophy of science. How else is one to decide whether microeconomic theory is even a theory?

Some of those most critical of traditional philosophy of science and most insistent on the need for a new empirical philosophy of science might object that we do not know enough philosophy now to understand the structure or methods of microeconomics. There is some merit in this objection, although I believe that it is overstated. It would help if we could begin with solid and well-confirmed philosophical theses. But no philosopher of science can now begin with these, since they are unavailable. A philosopher of economics studying economic theory is in the same philosophical position as any empirical philosopher of science seeking knowledge about the sciences. The only important difference is that philosophers of physics, for example, can begin with fewer doubts about the worth of the physics they study. Philosophers of physics are unlikely ever to conclude that Newton was a mediocre physicist. They can safely begin by regarding a large body of physics as "good physics." Revisions may of course be needed later. Philosophers of physics have, however, comparatively few practical problems deciding what to do when conventional philosophical wisdom does not fit

227

the "good physics" studied. The difficulties facing a philosopher of economics are much greater.

Yet I do not think that this contrast with philosophy of physics shows that we should postpone philosophical examination of more dubious sciences like economics. What we learn about knowledge acquisition in physics may not apply to economics. Even if it does, philosophers of economics will probably have to find this out through their investigations of economics. Furthermore, although the practical differences between the tasks of philosophers of economics and philosophers of physics are considerable, they are differences in degree, not in kind. Philosophers of physics can hardly assume that Newton or Einstein never blundered.

How are philosophers of economics to proceed, if they cannot simply import categories and theses concerning theories, laws, and so forth upon which philosophers agree? When microeconomics fails to fit current philosophical conceptions, philosophers cannot automatically conclude that something is wrong with microeconomics. Philosophers of economics will have to trim, revise, and even invent philosophical categories and theses in trying to make sense of economic theory. They can neither start from scratch nor rely on authoritative philosophical dicta. Cautiously and critically, the philosopher of economics must make use of the most plausible among current philosophical views of the sciences, as ill-founded and wrong-headed as they may be. There is no alternative.

To make sense of, for example, microeconomic theory, one needs not only philosophical apparatus to systematize what one finds, but also an idea of the sort of sense to make of the theory. Histories full of rational decision making and debate certainly make sense, but so do histories full of stupidity, stubbornness, dishonesty, and ideological distortion. When the economist's practice conflicts with the philosopher's dicta, which should be criticized? The question arises frequently. Controversies concerning the merits of economic theories often, for example, do not resemble philosophical models of how scientists assess competing theories. Should one "make sense" of such controversies as a different sort of rational debate or should one "make sense" of them by concluding that they are shot full of confusion, misunderstanding, and ideological distortion? Obvious answers may be deceptive. Perhaps there are unfamiliar methods or structures of sciences which are of great value. Yet we must make such assessments.

The difficulties are aggravated because we know that discussions of economic issues are often biased and distorted because of their importance to interests of individuals of various social groups. As Marx luridly put it: "In the domain of Political Economy, free scientific inquiry meets not merely the same enemies as in all other domains. The peculiar nature of the material it deals with summons as foes into the field of battle the most violent, mean and malignant passions of the human breast, the Furies of private interest" (1867, p. 10). Although I am skeptical of the possibility of finding a completely neutral starting point and of avoiding commitments, the philosopher of economics can address a broader audience and a wider spectrum of issues if he or she does not start by taking neoclassical (or Marxian, or institutionalist, or monetarist) economics as the paradigm for what economics should be. The philosophy of economics must struggle to avoid becoming apologetics for any school of economics.

My own work leads me to believe that the task of the philosopher of economics should be to show that the state and development of economics manifest imperfect rationality. The standard of scientific rationality comes, as it must, from existing philosophy of science, as inadequate as it may be. One should expect to find deviations because of the Furies' influence, but I believe that these will be important exceptions and complications, not the center of the story. If one succeeds in providing a compelling account that is in accordance with these expectations, one thereby provides evidence (not proof) that these expectations are correct.

Seeking to find imperfect rationality in economics comes down to looking for good reasons for whatever one finds unless there are specific grounds to expect or to substantiate bias. Given the dubiousness of many of the conclusions of economics, it is crucial to distinguish carefully between judging the enterprise to be rational and judging its results to be correct. When, according to the standards of accepted philosophy of science, some feature of, for example, microeconomics appears irrational, one should look both for ways of improving the philosophical model and for evidence of the influence of ideology or of simple error. I know of no precise rules to decide such cases.

5. CONCLUSION

The methodology of the philosophy of economics is thus vague and imprecise. It hardly evidences a dramatic new approach to the philosophy of science, such as the empirical approach might initially appear to be. What the empirical approach implies in practice are the following: (1) Philosophers should demand historical and psychological evidence for their conclusions and, insofar as that evidence is scanty (which it has been), should be hesitant about accepted philosophical "wisdom" concerning the sciences. (2) Philosophers of science should be more willing to study and to learn from particular sciences than they sometimes have been. Much can, I think, be learned by employing this homey advice.

17

Reflections on philosophy and economic methodology

Most methodological writing is by economists, and indeed almost all leading economists have tried their hand at it. The large literature concerned with economic methodology is of uneven quality, and there is striking disparity between the quality of the economic contributions and of the methodological reflections of major economists. If one read only their methodology, one would have a hard time understanding how Milton Friedman or Paul Samuelson could have won Nobel Prizes. It is less surprising that such economists scorn philosophizing than that they do so much of it.

Methodological reflections on economics pose other puzzles, too. Although this literature is heavily influenced by philosophy, it is not a part of philosophy. This quasi-autonomy is peculiar, since the methodological literature is concerned with apparently the same questions that occupy philosophers of science. Why is economic methodology a separate subdiscipline? Is it the same inquiry as philosophy of economics under another name? What are the prospects for bridging disciplinary boundaries and for strengthening the collaboration between economists and philosophers?

When I first started thinking about this question a dozen years ago, I was inclined to blame it all on the logical positivists. After all, up-to-date philosophers of science in the late 1970s blamed the logical positivists for everything else. From what I took to be the logical positivist's perspective, someone concerned with "economic methodology" must either be applying the general insights of the logical positivists, analyzing particular economic concepts, or doing some sort of applied psychology or sociology. No wonder, then, that reflection on economic methodology should be philosophically derivative.

I imagined that everything would change with the transcendence of logical positivism. But the hypothesis does not stand scrutiny. The divide between philosophy and methodology preceded logical positivism and has survived logical positivism's demise. Even on the narrowest version of logical positivism, lots of interesting work was left for those interested in economic methodology. Indeed, once the analysis of general scientific notions such as explanation or confirmation

A discussion with Larry Laudan and Gary Downing was instrumental in making me realize the point I try to argue in this essay. Comments and suggestions on a previous draft from Clark Glymour, Frederick Lee, Michael McPherson, Paul Thagard, and an audience at the 1984 meetings of the Philosophy of Science association were very helpful.

was complete, the only work remaining for those interested in philosophy of science would be to analyze concepts that figure in specific sciences such as economics. According to the positivists themselves, then, philosophy of science should dissolve into philosophy of the special sciences, and the only possible dividing line between economists interested in methodology and philosophers would lie between empirical study of research techniques and conceptual analysis. Revealed-preference theory hardly exhausts the possibilities for empiricist analyses of economic concepts. The puzzle remains.

As any sociologist who studies the institutionalization of academic disciplines can point out, there are numerous sociological barriers to effective collaboration between philosophers and economists. Just as one finds differences in, for example, the ways in which chemists and physicists study quantum mechanics, so one would expect to find differences in the way in which economists and philosophers reflect upon economic theory and the practice of economics.

But is there anything more? Are the only barriers to collaboration sociological? Are philosophers of science and economists interested in methodology prevented from dancing together by anything more than their clay feet? Subject to the limitations imposed by institutional barriers, can philosophers and economists now work hand-in-hand analyzing and overcoming the methodological difficulties economists confront?

I think not. For the aims and interests of philosophers and economists differ. Philosophers want to understand knowledge acquisition in economics mainly because of their general interest in the possibilities and limits of human knowledge. Economists want to understand knowledge acquisition in economics mainly because they want to improve the process and to reveal the blunders of those who pigheadedly adhere to a different approach to economic theorizing. While Karl Popper, for example, wanted to understand how knowledge can grow without the possibility of inductive proof, Popperian methodologists want clear-cut rules for economic theory acceptance and rejection. Can any single enterprise satisfy both these goals? Can philosophy of science be applied to economics without vulgarizing it and stripping it of its philosophical worth? Can methodological reflection on economics become philosophically sophisticated while remaining applicable?

The difficulties are instances of general problems concerning the applicability of theoretical knowledge and the relations between theory and practice. One finds the same conflicts of purpose and of criteria of success here that one finds between scientists and engineers, between moral theorists and social critics, or between economists themselves and bankers. The goal of achieving knowledge of a certain domain, which dominates the work of theorists, is at best an instrumental goal or an incidental outcome for those who have some practical purpose they want to achieve. The Copernican Revolution and the formulation of Newton's theory of

231

motion and gravitation could, for example, be epochal events in the development of science without, for a very long time, contributing anything significant to the practice of navigation. A hard-headed sailor might have wondered what all the fuss was about. Rawls's theory of justice (1971) was an important development in ethics regardless of whether it had any immediate application to questions of public policy. The entrepreneur's challenge to economics, "If you're so smart, why aren't you rich?" mistakes the aims of economic theorizing.[1] And so on. Even where the goal of theorizing is ultimately to assist practice, this conflict in immediate aims cannot be ignored.

The gap between theory and practice does not arise solely from this difference in aims, and it manifests itself in many ways. In some cases the gap may be unbridgeable: some theories may have no current practical applications. In other cases the gap may be only shakily bridged because the theoretical solution is too subtle and complex to be applied directly or because the theoretical solution is too simple and requires too many qualifications before it can be applied. In either of these cases the approximations that drive practice may have only a tenuous link to fundamental theory. There are also cases where a theory may be applicable to a practical problem yet not be applied. The theorist may not know of the practical problem or may not be interested in it, and those concerned with the problem may not understand the theory well enough to apply it.

One can find each of these gaps in the relations between philosophy of science and economic methodology. For example, the work of the later logical positivists (or so-called "logical empiricists") concerning the meaningfulness of terms that denote newly hypothesized and unobservable properties is largely irrelevant to much of economics, whose basic terms, such as "consumer," "commodity," or "preference" denote either observable things or properties of "unobservables" that humans have been referring to for millennia. Despite the philosophical cogency of the distinctions Uskali Mäki has drawn concerning types of realism and realisticness (1990), they do not provide an easily grasped tool that economists can use in the construction and criticism of economic analyses. Many standard philosophical accounts of theories, explanation, confirmation, and so forth are nearly inapplicable as well, sometimes because they are too subtle, but at least as often because they are too simple. Consider, for example, the deductive–nomological model of explanation (Hempel 1965). One can, I have argued, often fit explanations in economics into the model (1981a, pp. 148–50), but in doing so, one has said little about explanations in economics. Finally, recent work on confirmation

---

1 In pressing this question Donald McCloskey (1990) argues that new knowledge in economics and methodology is not to be had, because such knowledge would provide an opportunity for windfall profits, which, except by luck are not to be had. But even if new methodological and economic knowledge were *easy* to garner (which nobody believes), windfall profits would not be easily available, for the knowledge would be widely available.

theory, for example,[2] has found little application to economics because it is not yet understood by economists.

How closely can the efforts of writers on economic methodology and philosophers of science be linked, and how should their inquiries be related? First, the general division of labor, with philosophers as the "pure theorists" and methodologists as the "engineers" is basically sensible and bound to continue. It is utopian to expect more than a handful of philosophers interested in economics to become competent economists or for appreciable numbers of economists to become trained philosophers. And, in any case, I am arguing that philosophy and methodology are distinct tasks, not that philosophers and methodologists must be distinct persons. One can, however, still reasonably hope for more feedback from practice to theory and better communication between economic methodologists and philosophers of economics. For philosophical conclusions are not in general going to be well-confirmed apart from their attempted applications in disciplines such as economics, and philosophers hence cannot simply disregard problems of application. So economists potentially have important philosophical tasks, and philosophers can also do more to make their views applicable and to criticize misapplications. Working economists are going to rely on approximations that may seem crude to philosophers. But these approximations should simplify philosophical truth rather than philosophical error.

Second, a recognition of both the fallibility of philosophers and of the gap between philosophy and methodological practice gives those interested in methodology more responsibility. They have, I suspect, more to contribute when they focus on details of particular economic theories or inquiries without necessarily linking their conclusions to general philosophical views (for related claims see Caldwell 1982 and McCloskey 1985). No matter how greatly they despise philosophers, economists can never escape their influence entirely. But there is still an important difference between, on the one hand, attempting to look and see, however much the results may be biased by expectations and prior commitments, and, on the other hand, trying explicitly to apply a definite philosophical position.

Third, I remain enough of a conforming post-positivist philosopher of science to believe that progress in philosophy of science relies on close attention to scientific practice. However, when philosophers study specific disciplines, they should not, as I sometimes have, think of their task as directly helping scientists to go about their business. Sensible economists are not going to disregard the examples of their professors in favor of the conclusions defended in some book of philosophy, whose arguments will inevitably appear abstruse and hard to assess. Some good philosophy of science may be helpful to scientists, but not all of it will

2 Such as Glymour 1980, 1983. In an earlier version of this paper written in 1984, I gave the example of Mackie's analysis of causation (1974). But since then it has been picked up and applied by Daniel Hammond (1986) and Kevin Hoover (1990).

be or need be. Even the simplest philosophical message will require lots of mediation and interpretation before it will be usable. Those who hold positions in philosophy departments and have extensive philosophical education may devote themselves fruitfully to economic methodology, that is, to this mediation, but there are real advantages to not identifying such work with philosophy of economics itself. Better communication between philosophers and economic methodologists does not require conflating their tasks. On the contrary, it presupposes a clear recognition that the goals of the two inquiries are distinct. If one does not distinguish philosophy of economics from economic methodology, one will not have clear goals and clear criteria for success.

Philosophy is to economic methodology as science is to engineering or as economics and ethics are to public policy. Acquiring knowledge and applying knowledge are different tasks with different goals and different criteria for success, and application of knowledge is not just a trivial appendix to its acquisition. Even if those interested in economic methodology need to look to philosophers for general insights, they face serious and important problems of their own. And, unless one believes in an *a priori* path to philosophical truth, one must recognize that the general insights of philosophers are going to depend heavily on the applications of methodologists.

Where exactly does the philosopher *of economics* fit? Is there indeed any place for such a beast?[3] One might think of the philosopher interested in knowledge acquisition, the methodologist, and the economist as akin to the manufacturer, the retailer, and the consumer of some commodity. The philosopher of economics might then fit in as some sort of philosophical insight wholesaler. But the analogy is askew. For, as argued in the last essay, philosophical knowledge is produced by its consumers, retailers, and wholesalers. There are no independent manufacturers. Philosophers of economics and their brother and sister philosophers of physics, biology, nursing, and anthropology should replace all-purpose philosophers of science. There may be interesting and important comparisons and contrasts to be drawn between knowledge acquisition in different disciplines, and thus there will still be room for general philosophy of science. But general philosophy of science is not related to philosophy of economics or philosophy of psychology as theory to application. General philosophy of science is instead parasitic on philosophical study of specific cognitive activities, including scientific disciplines.

So philosophers of economics are philosophers of science who recognize that

---

3   The question is as ambiguous as is the term "philosophy of economics." Philosophers are not only interested in economics for epistemological reasons. Some who have no interest in issues of knowledge acquisition may, for example, study decision theory simply because they are themselves interested in it. "Philosophy of economics," includes parts of social and political philosophy, ethics, action theory, philosophy of mind, and metaphysics in addition to studies of knowledge acquisition. These other areas of overlap between economics and philosophy are not my concern here.

they had better know quite a lot about some specific science – in this case economics – if they are going to grapple productively with general philosophical problems concerning the possibilities of human knowledge and the means of acquiring it. Economic methodologists, while concerned with the same data, are more interested in contributing to the acquisition of economic knowledge. The two groups are natural partners: both will do better work with the help of the other. But there are two sets of questions and two activities here, not just one. The essays in this book all address issues in philosophy of economics, but many, especially in Part I, also address problems of economic methodology. I have straddled the fence between philosophy of economics and economic methodology, but I would not and could not knock it down.

Bibliography of relevant writings by
Daniel M. Hausman

BOOKS

1981b. *Capital, Profits and Prices: An Essay in the Philosophy of Economics.* New York: Columbia University Press.

1984d. *The Philosophy of Economics: An Anthology,* ed. New York: Cambridge University Press. Forthcoming in a Roumanian language edition, Bucharest: Editura Humanitas.

1992a. *The Inexact and Separate Science of Economics.* Cambridge: Cambridge University Press.

ESSAYS

1980. "How to Do Philosophy of Economics." In P. Asquith and R. Giere, eds. *PSA 1980.* East Lansing: Philosophy of Science Association, pp. 352–62; this volume, Chapter 16.

1981a. "Are General Equilibrium Theories Explanatory?" In J. Pitt, ed. *Philosophy in Economics.* Dordrecht: Reidel, pp. 17–32. Reprinted in Hausman 1984d, pp. 344–59.

1981c. "John Stuart Mill's Philosophy of Economics." *Philosophy of Science* 48: 363–85; this volume, Chapter 3.

1982a. "Causal and Explanatory Asymmetry." In P. Asquith and T. Nickels, eds. *PSA 1982,* vol. 1. East Lansing: Philosophy of Science Association, pp. 43–54.

1982b. "Constructive Empiricism Contested." *Pacific Philosophical Quarterly* 63: 21–28.

1983a. "Are There Causal Relations Among Dependent Variables?" *Philosophy of Science* 50: 58–81; this volume, Chapter 9.

1983b. "The Limits of Economic Science." In N. Rescher, ed. *The Limits of Lawfulness.* Pittsburgh: Center for Philosophy of Science, University of Pittsburgh, pp. 93–100; this volume, Chapter 8.

1984a. "Causal Priority." *NOUS* 18: 261–79.

1984b. "A Critique of Scientific Creationism." In J. Tabachnik, ed. *Scholar Program.* Chicago: Chicago Board of Rabbis, pp. 49–64.

1984c. "Defending Microeconomic Theory." *Philosophical Forum* 15: 392–404.

1985a. "Classical Wage Theory and the Causal Complications of Explaining Distribution." In J. Pitt, ed. *Change and Progress in Modern Science,* Dordrecht: Reidel, pp. 171–97; this volume, Chapter 10.

1985b. "Is Falsificationism Unpracticed or Unpractisable?" *Philosophy of the Social Sciences* 15: 313–19; this volume, Chapter 7.

1986a. "Causation and Experimentation." *American Philosophical Quarterly* 23: 143–54.

1986b. "Philosophy and Economic Methodology." In D. Asquith and P. Kitcher, eds. *PSA 1984,* vol. 2. East Lansing: Philosophy of Science Association, pp. 231–49.

1987. "Economic Methodology and Philosophy of Science." In R. Teichgraeber and G. Winston, eds. *The Boundaries of Economics.* Cambridge: Cambridge University Press, pp. 88–116.

BIBLIOGRAPHY

1988. "An Appraisal of Popperian Methodology." In N. de Marchi, ed. *The Popperian Legacy in Economics*. Cambridge: Cambridge University Press, pp. 65–86; this volume, Chapter 6.
1989a. "Arbitrage Arguments." *Erkenntnis* 30: 5–22; this volume, Chapter 13.
1989b. "Are Markets Morally Free Zones?" *Philosophy and Public Affairs* 18: 317–33.
1989c. "*Ceteris Paribus* Clauses and Causality in Economics." In A. Fine and J. Leplin, eds. *PSA 1988*, vol. 2. East Lansing: Philosophy of Science Association, pp. 308–17.
1989d. "Decision Theory and the Deductive Method." *Richerche Economiche* 43: 199–217.
1989e. "Economic Methodology in a Nutshell." *Journal of Economic Perspectives* 3: 115–27. Reprinted in B. Caldwell, ed. *The Philosophy and Methodology of Economics.* Cheltenham: Edward Elgar, 1992; this volume, Chapter 1.
1989f. "Explanatory Progress in Economics." *Social Research* 56: 361–81. Reprinted in B. Caldwell, ed. *The Philosophy and Methodology of Economics*. Cheltenham: Edward Elgar, 1992; this volume, Chapter 14.
1989g. "The Insufficiency of Nomological Explanation." *Philosophical Quarterly* 39: 22–35.
1989h. "On Justifying the Ways of Mammon to Man." In G. Feiwel, ed. *The Economics of Joan Robinson*. London: Macmillan, pp. 821–33.
1990a. "Agricultural Economics and the Chaos of Economic Methodology" (with Michael S. McPherson). *Journal of Agricultural Economics Research* 42, No. 2: 3–4. Reprinted in *Journal of Agricultural Economics Research Essays Supplement*, July 1991, pp. 24–5.
1990b. "The Deductive Method." *Midwest Studies in Philosophy* 15: 372–88; this volume, Chapter 4.
1990c. "Making Interpersonal Comparisons Coherently" (with Martin Barrett). *Economics and Philosophy* 6: 293–300.
1990d. "Supply and Demand Explanations and Their *Ceteris Paribus* Clauses." *Review of Political Economy* 2: 168–86; this volume, Chapter 11.
1990e. "What Are General Equilibrium Theories?" In W. Sieg, ed. *Acting and Reflecting*. Dordrecht: Kluwer, pp. 107–14; this volume, Chapter 12.
1991a. "On Dogmatism in Economics: The Case of Preference Reversals." *Journal of Socio-Economics* 20: 205–25; this volume, Chapter 15.
1992b. "When Jack and Jill Make a Deal." *Social Philosophy and Policy* 9: 95–113.
Forthcoming. "Taking Ethics Seriously: Economics and Contemporary Moral Philosophy" (with Michael S. McPherson) *Journal of Economic Literature*.

REVIEWS

of *Microeconomic Laws: A Philosophical Analysis* by Alexander Rosenberg, *NOUS* 13 (1979): 118–22.
of *Models of Man: Philosophical Thoughts on Social Action* by Martin Hollis, *Journal of Philosophy*, 76 (1979): 386–91.
of *The Rise and Decline of Nations* by Mancur Olson, *QQ: Report from the Center for Philosophy and Public Policy*, vol. 3 no. 2 (Spring 1983): 13–14.
of *Morality Within the Limits of Reason* by Russell Hardin, *Theory and Decision* 30 (1991): 273–78.

238

Bibliography of works by other authors

Adorno, T., ed. 1969. *Der Positivismusstreit in der Deutschen Soziologie*. Darmstadt: Hermann Luchterhand Verlag.

Akerlof, G. 1985. "Discriminatory, Status-based Wages among Tradition-oriented, Stochastically Trading Coconut Producers." *Journal of Political Economy* 93: 265–76.

Alam, S. 1970. "The Marginal Productivity Theory of Distribution – A Survey." *Indian Economic Journal* 18: 230–50.

Alchian, A. 1950. "Uncertainty, Evolution and Economic Theory." *Journal of Political Economy* 57: 211–21.

Ando, A. 1963. "Introduction." In A. Ando, F. Fisher, and H. Simon, eds. *Essays on the Structure of Social Science Models*. Cambridge, MA: MIT Press, pp. 1–4.

Anschutz, R. 1953. *The Philosophy of J. S. Mill*. Oxford: Clarendon Press.

Archibald, G. 1960. "Testing Marginal Productivity Theory." *Review of Economic Studies* 27: 210–13.

Arrow, K. and F. Hahn. 1971. *General Competitive Analysis*. San Francisco: Holden-Day.

Asher, H. 1976. *Causal Modeling*. Beverly Hills, CA: Sage Publications.

Aumann, R. 1964. "Markets with a Continuum of Traders." *Econometrica* 32: 39–50.

Ausubel, L. 1991. "The Failure of Competition in the Credit Card Market." *American Economic Review* 81: 50–81.

Bar Hillel, Y. 1974. "Popper's Theory of Corroboration." In Schilpp 1974, pp. 332–48.

Basmann, R. 1963. "The Causal Interpretation of Non-Triangular Systems of Economic Relations." *Econometrica* 31: 439–48.

Beauchamp, T. and A. Rosenberg. 1981. *Hume and the Problem of Causation*. Oxford: Oxford University Press.

Becker, G. 1957. *The Economics of Discrimination*. Chicago: University of Chicago Press.

Becker, G., M. deGroot, and J. Marschak. 1964. "Measuring Utility by a Single-Response Sequential Method." *Behavioral Science* 9: 226–32.

Bell, D. and I. Kristol, eds. 1981. *The Crisis in Economic Theory*. New York: Basic Books.

Bentzel, R. and B. Hansen. 1954. "On Recursiveness and Interdependency in Economic Models." *Review of Economic Studies* 22: 153–68.

Berg, J., J. Dickhaut, and J. O'Brien. 1985. "Preference Reversal and Arbitrage." In V. Smith, ed. *Research in Experimental Economics*, vol. 3. Greenwich: JAI Press, pp. 31–72.

Bicchieri, C. 1987. "Rationality and Predictability in Economics." *British Journal for the Philosophy of Science* 38:501–13.

Blalock, H. 1964. *Causal Inferences in Non-experimental Research*. Chapel Hill: University of North Carolina Press.

1968. "Theory Building and Causal Inferences." In H. Blalock and A. Blalock, eds. *Methodology in Social Research*. New York: McGraw-Hill.

For good bibliographies of works on economic methodology, see Caldwell, *Appraisal and Criticism in Economics* (1984b); Hausman, *The Philosophy of Economics* (1984d); and Redman, *Economic Methodology* (1989).

BIBLIOGRAPHY

1971. *Causal Models in the Social Sciences*. Chicago: Aldine.

Blalock, H. and Costner, H. 1972. "Scientific Fundamentalism and Scientific Utility: A Reply to Gibbs." *Social Science Quarterly* 52: 827–44.

Blaug, M. 1978. *Economic Theory in Retrospect*. 3rd edn. Cambridge: Cambridge University Press.

1980. *The Methodology of Economics: Or How Economists Explain*. Cambridge: Cambridge University Press.

Bliss, C. 1975. *Capital Theory and the Distribution of Income*. Amsterdam: North-Holland.

Böhm-Bawerk, E. 1889. *The Positive Theory of Capital*, trans. W. Smart. Repr. New York: G. E. Stechert & Co., 1923.

Boland, L. 1979. "A Critique of Friedman's Critics." *Journal of Economic Literature* 17: 503–22.

1982. *The Foundations of Economic Method*. London: Allen & Unwin.

Bonar, J. 1893. *Philosophy and Political Economy*. Reprint London: Allen & Unwin, 1967.

1911. *Disturbing Elements in the Study and Teaching of Economics*. Baltimore.

Brand, M., ed. 1976. *The Nature of Causation*. Urbana: University of Illinois Press.

Bray, J. 1977. "The Logic of Scientific Method in Economics." *Journal of Economic Studies* 4: 1–28.

Breit, W. 1967a. "Some Neglected Early Critics of the Wages Fund Theory." *Southwestern Social Science Quarterly* 48: 53–60.

1967b. "The Wages Fund Controversy Revisited." *Canadian Journal of Economics and Political Science* 33: 509–29.

Bromberger, S. 1966. "Why Questions." In R. Colodny, ed. *Mind and Cosmos: Essays in Contemporary Science and Philosophy*. Pittsburgh: University of Pittsburgh Press.

Bronfenbrenner, M. 1971. *Income Distribution Theory*. Chicago: Aldine.

Buchanan, J. 1958. "*Ceteris Paribus*: Some Notes on Methodology." *Southern Economic Journal* 24: 259–70.

1975. *The Limits of Liberty: Between Anarchy and the Leviathan*. Chicago: University of Chicago Press.

1979. *What Should Economists Do?* Indianapolis: Liberty Press.

Bunge, M. 1959. *Causality – the Place of the Causal Principle in Modern Science*. Cambridge, MA: Harvard University Press.

Bunzl, M. 1984. "A Causal Model of Causal Ordering." *Erkenntnis* 21: 31–44.

Cairnes, J. 1874. *Some Leading Principles of Political Economy*. Reprint. London: Harper and Brothers, 1900.

1875. *The Character and Logical Method of Political Economy*. 2nd edn. Reprint New York: A. M. Kelley, 1965.

Caldwell, B. 1982. *Beyond Positivism: Economic Methodology in the Twentieth Century*. London: Allen & Unwin.

1984. "Some Problems with Falsificationism in Economics." *Philosophy of the Social Sciences* 14: 489–95.

Caldwell, B. ed. 1984. *Appraisal and Criticism in Economics*. London: Allen & Unwin.

Cartwright, N. 1979. "Causal Laws and Effective Strategies." *Nous* 13: 419–37.

1980. "Do the Laws of Physics State the Facts?" *Pacific Philosophical Quarterly* 61: 75–84.

Carver, T. 1894. "The Theory of Wages Adjusted to Recent Theories of Value." *Quarterly Journal of Economics* 8: 377–402.

1904. *Distribution of Wealth*. New York: Macmillan.

Chamberlin, E. 1936. "Monopolistic Competition and the Productivity Theory of Distribution." Reprinted in Fellner and Haley 1946, pp. 143–57.

240

Chu, Y. and R. Chu. 1990. "The Subsidence of Preference Reversals in Simplified and Marketlike Experimental Settings: A Note." *American Economic Review* 80: 902–11.

Churchland, P. 1981. "Eliminative Materialism and Propositional Attitudes." *Journal of Philosophy* 78: 67–90.

Clark, J. B. 1902. *The Distribution of Wealth: A Theory of Wages, Interest and Profits.* New York: Macmillan.

Clark, J. M. 1931. "Distribution." Reprinted in Fellner and Haley 1946, pp. 58–71.

Collingwood, R. 1940. *An Essay on Metaphysics.* Oxford: Clarendon Press, pp. 285–327. Reprinted in Brand 1976, pp. 167–211.

Commons, J. 1893. *The Distribution of Wealth.* Reprint New York: A. M. Kelley, 1963.

Cox, J. and S. Epstein. 1989. "Preference Reversals Without the Independence Axiom." *American Economic Review* 79: 408–26.

Cyert, R., and J. March. eds. 1963. *A Behavioral Theory of the Firm.* Englewood Cliffs, NJ: Prentice-Hall.

Debreu, G. 1959. *Theory of Value.* New York: Wiley.

de Marchi, N. 1970. "The Empirical Content and Longevity of Ricardian Economics." *Economica* 37: 257–76.

1986. "Discussion: Mill's Unrevised Philosophy of Economics: A Comment on Hausman." *Philosophy of Science* 53: 89–100.

Dolan, E., ed. 1976. *The Foundations of Modern Austrian Economics.* Kansas City: Sheed & Ward.

Dorling, J. 1979. "Bayesian Personalism, The Methodology of Scientific Research Programmes, and Duhem's Problem." *Studies in the History and Philosophy of Science* 10: 177–87.

Douglas, P. 1927. "Elasticity of Supply as a Determinant of Distribution." In Hollander 1927, pp. 71–118.

Dray, W. 1957. *Laws and Explanation in History.* Oxford: Oxford University Press.

Duhem, P. 1906. *The Aim and Structure of Scientific Theories,* trans. P. Wiener. Princeton: Princeton University Press, 1954.

Dunlop, J., ed. 1957. *The Theory of Wage Determination.* London: Macmillan.

Durand, D. 1937. "Some Thoughts on Marginal Productivity, with Special Reference to Professor Douglas' Analysis." *Journal of Political Economy* 45: 740–58.

Earman, John, ed. 1983. *Testing Scientific Theories.* Minneapolis: University of Minnesota Press.

Eells, E. 1982. *Rational Decision and Causality.* Cambridge: Cambridge University Press.

Ehring, D. 1982. "Causal Asymmetry." *Journal of Philosophy* 79: 761–74.

Eichner, A. 1983. "Why Economics Is Not Yet a Science." In A. Eichner, ed. *Why Economics Is Not Yet a Science.* Armonk, New York: M.E. Sharpe, pp. 205–41.

Ekelund, R. 1976. "A Short-Run Classical Model of Capital and Wages: Mill's Recantation of the Wages Fund." *Oxford Economic Papers* 28: 66–85.

Elster, J. 1979. *Ulysses and the Sirens: Studies in Rationality and Irrationality.* Cambridge: Cambridge University Press.

Engle, R., D. Hendry, and J. Richard. 1983. "Exogeneity." *Econometrica* 51: 277–304.

Fawcett, H. 1883. *Manual of Political Economy.* London: Macmillan.

Fellner, W. and B. Haley, eds. 1946. *Readings in the Theory of Income Distribution.* Philadelphia: Blakiston.

Feyerabend, P. 1975. *Against Method: Outline of an Anarchistic Theory of Knowledge.* London: Verso Edition.

Fisher, F. 1966. *The Identification Problem in Econometrics.* New York: McGraw-Hill.

1969. "Causation and Specification in Economic Theory and Econometrics." *Synthese* 20: 489–500.

1971. "Aggregate Production Functions and the Explanation of Wages: A Simulation Experiment." *Review of Economics and Statistics* 53: 305–25.

Fisher, I. 1906. *The Nature of Capital and Income.* Reprint New York: A. M. Kelley, 1961.

1930. *The Theory of Interest.* New York: Macmillan.

Fisher, R. 1931. *The Genetical Theory of Natural Selection.* 2nd rev. edn. New York: Dover, 1958.

Friedman, Milton. 1953a. *Essays in Positive Economics.* Chicago: University of Chicago Press.

1953b. "The Marshallian Demand Curve." In Friedman 1953a, pp. 47–99.

1953c. "The Methodology of Positive Economics." In Friedman 1953a, pp. 3–43.

1962a. *Capitalism and Freedom.* Chicago: University of Chicago Press.

1962b. *Price Theory: A Provisional Text.* Rev. ed. Chicago: Aldine.

Garb, G. 1964. "The Problem of Causality in Economics." *Kyklos* 17: 594–611.

Gardner, M. 1979. "Realism and Instrumentalism in Nineteenth Century Atomism." *Philosophy of Science* 46: 1–34.

Gasking, D. 1955. "Causation and Recipes." Reprinted in Brand 1976, pp. 215–23.

Georgescu-Roegen, N. 1979. "Methods in Economic Science." *Journal of Economic Issues* 13: 317–28.

Geweke, J. 1982. "Causality, Exogeneity and Inference." In W. Hildenbrand, ed. *Advances in Econometrics.* Cambridge: Cambridge University Press.

1984. "Inference and Causality in Economic Time Series Models." In Z. Griliches and M. Intriligator, eds. *Handbook of Econometrics,* vol. 2. Amsterdam: North-Holland.

Gibbard, A. and H. Varian. 1978. "Economic Models." *Journal of Philosophy* 75: 664–77.

Giere, R. 1979, 1982. *Understanding Scientific Reasoning.* New York: Holt, Rinehart & Winston. 2nd edn. 1982.

Glymour, C. 1980. *Theory and Evidence.* Princeton: Princeton University Press.

1983. "On Testing and Evidence." In Earman 1983, pp. 3–26.

Goldstein, L. 1967. "Theory in Anthropology: Developmental or Causal." In Gross 1967, pp. 153–80.

Gordon, S. 1973. "The Wage-Fund Controversy: The Second Round." *History of Political Economy* 5: 14–35.

1982. "Why Did Marshall Transpose the Axes?" *Eastern Economic Journal* 8: 31–45.

Gorovitz, S. 1969. "Aspects of the Pragmatics of Explanation." *NOUS* 3: 61–72.

Granger, C. 1969. "Investigating Causal Relations by Econometric Models and Cross-Spectral Methods." *Econometrica* 37: 424–38.

1980. "Testing for Causality: A Personal Viewpoint." *Journal of Economic Dynamics and Control* 2: 329–52.

1985. "Causality Testing in a Decision Science." Department of Economics, University of California, San Diego Discussion Paper No. 85-19.

Green, E. 1981. "On the Role of Fundamental Theory in Positive Economics." In Pitt 1981, pp. 5–15.

Grether, D. and C. Plott. 1979. "Economic Theory of Choice and the Preference Reversal Phenomenon." *American Economic Review* 69: 623–38.

1982. "Economic Theory of Choice and the Preference Reversal Phenomenon: Reply." *American Economic Review* 72: 575.

Gross, L., ed. 1967. *Sociological Theory: Inquiries and Paradigms.* New York: Harper & Row.

Grünbaum, A. 1976. "Is Falsifiability the Touchstone of Scientific Rationality? Karl

Popper Versus Inductivism." In R. Cohen, P. Feyerabend, and M. Wartofsky, eds. *Essays in Memory of Imre Lakatos*. Dordrecht: Reidel, pp. 213–52.

Hahn, F. 1972. *The Share of Wages in the National Income. An Enquiry into the Theory of Distribution*. London: London School of Economics and Political Science.

1973. "The Winter of Our Discontent." *Economica* 40: 322–30.

Hamilton, W. 1967. "Extraordinary Sex Ratios." *Science* 156: 477–88.

Hammond, J.D. 1986. "Monetarist and Antimonetarist Causality." *Research in the History of Economic Thought and Methodology* 4: 109–26.

unpublished 1991. "Early Drafts of Friedman's Methodological Essay." Delivered at the History of Economics Society Meetings, June.

Hands, D. 1984. "What Economics Is Not: An Economist's Response to Rosenberg." *Philosophy of Science* 51: 495–503.

1985a. "Karl Popper and Economic Methodology." *Economics and Philosophy* 1: 83–100.

1985b. "The Structuralist View of Economic Theories: The Case of General Equilibrium in Particular." *Economics and Philosophy* 1: 303–36.

Harcourt, G. 1975. *Some Cambridge Controversies in the Theory of Capital*. Cambridge: Cambridge University Press.

Harris, M. 1966. "The Cultural Ecology of India's Sacred Cattle." *Current Anthropology* 7: 51–59.

Harsanyi, J. 1977. *Rational Behavior and Bargaining Equilibrium in Games and Social Situations*. Cambridge: Cambridge University Press.

Hegel, G. 1817. *Encyklopädie der Philosophischen Wissenschaften in Grundrisse*. Erster Teil. Heidelberg: A. Oswald. Trans. W. Wallace as *Hegel's Logic* (Part One of the *Encyclopedia of the Philosophical Sciences*). Oxford: Clarendon Press, 1975.

Hempel, C. 1965. *Aspects of Scientific Explanation and Other Essays in the Philosophy of Science*. New York: Free Press.

1966. *Philosophy of Natural Science*. Englewood Cliffs, NJ: Prentice-Hall.

Hempel, C. and Oppenheim, P. 1948. "Studies in the Logic of Explanation," Reprinted in Hempel 1965, pp. 245–96.

Hesse, M. 1974. *The Structure of Scientific Inference*. Cambridge: Cambridge University Press.

Hicks, J. 1932. *The Theory of Wages*. London: Macmillan.

1946. *Value and Capital*. 2nd edn. Oxford: Oxford University Press.

1979. *Causality in Economics*. New York: Basic Books.

Hirsch, A. and N. de Marchi. 1986. "Making a Case When Theory Is Unfalsifiable: Friedman's Monetary History." *Economics and Philosophy* 2: 1–22.

1990. *Milton Friedman: Economics in Theory and Practice*. Ann Arbor: University of Michigan Press.

Hirschman, A. 1977. *The Passions and the Interests: Political Arguments for Capitalism Before Its Triumph*. Princeton: Princeton University Press.

Hobson, J. 1904. "Marginal Units in the Theory of Distribution." *Journal of Political Economy* 12: 449–72.

Hollander, J., ed. 1927. *Economic Essays Contributed in Honor of John Bates Clark*. New York: Macmillan.

Hollander, S. 1968. "The Role of Fixed Technical Coefficients in the Evolution of the Wages Fund Controversy." *Oxford Economic Papers* 20: 320–41.

1987. *Classical Economics*. Oxford: Blackwell.

Hollis, M. and E. Nell. 1975. *Rational Economic Man: A Philosophical Critique of Neo-Classical Economics*. London: Cambridge University Press.

Holt, C. 1986. "Preference Reversals and the Independence Axiom." *American Economic Review* 76: 508–15.

Hood, W. and T. Koopmans, eds. 1953. *Studies in Econometric Method.* New York: John Wiley.

Hoover, K. 1990. "The Logic of Causal Inference: Econometrics and the Conditional Analysis of Causation." *Economics and Philosophy* 6: 207–34.

Horwich, P. 1982. *Probability and Evidence.* Cambridge: Cambridge University Press.

Howson, C. and P. Urbach. 1989. *Scientific Reasoning: The Bayesian Approach.* LaSalle, IL: Open Court.

Hume, D. 1748. *An Inquiry Concerning Human Understanding.* Reprint Indianapolis: Bobbs-Merrill, 1955.

Hutchison, T. 1938. *The Significance and Basic Postulates of Economic Theory.* Reprint with a new Preface. New York: A. M. Kelley, 1960.

1953. *A Review of Economic Doctrines, 1870–1929.* Oxford: Clarendon Press.

1977. *Knowledge and Ignorance in Economics.* Chicago: University of Chicago Press.

1978. *On Revolutions and Progress in Economic Knowledge.* Cambridge: Cambridge University Press.

1981. *The Politics and Philosophy of Economics: Marxians, Keynesians and Austrians.* Oxford: Basil Blackwell.

Jaffé, W. 1954. "Translator's Notes." In L. Walras, *Elements of Pure Economics* [1926], trans. W. Jaffé. Homewood, IL: Richard D. Irwin 1954, pp. 497–588.

Jeffrey, R. 1983. "Bayesianism with a Human Face." In Earman 1983, pp. 133–56.

Jevons, W. 1888. *The Theory of Political Economy.* Reprint New York: A. M. Kelley, 1965.

Kahneman, D., J. Knetsch, and R. Thaler. 1990. "Experimental Tests of the Endowment Effect and the Coase Theorem." *Journal of Political Economy* 98: 1325–48.

Kaldor, N. 1955–56. "Alternative Theories of Distribution." *Review of Economic Studies* 23: 83–100.

Kaplan, A. 1965. "Noncausal Explanation." In Lerner 1965, pp. 144–55.

Kaplan, M. 1983. "Decision Theory as Philosophy." *Philosophy of Science* 50: 549–77.

1989. "Bayesianism without the Black Box." *Philosophy of Science* 56: 48–69.

Karni, E. and Z. Safra. 1987. " 'Preference Reversal' and the Observability of Preferences by Experimental Methods." *Econometrica* 55: 675–85.

Keynes, J. N. 1917. *The Scope and Method of Political Economy.* 4th edn. (1st edn. 1891) Reprint New York: A. M. Kelley, 1955.

Kincaid, H. 1989. "Confirmation, Complexity and Social Laws." In A. Fine, ed. *PSA 1988,* vol. 2. East Lansing: Philosophy of Science Association, pp. 299–307.

Klant, J. 1984. *The Rules of the Game.* Cambridge: Cambridge University Press.

Knight, F. 1921a. "Traditional Economic Theory – Discussion." *American Economic Review Papers and Proceedings* 22: 143–6.

1921b. *Risk, Uncertainty and Profit.* Chicago: University of Chicago Press, 1971.

1935. *The Ethics of Competition and Other Essays.* New York and London: Harper and Brothers.

1936. "The Quantity of Capital and the Rate in Interest." *Journal of Political Economy* 44: 433–463, 612–642.

1940. "What Is 'Truth' in Economics?" *Journal of Political Economy* 48: 1–32.

Koopmans, T. 1949. "Identification Problems in Economic Model Construction." *Econometrica* 17: 125–44.

1957. *Three Essays on the State of Economic Science.* New York: McGraw-Hill.

Kuenne, R. 1971. *Eugen von Böhm-Bawerk.* New York: Columbia University Press.
Kuhn, T. 1970. *The Structure of Scientific Revolutions.* 2nd edn. Chicago: University of Chicago Press.
Lakatos, I. 1968. "Criticism and the Methodology of Scientific Research Programs." *Proceedings of the Aristotelian Society* 69: 149–86.
    1970. "Falsification and the Methodology of Scientific Research Programmes," in Lakatos and Musgrave 1970, pp. 91–196; and in Lakatos, 1978, vol. 1, pp. 8–101.
    1974. "Popper on Demarcation and Induction." In P. Schilpp, ed. *The Philosophy of Karl Popper.* LaSalle, IL: Open Court, pp. 241–73. Reprinted in Lakatos 1978, vol. 1, pp. 139–67.
    1978. *Philosophical Papers.* 2 vols. Cambridge: Cambridge University Press.
Lakatos, I. and A. Musgrave, eds. 1970. *Criticism and the Growth of Knowledge.* Cambridge: Cambridge University Press.
Latsis, S., ed. 1976. *Method and Appraisal in Economics.* Cambridge: Cambridge University Press.
Laudan, L. 1977. *Progress and Its Problems.* Berkeley: University of California Press.
Leamer, E. 1984. "Vector Autoregressions for Causal Inference?" Paper delivered at 1984 Carnegie-Rochester Conference.
Leijonhufvud, A. 1974. "The Varieties of Price Theory: What Microfoundations for Macrotheory?" UCLA Discussion Paper Number 44.
    1983. "What Was the Matter with IS-LM?" In J. Fitousse, ed. *Modern Macroeconomic Theory.* Oxford: Blackwells, pp. 64–90.
Leontief, W. 1971. "Theoretical Assumptions and Nonobserved Facts." *American Economic Review* 61: 1–7.
Lerner, D., ed. 1965. *Cause and Effect.* New York: Free Press.
Lester, R. A. 1946. "Shortcomings of Marginal Analysis for Wage-Employment Problems." *American Economic Review* 36: 62–82.
    1947. "Marginalism, Minimum Wages, and Labor Markets." *American Economic Review* 37: 135–48.
Levi, I. 1967. *Gambling with Truth.* Cambridge, MA: MIT Press.
    1980. *The Enterprise of Knowledge.* Cambridge, MA: MIT Press.
    1986. "The Paradoxes of Allais and Ellsberg." *Economics and Philosophy* 2: 23–53.
Levi, I. and S. Morgenbesser. 1964. "Beliefs and Dispositions." *American Philosophical Quarterly* 1: 221–32.
Levison, A. 1974. "Popper, Hume, and the Traditional Problem of Induction." In Schilpp 1974, pp. 322–31.
Lewis, D. 1973a. "Causation." *Journal of Philosophy* 70: 556–67.
    1973b. *Counterfactuals.* Cambridge, MA; Harvard University Press.
Lichtenstein, S. and P. Slovic. 1971. "Reversals of Preference Between Bids and Choices in Gambling Decisions." *Journal of Experimental Psychology* 89: 46–55.
    1973. "Response-Induced Reversals of Preference in Gambling: An Extended Replication in Las Vegas." *Journal of Experimental Psychology* 101: 16–20.
Lieberson, J. 1982a. "Karl Popper." *Social Research* 49: 68–115.
    1982b. "The Romantic Rationalist." *New York Review of Books* 29 (December 2).
Lindman, H. 1971. "Inconsistent Preferences Among Gambles." *Journal of Experimental Psychology* 89: 390–7.
Longe, F. 1866. *A Refutation of the Wage Fund Theory of Modern Political Economy as Enunciated by Mr. Mill and Mr. Fawcett.* Reprinted in J. Hollander, ed. *A Reprint of Economic Tracts.* Baltimore: Johns Hopkins Press, 1903 (original pagination).

Loomes, G. and R. Sugden. 1982. "Regret Theory: An Alternative Theory of Rational Choice under Uncertainty." *Economic Journal* 92: 805–24.

1983. "A Rationale for Preference Reversal." *American Economic Review* 73: 428–32.

Loomes, G., C. Starmer, and R. Sugden. 1989. "Preference Reversal: Information-Processing Effect or Rational Nontransitive Choice." *Economic Journal* (Conference Supplement) 99: 140–51.

McClelland, P. 1975. *Causal Explanation and Model Building in History, Economics and the New Economic History.* Ithaca: Cornell University Press.

McClennen, E. 1990. *Rationality and Dynamic Choice: Foundational Explorations.* Cambridge: Cambridge University Press.

McCloskey, D. 1985. *The Rhetoric of Economics.* Madison: University of Wisconsin Press.

1990. *If You're So Smart: The Narrative of Economic Expertise.* Chicago: University of Chicago Press.

McCormick, B. 1969. *Wages.* Baltimore: Penguin.

Machina, M. 1987. "Choice under Uncertainty: Problems Solved and Unsolved." *Journal of Economic Perspectives* 1: 121–54.

Machlup, F. 1946. "Marginal Analysis and Empirical Research." *American Economic Review* 36: 519–54.

1947. "Rejoinder to an Antimarginalist." *American Economic Review* 37: 148–54.

1955. "The Problem of Verification in Economics." *Southern Economic Journal* 22: 1–21.

1956. "Rejoinder to a Reluctant Ultra-Empiricist." *Southern Economic Journal* 22: 483–93.

1960. "Operational Concepts and Mental Constructs in Model and Theory Formation." *Giornale Degli Economisti* 19: 553–82.

1963. "Reply to Professor Takata." In M. Miller, ed. *Essays in Economic Semantics.* Englewood Cliffs: Prentice-Hall, pp. 207–10.

Mackie, J. 1974. *The Cement of the Universe.* Oxford: Oxford University Press.

Mäki, U. 1990. *Studies in Realism and Explanation in Economics.* Helsinki: Suomalainen Tiedeakatemia.

Malinvaud, E. 1972. *Lectures on Microeconomic Theory,* trans. A. Silvey. Amsterdam: North-Holland.

Marschak, J. 1950. "Statistical Inference in Economics: An Introduction," In T. Koopmans, ed. *Statistical Inference in Dynamic Economic Models.* New York: John Wiley, pp. 1–50.

1953. "Econometric Measurements for Policy and Prediction." In Hood and Koopmans 1953, pp. 1–26.

Marshall, A. 1885. "The Present Position of Economics." Reprinted in A. Pigou, ed. *Memorials of Alfred Marshall.* London: Macmillan, 1925, pp. 152–74.

1930. *Principles of Economics.* 8th edn. London: Macmillan.

Marx, K. 1867. *Capital,* vol. 1, trans. S. Moore and E. Aveling. New York: International Publishers, 1967.

Mill, James. 1820. *An Essay on Government,* ed. Currin V. Shields. Indianapolis: Bobbs-Merrill, 1955.

Mill, J. S. 1836. "On the Definition of Political Economy and the Method of Investigation Proper to It." Reprinted in *Collected Works of John Stuart Mill,* vol. 4, J. Robson, ed. Toronto: University of Toronto Press, 1967.

1843. *A System of Logic.* London: Longmans, Green & Co., 1949.

1844. *Essays on Some Unsettled Questions of Political Economy.* Reprinted in *Collected Works of John Stuart Mill,* vol. 4, J. Robson, ed. Toronto: University of Toronto Press, 1967.

246

1869. "Thornton on Labour and Its Claims." *Fortnightly Review*, n.s. V, pp. 505–18, 680–700. Reprinted in *Essays on Economics and Society, Collected Works of John Stuart Mill*, vol. 5, J. Robson, ed. Toronto: University of Toronto Press, 1967.

1871. *Principles of Political Economy*. 7th edn., W. Ashley, ed. (1909). Reprint New York: A. M. Kelley, 1976.

1873. *Autobiography*. Reprint New York: New American Library.

Miller, A. 1971. "Logic of Causal Analysis: From Experimental to Non-Experimental Design." In Blalock 1971, pp. 273–94.

Miller, D. 1974. "Popper's Qualitative Theory of Verisimilitude." *British Journal for the Philosophy of Science* 25: 166–77.

1982. "Conjectural Knowledge: Popper's Solution to the Problem of Induction." In P. Levinson, ed. *In Pursuit of Truth: Essays in Honor of Karl Popper's 80th Birthday*. Hassocks: Harvester, pp. 17–49.

Mirowski, P. 1990. *More Heat than Light*. Cambridge: Cambridge University Press.

Morgenbesser, S. 1969. "The Realist–Instrumentalist Controversy." In S. Morgenbesser, P. Suppes, and M. White, eds. *Philosophy, Science, and Method*. New York: St. Martin's, pp. 200–18.

1970. "Is It a Science?" In D. Emmett and A. MacIntyre, eds. *Sociological Theory and Philosophical Analysis*. New York: Macmillan, pp. 20–35.

Mowen, J. and J. Gentry. 1980. "Investigation of the Preference-Reversal Phenomenon in a New Product Introduction Task." *Journal of Applied Psychology* 65: 715–22.

Muth, J. 1961. "Rational Expectations and the Theory of Price Movements." *Econometrica* 29: 315–35.

Nagel, E. 1961. *The Structure of Science*. New York: Harcourt, Brace & World.

Nelson, A. 1986. "New Individualistic Foundations for Economics." *Noûs* 20: 469–90.

Nisbett, R. and P. Thagard. 1982. "Variability and Confirmation." *Philosophical Studies* 42: 379–94.

Nooteboom, B. 1986. "Plausibility in Economics." *Economics and Philosophy* 2: 197–224.

Orcutt, G. 1952. "Actions, Consequences and Causal Relations." *Review of Economics and Statistics* 34: 305–13.

Patinkin, D. 1956. *Money, Interest and Prices*. Evanston, IL: Row, Peterson and Co.

Phelps Brown, E. 1962. *Economics of Labor*. New Haven: Yale University Press.

Pierson, F. 1965. "An Evaluation of Wage Theory." In R. Lester, ed. *Labor: Readings on Major Issues*. New York: Random House, pp. 264–91.

Pigou, A. 1949. "Mill and the Wages Fund." *Economic Journal* 59: 171–80.

Pitt, J., ed. 1981. *Philosophy in Economics*. Dordrecht: Reidel.

Pommerehne, W., F. Schneider, and P. Zweifel. 1982. "Economic Theory of Choice and the Preference Reversal Phenomenon: A Reexamination." *American Economic Review* 72: 569–74.

Popper, K. 1957. *The Poverty of Historicism*. New York: Harper & Row.

1966. *The Open Society and Its Enemies*, vol. II, 5th edn. Princeton: Princeton University Press.

1968. *The Logic of Scientific Discovery*. Rev. edn. London: Hutchinson & Co.

1969a. *Conjectures and Refutations; The Growth of Scientific Knowledge*. 3rd edn. London: Routledge & Kegan-Paul.

1969b. "Die Logik der Sozialwissenschaften." In Adorno 1969, pp. 103–23.

1972. *Objective Knowledge; An Evolutionary Approach*. Oxford: Clarendon Press.

1974. "Replies to My Critics." In Schilpp 1974, pp. 961–1200.

1979. *Die Beiden Grundprobleme der Erkenntnistheorie*. Tubingen: Mohr-Siebeck.

1983. *Realism and the Aim of Science; From the Postscript to the Logic of Scientific Discovery*, ed. W. Bartley, III. Totowa, NJ: Rowman and Littlefield.

Putnam, H. 1974. "The 'Corroboration' of Theories." In Schilpp 1974, pp. 221–40.

Puu, T. 1969. "Causal Versus Teleological Explanation in Economics." *Swedish Journal of Economics* 71: 111–26.

Quine, W. 1960. *Word and Object*. Cambridge, MA: MIT Press.

1969. "Epistemology Naturalized." In *Ontological Relativity and Other Essays in the Philosophy of Science*. New York: Columbia University Press, pp. 69–90.

Rawls, J. 1971. *A Theory of Justice*. Cambridge, MA: Harvard University Press.

Reddaway, W. 1959. "Wage Flexibility and the Distribution of Labor." *Lloyd's Bank Review* 54 (October): 32–48.

Redman, D. 1989. *Economic Methodology: A Bibliography with References to Works in the Philosophy of Science, 1860–1988*. New York: Greenwood Press.

Reilly, R. 1982. "Preference Reversal: Further Evidence and Some Suggested Modifications in Experimental Design." *American Economic Review* 72: 576–84.

Rescher, N. 1970. *Scientific Explanation*. New York: Macmillan.

Ricardo, D. 1817. *On the Principles of Political Economy and Taxation*. Vol. 1 of *The Collected Works of David Ricardo*, P. Sraffa and M. Dobb, eds. Cambridge: Cambridge University Press, 1951.

Robbins, L. 1932, 1935. *An Essay on the Nature and Significance of Economic Science*. 2nd edn. London: Macmillan, 1935.

Robertson, D. 1931. "Wage Grumbles." In Fellner and Haley 1946, pp. 221–36.

Rosenberg, A. 1976. *Microeconomic Laws: A Philosophical Analysis*. Pittsburgh: University of Pittsburgh Press.

1980. *Sociobiology and the Preemption of the Social Sciences*. Baltimore: Johns Hopkins University Press.

1983. "If Economics Isn't a Science: What Is It?" *Philosophical Forum* 14: 296–314.

1986. "What Rosenberg's Philosophy of Economics Is Not." *Philosophy of Science* 53: 127–32.

Rosenkranz, R. 1977. *Inference, Method and Decision*. Dordrecht: Reidel.

Roth, A. 1988. "Laboratory Experimentation in Economics: A Methodological Overview." *Economic Journal* 98: 974–1031.

Rothschild, K. 1954. *The Theory of Wages*. New York: Macmillan.

Ryan, A. 1974. *J. S. Mill*. London: Routledge.

Safra, Z., U. Segal, and A. Spivak. 1990. "Preference Reversal and Nonexpected Utility Behavior." *American Economic Review* 80: 922–30.

Salmon, W. 1981. "Rational Prediction." *British Journal for the Philosophy of Science* 32: 115–25.

Samuels, W., ed. 1980. *The Methodology of Economic Thought: Critical Papers from the Journal of Economic Thought {Issues}*. New Brunswick: Transaction Books.

Samuelson, P. 1947. *Foundations of Economic Analysis*. Cambridge, MA: Harvard University Press.

1951. "Economic Theory and Wages." In D. Wright, ed. *The Impact of the Union*. New York: Kelley and Millman, pp. 312–42.

1958. "An Exact Consumption-Loan Model of Interest with or without the Social Contrivance of Money." *Journal of Political Economy* 66: 467–482.

1963. "Problems of Methodology – Discussion." *American Economic Review Papers and Proceedings* 53: 232–36.

1965. "Causality and Teleology in Economics." In Lerner 1965, pp. 99–143.

1973. *Economics.* 9th ed. New York: McGraw-Hill.

Sanford, D. 1976. "The Direction of Causation and the Direction of Conditionship." *Journal of Philosophy* 73: 193–207.

Schick, F. 1987. "Rationality: A Third Dimension." *Economics and Philosophy* 3: 49–66.

Schilpp, P. 1974. *The Philosophy of Karl Popper.* La Salle, IL: Open Court.

Schkade, D. and E. Johnson. 1989. "Cognitive Processes in Preference Reversals." *Organizational Behavior and Human Performance* 44: 203–31.

Schultz, H. 1929. "Marginal Productivity and the General Pricing Process." *Journal of Political Economy* 37: 505–51.

Schumpeter, J. 1954. *History of Economic Analysis.* New York: Oxford University Press.

Schwartz, P. 1972. *The New Political Economy of John Stuart Mill.* Durham, NC: Duke University Press.

Segal, U. 1988. "Does the Preference Reversal Phenomenon Necessarily Contradict the Independence Axiom?" *American Economic Review* 78: 233–6.

Senior, N. 1830. *Three Lectures on the Rate of Wages.* London: John Murray.

1836. An *Outline of the Science of Political Economy.* Reprint New York: A. M. Kelley, 1965.

Settle, T. 1974. "Induction and Probability Unfused." In Schilpp 1974, pp. 697–749.

Shapere, D. 1969. "Towards a Post-positivistic Interpretation of Science." In P. Achinstein and S. Barkers, eds. *The Legacy of Logical Positivism.* Baltimore: Johns Hopkins University Press, pp. 115–60.

Simon, H. 1953. "Causal Ordering and Identifiability." Reprinted in Simon 1977, pp. 53–80.

1954. "Spurious Correlation: a Causal Interpretation." Reprinted in Simon 1977, pp. 93–106.

1955. "Causality and Econometrics: Comment." *Econometrica* 28: 428–42.

1959. "Theories of Decision-Making in Economics and Behavioral Science." *American Economic Review* 49: 253–83.

1976. "From Substantive to Procedural Rationality." In Latsis 1976, pp. 129–48.

1977. *Models of Discovery and Other Topics in the Methods of Science.* Dordrecht: D. Reidel.

1979. "On Parsimonious Explanations of Production Relations." *Scandinavian Journal of Economics* 81: 459–74.

Sims, C. 1972. "Money, Income and Causality." *American Economic Review* 62: 540–52.

1977. "Exogeneity and Causal Orderings in Macroeconomic Models." In C. Sims, ed. *New Methods in Business Cycle Research.* Minneapolis: Federal Reserve Bank, pp. 23–43.

1980. "Macroeconomics and Reality." *Econometrica* 48: 1–48.

1981. "What Kind of Science Is Economics? A Review Article on *Causality in Economics* by John R. Hicks." *Journal of Political Economy* 89: 578–83.

Slovic, P., D. Griffin, and A. Tversky. 1990. "Compatibility Effects in Judgment and Choice." In R. M. Hogarth, ed. *Insights in Decision Making: Theory and Applications.* Chicago: University of Chicago Press, pp. 5–27.

Slovic, P. and S. Lichtenstein. 1968. "Relative Importance of Probabilities and Payoffs in Risk Taking." *Journal of Experimental Psychology Monograph* 78, Pt. 2: 1–18.

1983. "Preference Reversals: A Broader Perspective." *American Economic Review* 73: 596–605.

Smith, A. 1776. *An Inquiry into the Nature and Causes of the Wealth of Nations.* London: J. M. Dent, 1910.

Sneed, J. 1971. *The Logical Structure of Mathematical Physics.* Dordrecht: Reidel.

Sober, E. 1983. "Equilibrium Explanation." *Philosophical Studies* 43: 201–10.

Stegmueller, W. 1976. *The Structure and Dynamics of Theories*, trans. William Wohlhueter. New York: Springer-Verlag.

1979. *The Structuralist View of Theories*. New York: Springer-Verlag.

Stegmueller, W., W. Balzer, and W. Spohn, eds. 1982. *Philosophy of Economics: Proceedings, Munich, July 1981*. New York: Springer-Verlag.

Steward, I. 1979. *Reasoning and Method in Economics. An Introduction to Economic Methodology*. London: McGraw-Hill.

Stigler, G. 1941. *Production and Distribution Theories: The Formative Period*. New York: Macmillan.

1947. "Professor Lester and the Marginalists." *American Economic Review*, 37: 154–7.

Stiglitz, J. 1982. "Ownership, Control, and Efficient Markets: Some Paradoxes in the Theory of Capital Markets." In K. Boyer and W. Shepherd, eds. *Economic Regulation: Essays in Honor of James R. Nelson*. Ann Arbor: University of Michigan Press, pp. 311–40.

Stirling, J. 1869. *Trade Unionism with Remarks on the Report of the Commissioners on Trade Unions*. Glasgow.

Strotz, R. 1960. "Interdependence as a Specification Error." *Econometrica* 28: 428–42.

Strotz, R. and H. Wold. 1960. "Recursive vs. Non-recursive Systems: An Attempt at Synthesis." *Econometrica* 28: 417–27.

Suppe, F. 1974. "Theories and Phenomena." In W. Leinfeller and W. Kohler, eds. *Developments in the Methodology of Social Science*. Dordrecht: Reidel, pp. 45–92.

1976. "Theoretical Laws." In M. Przłecki, K. Szaniawski, and R. Wojcicki, eds. *Formal Methods in the Methodology of Empirical Science*. Wrocław: Ossolineum, pp. 247–67.

Suppe, F., ed. 1977. *The Structure of Scientific Theories*. 2nd edn. Urbana: University of Illinois Press.

Suppes, P. 1957. *Introduction to Logic*. New York: Van Nostrand-Reinhold.

Taussig, F. 1896. *Wages and Capital: An Examination of the Wages Fund Doctrine*. New York: D. Appleton and Co.

1939. *Principles of Economics*. 4th edn. New York: Macmillan.

Thagard, P. and R. Nisbett. 1982. "Variability and Confirmation." *Philosophical Studies* 42: 379–94.

Theodorson, G. 1967. "The Uses of Causation in Sociology." In Gross 1967, pp. 131–53.

Thornton, W. 1870. *On Labour, Its Wrongful Claims and Rightful Dues, Its Actual Present and Possible Future*. 2nd ed. London: Macmillan.

Thurow, L. 1975. *Generating Inequality: Mechanisms of Distribution in the U.S. Economy*. New York: Basic Books.

Tichy, P. 1974. "On Popper's Definition of Verisimilitude." *British Journal for the Philosophy of Science* 25: 155–60.

Tversky, A., P. Slovic, and D. Kahneman. 1990. "The Causes of Preference Reversal." *American Economic Review* 80: 204–17.

Tversky, A. and R. Thaler. 1990. "Preference Reversals." *Journal of Economic Perspectives* 4: 201–11.

Valk, W. 1928. *The Principles of Wages*. London: P. S. King & Son.

van Fraassen, B. 1980. *The Scientific Image*. Oxford: Oxford University Press.

Veblen, T. 1898. "Why Is Economics Not an Evolutionary Science?" *Quarterly Journal of Economics* 12: 373–97.

von Mises, L. 1981. *Epistemological Problems of Economics*, trans. G. Reisman. New York: New York University Press.

von Wright, G. 1975. *Causality and Determinism*. New York: Columbia University Press.

Walker, F. 1876. *The Wages Question: A Treatise on Wages and the Wages Class*. New York: Henry Holt.

Walras, L. 1926. *Elements of Pure Economics,* trans. W. Jaffé. Homewood, IL: Richard D. Irwin, 1954.

Watkins, J. 1984. *Science and Scepticism*. Princeton: Princeton University Press.

Weber, M. 1904. " 'Objectivity' in Social Science and Social Policy." In Weber 1949, pp. 49–112.

1949. *The Methodology of the Social Sciences,* E. Shils and H. Finch, trans. and ed. New York: Macmillan.

Weintraub, E. R. 1985a. "Appraising General Equilibrium Analysis." *Economics and Philosophy* 1: 23–38.

1985b. *General Equilibrium Analysis: Studies in Appraisal*. Cambridge: Cambridge University Press.

Weintraub, S. 1958. *An Approach to the Theory of Income Distribution*. Philadelphia: Chilton Company.

Wicksell, K. 1911: *Lectures on Polititcal Economy,* trans. W. Claussen; L. Robbins, ed. Reprint New York: A. M. Kelley, 1967.

Wicksteed, P. 1894. *An Essay on the Coordination of the Laws of Distribution*. London: Macmillan.

Williams, M. 1977. *Groundless Belief*. New Haven: Yale University Press.

Winter, S. 1962. "Economic 'Natural Selection' and the Theory of the Firm." *Yale Economic Essays* 4: 255–72.

Wold, H. 1954. "Causality and Econometrics." *Econometrica* 22: 162–77.

1955. "Causality and Econometrics: Reply." *Econometrica* 23: 196–7.

1960. "A Generalization of Causal Chain Models." *Econometrica* 28: 443–63.

1969: "Mergers of Economics and Philosophy of Science." *Synthese* 20: 427–82.

Wolfson, R. 1970. "Points of View, Scientific Theories and Econometric Models." *Philosophy of Science* 37: 249–60.

Wood, S. 1889. "The Theory of Wages." *Publications of the American Economic Association* 4: 5–35.

Yeager, L. 1960. "*Methodenstreit* over Demand Curves." *Journal of Political Economy* 68: 53–64.

Zahar, E. 1983. "The Popper-Lakatos Controversy in the Light of 'Die Beiden Grundprobleme der Erkenntnistheorie.' " *British Journal for the Philosophy of Science* 34: 149–74.

251

Index

Printed in the United Kingdom
by Lightning Source UK Ltd.
131385UK00002B/56/A